COURTROOM
AVENGER

KURT CHANDLER

COURTROOM AVENGER

THE CHALLENGES AND TRIUMPHS OF
ROBERT HABUSH

Cover design by Elmarie Jara/ABA Publishing.

Printed in the United States of America.

18 17 16 15 14   5 4 3 2

Library of Congress Cataloging-in-Publication Data

Chandler, Kurt, author.
  Courtroom avenger : the challenges and triumphs of Robert Habush / by Kurt Chandler.
    pages cm
  Includes index.
  ISBN 978-1-62722-308-9 (alk. paper)
  1. Habush, Robert L. 2. Lawyers--Wisconsin--Milwaukee--Biography. I. Chandler, Kurt, author. II. Title.
  KF373.H22A3 2014
  340.092--dc23
  [B]
                        2014002101

Discounts are available for books ordered in bulk. Special consideration is given to state bars, CLE programs, and other bar-related organizations. Inquire at Book Publishing, ABA Publishing, American Bar Association, 321 N. Clark Street, Chicago, Illinois 60654-7598.

www.ShopABA.org

Contents

CHAPTER ONE

The Avenger

It was the biggest case of his life, the pinnacle of a long and brilliant career. Trial lawyer Bob Habush had sued Mitsubishi Heavy Industries America on behalf of the widows of three ironworkers who had been killed during the construction of Miller Park stadium in Milwaukee. Mitsubishi had been hired to build a retractable roof for the new ballpark, and on July 14, 1999, a giant crane nicknamed Big Blue lifted 450 tons of steel in heavy winds and cracked in half, toppling into the bowl of the unfinished stadium. Sixteen months later, in a grueling, tumultuous trial, Habush argued that Mitsubishi was negligent and that the company's management had ignored warnings of unsafe working conditions. Now the case finally was in the hands of the jury.

The courtroom was packed, standing room only. Families of the ironworkers huddled together. Courthouse lawyers and law clerks lined the walls. Curious spectators craned their necks to get a better look as TV cameras hummed.

"Has the jury reached a verdict, Mr. Foreman?" the judge asked.

"Yes, sir," said the foreman. He handed the verdict to the bailiff, who passed it to the judge.

The wait was never ending, an eternity to Habush as he sat at the plaintiff's table. His heart pounded. His legs felt weak. Sweat poured down his back. After more than one hundred jury trials, it never got easier.

"Why do I keep torturing myself?" he wondered, shaking his head from side to side.

He knew the answer all too well.

1

* * *

It was a personal tragedy earlier in his life that unleashed an uncompromising drive for vengeance and shaped his career as a trial lawyer. Bob Habush was in his second year of law school at the University of Wisconsin when his wife, Mimi, gave birth to their first child, a healthy baby girl. Born on April 29, 1960, Sherri showed no signs of complications following the delivery. When her proud parents took her home, their small Madison apartment was filled with warmth and joy.

When Sherri was two months old, she was inoculated for diphtheria, pertussis, and tetanus, a routine procedure. At the time, the standard triple-antigen vaccination was given two injections that also included a fourth antigen to prevent polio. A DPT "polio-plus" vaccine, a quadruple antigen called Quadrigen, was new on the market, developed and sold by the pharmaceutical giant Parke-Davis. The Habushes' pediatrician recommended the new vaccination.

"After she had her first shot, we noticed that her head started to drop to the side a little bit," recalls Bob Habush. "She'd be sitting in the high chair and there was this kind of subtle staring. We took her to the pediatrician and he said not to worry, she's fine. So he gave her the second shot."

Within days, Sherri started having seizures. Her arms jerked sporadically while she lay awake or fed from a bottle. Her movements were out of control. Bob and Mimi rushed her to Wisconsin General Hospital and met with the chief of pediatric neurology, who diagnosed Sherri with myoclonic epilepsy. She was admitted to the hospital and put on sedatives to stop the seizures, but they continued, shaking the child mercilessly. It was not epilepsy.

The Habushes were sure their daughter was going to die. Sick with guilt, they felt alone and helpless. "What's wrong with us? What caused this?" they asked the neurologist. The doctor shook his head. "These things happen," he said.

They learned of an emergency treatment at the Mayo Clinic, given by the pediatric neurologist Gordon Millichap, that involved ACTH, a synthetic hormone used to treat other medical conditions. They drove to Rochester, Minnesota, to meet the doctor. "He was a small man and British, with a very distinct British accent," says Habush. "At the time he seemed compassionate and caring."

Dr. Millichap started Sherri on the drug, and the seizures stopped. The Habushes' relief, though, was short-lived. An electroencephalogram showed abnormal brain-wave deviation. The harm had been done.

"She had brain damage," Habush says. "We didn't know to what extent. We had no idea whether she would ever sit up, whether she would talk or walk. We just didn't know."

The heartsick young parents went home without any answers. "We just sobbed and sobbed and sobbed," says Habush. "I never felt that bad before, and I have never felt that bad since. The idea of having your first baby, a little innocent baby, devastated neurologically . . . We thought maybe there was something genetically wrong with us and that we caused it. It was awful. But at that point there was no blaming anyone other than ourselves."

The Habushes' pediatrician offered some chilling advice: "Put her in an institution and forget about her. She's going to ruin your life."

The couple was stunned. "There is no way we're going to put Sherri away," Habush said to his wife. "We're going to take care of this child. I [don't] know how. I'm still in law school, and we don't have any money or health insurance. But we'll find a way."

Beneath Habush's frustration and despair, an anger churned. On the day Sherri was admitted to Wisconsin General Hospital, he visited the pediatric ward. Parents stood silently beside their children's hospital beds. "What a terrible community of sorrow, of anguish," Habush remembers thinking. "'There is no God,' I told myself. 'All these innocent kids, suffering. No good God could ever do this.' The anger bubbled over. I wanted to kill somebody. I just didn't know *who*."

It would be some time before he would find out.

✳ ✳ ✳

Bob Habush has known this feeling of simmering rage for nearly as long as he can remember. When faced with a fight-or-flight choice, his instinct is to fight. When provoked or wronged, rather than turn the other cheek, he'll strike back at whoever delivers the harmful blow. It's an anger born out of an unsuppressed drive to right a wrong, to get even. "It's a quiet sort of intensity," he says. "A restlessness, a will to fight to the end."

That will to fight has served Habush well in his fifty years as a personal injury attorney. He was able to harness his rage and put it to good use as he rose to become one of the most respected trial lawyers in the United States. In his own words, "I'm good at what I do, and when I'm angry, I'm *really* good."

His quest for revenge goes hand in hand with his ability to empathize with those who have suffered tragedy or injustice. "I've lived through enough personal tragedy in my life that I can identify with people who have been injured and are in a bad way through the fault of others—which gets me angry," he says. "It shows, and that's an attribute as a trial lawyer."

Representing the underdog, he has taken on giants, such as automobile manufacturers, the chemical industry, heavy-machinery makers, Big Pharma, and Big Tobacco, as well as bad drivers and bad doctors, making changes in the safety of everyday products and in laws that continue to protect consumers today. Chrysler, Toyota, Dow Chemical, International Harvester—Habush doesn't flinch at the size or legal firepower of his opponents.

He took on Volkswagen, representing Larry Totsky, who suffered permanent injuries after crashing his VW Beetle. Habush, investigating the crash as part of the discovery process, proved that a chunk of concrete had fallen from the ceiling in a German assembly plant and gotten lodged inside the steering gearbox of Totsky's vehicle as it was being built. The encapsulated concrete years later had worked its way into the gears and impaired the Beetle's steering system while Totsky was driving along a freeway one night. Suddenly he could not steer. His car left the road and rolled several times, leaving him permanently paralyzed from the neck down. In January 1975, a Wisconsin jury awarded him $1.86 million, the largest personal injury award in the state at the time.

Habush took on the British company Smith & Nephew, one of the world's largest manufacturers of medical devices, for making latex gloves that caused a near-fatal allergic reaction in a hospital worker. He represented the radiologic technician Linda Green, who, years before the medical industry became aware of latex allergies, developed an inexplicable skin rash, respiratory complications, and symptoms that resembled anaphylactic shock. In one of the only such trials in the country, Habush showed that the manufacturing process used at a Smith & Nephew plant in Malaysia failed to remove excessive latex proteins from the gloves, which caused allergies in Green and thousands of other health-care workers. The case went to the Wisconsin Supreme Court, which sided with Green and affirmed a jury's verdict of $1 million. The U.S. Food and Drug Administration ordered manufacturers to attach warning labels to their latex products. Soon after, latex gloves were restricted in medical centers.

In another case, Habush went head-to-head with corporate giant Firestone following the explosion of a fifty-five-gallon drum of methanol, which severely burned and permanently disfigured two employees of a service station. The jury decided Firestone had failed to properly label the drum with a warning and awarded $942,000 in the verdict.

Habush took on Costco Wholesale Corporation for making high chairs that failed to prevent small children from slipping under the food tray and getting hung on the strap underneath. He represented the family of Nathan Heintz, a four-year-old boy who suffered brain damage because of a chair's poorly designed restraint. The lawsuit led to a $2.7 million settlement and a drastic reduction in the number of deaths and injuries after manufacturers were compelled to redesign the chairs.

High chairs, latex gloves, seat belts, car seats, camp stoves, bottle caps, extension cords, forklifts, farm machines, rearview mirrors, air bags, bicycles, and children's vaccinations: that's a long list of products that were unsafe and have since been redesigned or recalled because of the efforts of Habush and a select group of other plaintiff's lawyers.

"In cases like these, I'm representing people who have been devastated by injury," he says. "Their lives have been turned on their heads, and they're out of money and they've got no future. When you dig into these cases, when you see what I see, you discover that these companies knew their products were hurting people—but not *enough* people. The body count hadn't gotten high enough for them to do anything about it. They believe it will cost too much money to add the safeguards. It's about profits before safety."

Habush has won landmark cases. In 1988, he sued the Blood Center of Southeastern Wisconsin for failing to test blood for HIV contamination, a first-of-its-kind case that netted his client $3.9 million and caused the nation's blood banks to correct faulty inventory practices.

His fighting instinct also launched him into the role of political activist. For years, as a board member and then president of the American Trial Lawyers Association (ATLA), Habush fought tort reform in Congress and across the country, going head-to-head against a movement that had tried for decades to undermine laws that provide legal recourse when people have been unjustly treated, injured, or killed. "Bob Habush is a giant among the nation's trial lawyers," says Leo Boyle, a Boston attorney and past president of ATLA, which is now known as the American Association for Justice.

During his term as ATLA president, Habush formed working partnerships state by state with public interest groups—consumer groups, education groups, environment groups, senior groups, labor organizations—to develop strategies to repel the tort reformers' attacks. In those days, "ATLA was the strongest political lobbying force of Congress," says Russ Herman, a New Orleans attorney who served on the ATLA executive committee during Habush's two-year presidency and subsequently was elected president of the association. "The first piece of legislation that ATLA had to fight on the floor of the Congress was defeated through Bob's leadership."

Habush was also a pioneer in courtroom practice, adds Herman. "He is extraordinarily gifted. Bob is a very dynamic fellow, very thoughtful, and very focused. And, of course, he's very persuasive. Yet he never learned how to practice law on his knees. You can't intimidate him. So here you have the trial lawyer who was schooled in politics, an effective leader, and a great courtroom trial lawyer. He's a complete package. And that doesn't come along very often."

Above all, Habush seems to relish the roles of protector and avenger. It's what drives him to continue practicing law, now in his sixth decade. "To me, it's not just another case to work on," he explains. "It's about getting even. It's about the fight."

* * *

Robert Lee Habush was born on March 22, 1936, the middle child of three, the brother of two sisters. Both of his parents were raised in Milwaukee and were children of European immigrants. His mother, Beatrice, was a loving and nurturing mother and housewife.

"During World War II, she planted a victory garden in our yard—peas, beans, potatoes, and cucumbers, which she canned to make dill pickles," Habush remembers. "She was a wonderful mother. She stood about five feet tall and limped badly. She told my sisters and me that she was pushed down a fire escape as a child and broke her hip. Later we learned that she was born with a congenital hip deformation, and at the time the doctors didn't know how to fix it. She had a hard time getting around and must have been ashamed of it. But she was quite beautiful."

His father, Jesse Habush, was a lawyer. Slim and handsome, he sold shoes while working his way through Marquette University and Marquette Law School. After graduating in 1930, Jesse began his practice during the early years of the Great Depression. "At that time, lawyers had a hard time making a living," says Habush. "The money wasn't there. Lawyers were starving. My father was Jewish, and none of the big law firms would hire him, so he had to hustle to scrape by, going bar to bar, handing out his calling cards, making friends with bartenders, cops, hospital nurses, and ambulance drivers, looking for business. He would take any case he could get, and all these assholes in the big firms looked down their noses at him as an ambulance chaser. It was a tough life. No one ever gave him anything."

Jesse kept a small notebook in his desk drawer during those years and recorded how much he made on each case—$1.50, $2.50, $7.50—page after page of the fees he collected. It wasn't until World War II that he finally began making a livable wage.

From Habush's birth until he was eleven, his parents rented a house north of Milwaukee in the suburb of Whitefish Bay, where they raised their family. "We lived in a three-bedroom rental, a red brick house," he recalls. "There was a vacant lot next door and other empty lots all through the neighborhood where I would play. You could see dozens of excavations that never were finished. This was during World War II, when housing construction came to a halt."

His father, at six feet tall, seemed like a giant to the young boy. "He was aloof and a strict disciplinarian," Habush says, "who never was reluctant to slap my sisters and me if we got into some kind of mischief. When I broke the neighbor's window with a baseball, my mother protected me by not telling my father. He terrified me, and I never felt that he loved me. All in all, I remember those days in that red brick house as generally happy ones because my mother filled what void emotionally my father had left."

The Village of Whitefish Bay hugs the western shoreline of Lake Michigan, eight miles north of Milwaukee's city limits, insulated from the big-city problems. The small, close-knit community is predominantly white, and a significant percentage—nearly 60 percent—is Roman Catholic. Today, minorities make up about 10 percent of the population, and the city's median household income stands around $102,000, more than double that of the state's median income.

Demographics were of little interest to a boy whose day-to-day world stretched no farther than his leafy backyard and grade-school playground. The surroundings were idyllic. Yet very early in his life, Habush sensed he was somehow different, separate from his friends and classmates, a social outlander. The feeling, little more than amorphous at first, was thrown into stark relief when he was in kindergarten.

"I had a friend named Norman," he says. "He lived four houses down from me. Norman and I played together every day. He was my best friend, my only friend."

One day they were outside, playing near Norman's house, and it started to rain.

"Let's go inside," Habush said, and the two boys ran to Norman's backyard.

"Wait here," Norman said and went inside the house. A minute or two later, he came back, closing the door behind him. "Bobby, you can't come in," he said.

"Why?" Habush asked.

"Because you killed Jesus."

Habush didn't understand. "No, I didn't. What are you talking about? What do you mean?"

"My brother says the Jews killed Jesus and my family doesn't want you in my house."

Habush ran home and burst into the kitchen, crying.

"What's the matter?" said his mother.

"Norman doesn't want to play with me anymore," he told her.

"Well, why not?"

"He said I killed Jesus, and when I went over to his house, his family wouldn't let me in. Why did he say I killed Jesus? Who is Jesus?"

His mother sat him down and explained. "Some people believe Jesus was God. Jewish people believe there was a Jesus but that he wasn't God. And there are some bad people who blame Jewish people for killing Jesus. Those people are still mad at us."

"Well, can I still play with Norman?" he asked.

"Yes, of course you can still play with Norman."

Looking back, Habush says that from that point on, he knew Norman thought he was different. "That was a seed that got planted. I remember how bad I felt and how shocked I was, because I didn't *feel* different."

Habush went to Henry Clay Elementary, a two-story public school a block from the high school. Although he didn't know it at the time, Habush was the only Jewish boy at Clay Elementary when he entered first grade. "I'd go out on the playground and the other boys would say, 'There's a Jew. There's a Jew. Let's get the Jew.' And I was bewildered. I hadn't done anything wrong."

Habush lived twelve blocks from the school and would walk home every day. One day, he was confronted by a gang of grade-school toughs. "The leader was a kid called Pudge," he remembers. "He lived on the next street over from me. They saw me walking home, and Pudge yelled, 'Let's get him!' About five or six of them jumped me. They kicked me and beat on me. 'Dirty Jew!' they screamed. 'You killed Christ. We're gonna kill you!' I remember coming home with a bloody nose and bruises. My mother, of course, felt badly about it.

"'What should I do?' I asked her as she patched me up. She said, 'Just find a different way home so they can't find you.'"

It didn't work. The bullying continued until he'd finally had enough. On a Saturday, he made the short walk to Pudge's house and waited for him in the yard. "When he came out, I walked right up and punched him, as hard as I could, in the nose," says Habush. "Blood started pouring out, and he started crying—which made me feel really good. I got back at every one of those kids. I would wait for them after school as they were walking home.

I'd tap them on the shoulder and, when they turned around, smash them as hard as I could in the nose."

That ended the neighborhood bullying of Bobby Habush. Banned from his friend Norman's house and beaten up because he was Jewish, Habush had tasted revenge, a taste that was satisfying yet bittersweet. "There was a newfound respect for me," he says. "But I was still different. I was the still 'the Jew.' And from that point on, I was an outsider."

He had won the battle, but the war would never end. Vengeance would now become self-fulfilling. It was part of his DNA.

Habush nonetheless tried to fit in at Henry Clay Elementary. He played team sports—football, basketball, track—and studied hard to get good grades, earning A's and B's in each class, which pleased his teachers. But being Jewish had cast him as odd man out. Occasionally new students would transfer into his school. Some of them would find a reason to belittle Habush, and their offhand insults would ignite his tinderbox temper. He remembers one day in sixth grade: "We were rehearsing for a play, and I blew one of my lines. This new kid said, 'You dizzy Jew,' and, whop, I knocked him right out of his chair. The kids in the classroom started screaming, and out I went to the principal's office. My father, much to his dismay, had to come to school, and I had to promise the principal that it would never happen again. But as I walked out of the office with my father, he said to me, 'Anytime someone says something like that again, you knock him down.' He was very supportive of what I'd done. In fact, when I think back about my relationship with my father, that is one of my clearest memories. But that was the only thing my father ever praised me for. Not the grades, not my athletic prowess, but defending myself, which of course stuck in my mind."

Habush was a talented athlete in the seventh and eighth grades. He was a running back on the football team, a guard on the basketball team, and a high jumper on the track team. "Excelling at sports made me accepted by my peers," he says. "But I never really felt comfortable."

On the track field in those days, there were no protective pads around the sand pit where the high jumper landed. At one meet, just before the end of his last year at Henry Clay, Habush completed a jump and fell hard on the wooden frame bordering the pit. "I dislocated my wrist and broke both bones in my left arm," he says. "A very bad break and a very bad dislocation."

The following year, Habush entered Whitefish Bay High School, the city's only public high school. He was among a dozen other Jewish boys and girls there, yet he still had the reputation of an outsider, a scrappy fighter who wouldn't tolerate insults. The anti-Semitism persisted, albeit less conspicuously.

Habush tried out for the freshman football team, the Whitefish Bay Blue Dukes. With his arm still weak from the track accident, he decided not to go out for running back and approached the coach one day during practice.

"Coach, I'd like to play quarterback," he said.

The coach looked the freshman over. "Habush," he replied, "if you're a quarterback, I'm the Pope."

There was no arguing. The coach's mind was made up. "Well, he sure wasn't the Pope," Habush says, looking back. "But I really loved football. So I settled for playing end and linebacker that season. But I was still a starting player."

In his sophomore year, Habush decided to try out for wide receiver. His arm had healed and his confidence had returned. The junior varsity coach, Marshall Riebolt, assigned him to the position.

The first game of the season was scheduled for a Friday night, which posed a problem for Habush. It was the first night of Yom Kippur, the holiest of all nights for Jews, a day of atonement.

"You're not playing football tonight. You're going to temple," Habush's father told him.

"No, Dad. I'm playing football. I'm on the team. It's our first game of the season. I've gotta play."

Jesse Habush wouldn't budge. "You are not playing football!" he yelled. "As long as you live in my house, you do what I say. Or you can move out."

Back and forth they argued, storming from room to room, until Beatrice began crying, pleading with her son to listen to his father.

"Bobby, you'll miss one game," she said. "It's no big deal."

But it *was* a big deal to the starting wide receiver. The following Monday, Coach Riebolt stopped him in the hallway at school. "Habush, where were you Friday? Why weren't you at the game?"

"I had to go to temple, Coach. It was Yom Kippur."

Riebolt was unforgiving. "Well, you decide whether you want to be a rabbi or a football player. Until you do, you're no longer the starting wide receiver."

Habush couldn't believe it. As he recalls, "I felt like I had gotten hit by a four-hundred-pound defensive tackle. But there was nothing I could do. I was on his shit list and I was staying there."

Habush today sees the demotion as an anti-Semitic put-down. He intellectualized it as such when he was in high school, but the incident made an impression, adding to his anger and feeling of being isolated. He could have quit the team. But the coach's comment only made him more defiant. He dug in his heels and finished out the season, most of the time sitting on the bench.

In his senior year, however, he grew tired of being a benchwarmer. "I never got off third string," he says, "so I thought, 'Screw it.' I quit the team." He tried out for a role in the senior class play, trading his shoulder pads for cue cards.

Throughout high school, it never crossed his mind to hide the fact that he was Jewish. "Never. It was always 'Come on. Do you want to see if a Jew is weak? Do you want to see if a Jew can't fight?' There was a lot of that going around at the time, particularly during World War II. [People would say,] 'Jews didn't go into combat. Jews were put in the finance corps instead because Jews couldn't fight'—that sort of thing.

"Following the Holocaust, when it was discovered that six million Jewish souls were rounded up, marched into the freight cars, and murdered by the Nazis, people asked, 'Why didn't they fight? Why didn't they resist?' But people had forgotten the Jewish rebellion in the Warsaw ghetto, and the uprising at the Treblinka death camp, and the resistance groups in Germany, France, and Belgium. There was defiance, and there were fighters. But there was this common misbelief, this class libel, that Jews were not fighters."

When provoked, no matter what the circumstances, Habush would come out swinging, defiant and defensive. "I couldn't overcome my feeling of being on the outside," he says. "There was always that big chip on my shoulder waiting for someone to knock it off. And my reaction was abrupt."

That mixture of brashness and reserve, combined with his engaging smile, crew cut, and athletic build, made Habush popular among the girls at Whitefish Bay High School. He was oblivious of his good looks. In fact, he suffered a measure of insecurity, thinking he was awkward and unattractive. That self-consciousness turned into a hotheaded possessiveness when he began dating a girl named Mimi Friedman.

The two met in the summer of 1953. Habush was going into his senior year at Whitefish Bay. Mimi, two years younger, was a sophomore at Washington High School, across town. They both went to a picnic one day at Milwaukee's McGovern Park. Habush sat by the swimming pool with Jerry Friedman, Mimi's cousin, and stared at Mimi, who was sunning herself. At five feet four, with dark brown hair cut into a ducktail style, she was a young beauty.

"Your cousin Mimi's really a great-looking girl," Habush said. "I'd like to ask her out."

"Forget about it. She's going steady," Friedman said.

"Maybe I can put an end to that," Habush said as he stood up. Though he couldn't swim, he jumped into the shallow end of the pool and pretended to do the crawl, walking through the water toward Mimi.

"I'm Bob," he said to her. "How would you like to go out sometime?"

"I can't," she replied, eyeing him curiously. "I'm going steady."

"Well, maybe you should break up," he said, grinning. "Just let me know when you're ready." Then he "swam" back to the other side of the pool.

Sitting down next to Mimi's cousin, he made a pledge. "I'm going to marry that girl."

Later that night, Mimi confided to her mother about her soon-to-be ex-boyfriend, "You know, I think I'm going to break up with Bernie."

Despite their ensuing steady relationship, Habush was insecure about Mimi. "That continued throughout college, and forever, really," he says. "When she became my girlfriend, I was jealous of every guy who looked at her. The hairs on the back of my neck would stand on end. I was convinced she would want to go out with someone else and break up with me. And that translated into a problem.

"One time we were out ice-skating. I kept falling down, and then I'd get up and she'd laugh. And some guy came around and pushed me down and took her hand and started skating away with her. I went off the ice, took off my skates, waited for him to come around, grabbed him, pulled him off the ice, and decked him with one punch.

"Mimi was very upset. But this was me. This was Bobby Habush. I was afraid of nothing. I was afraid of nobody—bigger guys, smaller guys, one guy, two guys, I didn't care. It made no difference to me. What started to develop was a fearlessness, an attitude that I was not afraid of the consequences. I just acted impulsively. It just happened. And I was not afraid of getting beat."

* * *

In 1954, after graduating from high school, Habush enrolled at the University of Wisconsin in Madison. He was ninety miles away from home. And Mimi. "My girl is back in Milwaukee and I'm in Madison, worrying twenty-four hours a day that she's dating someone else," he recalls.

At UW, he joined Phi Sigma Delta, a Jewish fraternity, although he admits, "I was the worst possible person to ever join a fraternity because I don't like people telling me what to do when I don't want to do it." He signed on as a pledge and ran into trouble right away. One weekend, he wanted to go home to visit Mimi. The active fraternity brothers ordered him to remain at the frat house and shine their shoes. "Go screw yourself," he told them and caught a bus to Milwaukee.

"Well, a pledge is not supposed to talk like that to an active," he says now. "They didn't take kindly to that. But the fraternity had just bought a house and needed all the money they could get from their new pledge class, and they couldn't afford to kick me out."

The insolent pledge was pushed to the limit during Hell Week, when pledges had to pass initiations to rise to the status of active members. One of the initiations required them to drink milk out of bottles fitted with nipples, like baby bottles. When one active made a crude remark regarding Habush's girlfriend, he let loose: "The story is I choked him into unconsciousness until someone hit me over the head with a chair and knocked me out. . . . That was my temperament through my college days. I hadn't changed a bit from my high school days."

At UW, Habush also had signed up for the Army ROTC (Reserve Officers' Training Corps) a college-based program for training commissioned officers. From 1948 to 1973, in times of peace and war, men were drafted to fill vacancies in the armed forces that could not be filled by volunteers. College students were granted deferments. Habush had no objection to serving, but instead of being drafted and ranked as a private, he decided to join the ROTC and become an officer.

He signed on for the military police. "Because I was going to law school, I thought—mistakenly—that the military police would have the potential of participating in court martials," he says.

Following basic training and infantry training, Habush was assigned to the military police center in Fort Gordon, Georgia, near Augusta, for six months of active duty. There, as an officer, he was tasked with training a battalion of young soldiers. His athleticism, combined with his pugnacious, never-back-down personality, meshed perfectly with the leadership role of turning fresh draftees into military cops.

"I was a second lieutenant," remembers Habush, "and I put them through self-defense courses and other very physical things. I had to teach them how to fight, but the fighting was not boxing. It was how to hurt people and, if necessary, kill people with your hands. This was no sport. It was how to put them unconscious by a blow to the back of the ear, how to bring them down with a knee."

Some of the soldiers in the battalion were social misfits who needed more discipline and direction in their lives. Habush was just the guy to provide it. "I had a bunch of kids from New York and New Jersey who thought they were pretty tough," he says. "They were an unruly bunch. Totally undisciplined. Never took an order from anybody. They had no fathers and no male influence, and they didn't like taking commands. These guys were troublemakers. My job was to take some of the starch out of them. Little by little, they finally learned how to march and how to salute and how to behave themselves."

The army clearly suited him. For the first time, he had found a very legitimate way to channel his combative nature. "I loved the training. I just loved it," he admits. "It released some of my frustration, and I enjoyed the discipline, the regimentation, the rules and regs. The whole physicality of being in school sports had fit perfectly for me. I was never afraid of a fight. The army was an extension of that."

This was in the 1950s and early 1960s, after the Korean War had ended and before Vietnam began to heat up, so Habush did not serve in combat or overseas. But after the ROTC, he continued in the Army Reserve for close to ten years before retiring as a captain. "When I tell people I loved the army, they think I'm totally insane."

* * *

Throughout their early twenties, Bob and Mimi's marriage remained on solid ground, despite the guilt and anger that had swept over them after learning of their daughter Sherri's brain damage. "We'd been together since high school, and our roots were so deep that the tree just never got blown over," Habush says. There were no special education classes offered in public school at the time, although he would later work to change that. Sherri attended Montessori School with nondisabled children. Mimi, though, was reluctant to have her play with other kids or go to birthday parties.

Suddenly, one day Mimi received a phone call. "Hello, Mrs. Habush, my name is Marjorie Grant," said the caller. "I got your name from our doctor, Gordon Millichap, at the Mayo Clinic. Several years ago, my son Scotty had the same vaccination as your daughter, and like your daughter, he was brain damaged too. I found out that Quadrigen was the shot that caused brain damage to Scotty. I'm sorry to bring it up, but I thought you ought to know."

Mimi was stunned. She thanked Marjorie for calling, hung up, and waited anxiously for her husband to come home from work. When she told him the news, Habush was ambivalent, unsure whether he wanted to open old wounds. "Come on, Mimi. Forget it," he said. "It's taken us seven years to try to deal with this and get over the terrible guilt. Let's not walk down that path."

But Mimi insisted that he look into Marjorie Grant's claim. "You're a lawyer. You've got to do this," she pressed. "Mrs. Grant said there were other cases against the drug company. You've got to find out the truth."

Habush eventually agreed. He began researching the drug company, Parke-Davis. Founded after the Civil War, the Detroit pharmaceutical firm was a leader in the field of vaccination development and had been one of several manufacturers contracted to produce the Salk vaccine for the polio virus in the 1950s. Parke-Davis had developed Quadrigen in 1954 and, with FDA approval, had begun distributing the vaccine five years later.

Habush discovered a lawsuit against Parke-Davis that had been tried in federal court in North Dakota in 1966. Four-month-old Shane Stromsodt had been given Quadrigen by his family's doctor in October 1959, just months before the vaccine had been administered to Sherri. The baby boy began suffering severe convulsions and was left permanently brain damaged, like Sherri. The court had awarded the Stromsodts $500,000.

Then a second Quadrigen case surfaced, *Tinnerholm v. Parke-Davis & Co.*, this one in New York City. In November 1959, again an infant was given the vaccine and suffered convulsions, mental retardation, and paralysis, strikingly similar to the effects suffered by Shane Stromsodt and Sherri. The *Tinnerholm* award was $610,000.

"Both were brain-damaged kids. Both had received Quadrigen. Both got verdicts against Parke-Davis," says Habush. Evidence from the two trials had exposed Parke-Davis's Quadrigen as a dangerously crippling drug.

Habush began to build his case, gathering transcripts from the trials and appellate briefs: "I read through both cases, boxes and boxes of files. I was convinced there was something there and that the doctors had lied to us. They refused to tell us what they already knew—that the vaccine was defective. The doctors damn well *knew* that. They knew from tests and clinical studies that this was a potential danger, and they never warned anyone about it. My child had been brain damaged by a drug company that put out a defective product."

Habush could feel the rage begin to crest. "I mean, the top of my head was ready to come off. I was this fighting guy, this angry guy, and now beside himself, consumed with getting even."

Habush decided to contact Dr. Millichap, the pediatric neurologist. He wanted to confront him face-to-face. Millichap by then had left the Mayo Clinic and was the chief of pediatric neurology at Children's Memorial Hospital in Chicago. Habush drove from Milwaukee to Chicago to see him.

Standing in the doctor's dimly lit office, Habush felt nervous, unsure how to confront Millichap without losing his temper. With a few years of litigating under his belt, though, he knew how to present himself forcefully and intensely, yet in a calm and controlled way.

"Hello, Mr. Habush," said Dr. Millichap, extending his right hand. "How is Sherri doing?"

Habush stared at him, his own right hand still at his side, and then said, "You lied to us, doctor. You knew all along it was the vaccination that caused her seizures and her brain damage, didn't you?"

Millichap was taken aback. "Yes," he admitted in a whisper.

"Why didn't you tell us?" Habush asked. "We postponed having another child because we blamed ourselves. We were filled with guilt, and we were angry at each other. Why didn't you tell us?"

Millichap was at a loss for words. "I couldn't tell you . . . The Mayo Clinic . . . the policy was not to encourage litigation. Parke-Davis, the drug manufacturer, they were a big grant giver to the clinic. I would have been fired if I had told you."

The explanation wasn't enough. "Dr. Millichap," said Habush, his heart pounding, "you owe me. You owe Mimi and you owe Sherri. You ruined our lives. I'm now going to sue the drug company, and your payback will be to agree to be my expert witness against Parke-Davis."

The doctor considered the veiled demand and then nodded. "OK. I will testify."

Habush nodded back. "My lawyer will be in touch with you," he said and walked out of the office.

He had nailed down his expert witness, an important first step. Next he needed a lawyer to run the case. He was a client at this point, the father of the injured girl. He called upon the attorneys for the plaintiffs in the two previous Quadrigen cases. Jack Fuchsberg, a legendary trial lawyer in New York City and the first attorney in the United States to win a personal injury verdict of more than $1 million, had represented the Tinnerholms. The California torts attorney Melvin Belli had represented the Stromsodts in North Dakota.

Referred to in some quarters as Bellicose Belli for his relentlessly aggressive style, Belli was a brilliant lawyer. Over the years, he had represented a string of high-profile clients, including Mae West, Errol Flynn, Muhammad Ali, and the Rolling Stones. In his best-known case, Belli represented Jack Ruby, who was on trial for killing Lee Harvey Oswald, John F. Kennedy's assassin. But Belli also was also a champion of consumer rights law. "They called him the King of Torts," Habush recalls. "There's never been anyone since like him. He invented demonstrative evidence—how to use charts, models, graphs, photographs, and the like."

Habush hired Belli, and the two began preparing a lawsuit against Parke-Davis. They discussed how they would frame the drug company's negligence. Says Habush, explaining the science behind the case: "When Parke-Davis added the poliomyelitis vaccine, it aggravated the pertussis vaccine. With some infants, the vaccine for pertussis, or whooping cough, can cause encephalitis, brain inflammation. A preservative agent in Quadrigen altered the cellular structure of the pertussis bacteria, which caused hyper-pertussis encephalitis. That's what happened with Sherri. She had encephalitis, which caused brain damage. And Sherri wasn't the only one. Countless kids were brain damaged . . . thousands."

Sherri's case never went to trial. Instead, Parke-Davis offered to settle. "They paid a sum in the mid–six figures, which at that time was a lot of money," Habush says. "Mimi and I put it in a trust for Sherri, which still exists today. The trust has grown tremendously, so if anything happens to us she will always have enough money to be taken care of."

Soon after, in 1968, Parke-Davis removed Quadrigen from the market.

It was dramatic victory for Habush. No other children would be subjected to the risks of the defective vaccine. And while he and Mimi could never turn back the clock, the blame for their daughter's disability was finally lifted from their shoulders.

Habush decided not to sue Sherri's pediatrician, the doctor who had administered the Quadrigen. In the course of his investigation, he had acquired the pediatrician's medical files and knew without a doubt that the doctor should not have given Sherri that second shot. Yet he thought a lawsuit against the drug manufacturer would have a greater impact than a lawsuit against the doctor.

But years later, when Sherri was eighteen, a strange coincidence occurred. "Sherri was in the Special Olympics," Habush recalls. "She was a swimmer, very strong, just terrific. She was winning gold medals in the local and then regional Olympics. One day we were in Madison for the state finals. I'm sitting in the stands, reading the program before Sherri's event, and there in the program, listed as medical adviser to the Special Olympics in Madison, is her pediatrician from when she was an infant. I look across the pool to the officials' table, but I don't remember clearly what the doctor looked like. So I walk over to the table and someone points him out to me."

Habush tapped the doctor on the shoulder and, when he turned around, asked, "Remember me?"

The pediatrician froze. "Yes, I remember you, Mr. Habush."

"I see you're the doctor for these handicapped children," Habush said, holding back his anger. "I find that kind of interesting. Ironic, wouldn't you say?"

The other man was remorseful. "I never forgave myself for what I had done," he said. "I can't tell you how many times I wanted to pick up the phone and call you and your wife to say I'm sorry. Since then, I've dedicated myself to handicapped children and to children injured in accidents."

Swimmers were warming up in the pool, preparing for the next event. "I saw Sherri's name in the program," said the doctor. "I knew she was here."

"Then why didn't you come over to meet her?" Habush said.

"For the same reason I never called you. I felt guilty."

Habush gazed at Sherri as she swam a lap. "Well, Doctor, she's doing fine now. Look at her swim. She's like a fish in water."

The sounds of dozens of excited swimmers and their fans echoed in the cavernous room. "I'm very glad to hear you learned your lesson," Habush said. "And I'm very glad that you're a better doctor now than you were back in 1960."

Below the surface, his anger still simmered. He wanted to take a swing at the guy, but he didn't. He turned and walked back to the other side of the pool to watch his daughter's race—his anger controlled, reserved for another battle, another time.

The war wasn't over. The damage wasn't forgotten. Neither the pediatrician's long-overdue apology nor the compensation from Parke-Davis could diminish Robert Habush's sense of outrage over the harm to his daughter and to thousands of other children who had been injected with Quadrigen. There was closure for his wife. But not for him.

"It's a hundred-year war," he says today. "There's not going to be an armistice. There's not going to be a peace treaty. As long as I'm drawing breath I will get even, I will make them pay: the malpracticing doctors, the defective manufacturers, the companies who sell unsafe products. That's the way I am. There is no forgiveness in my heart. There is no turning the other cheek. There never was and there never will be."

CHAPTER TWO

Breaking Out

In his senior class play in high school, Bob Habush played the defense attorney in Ayn Rand's courtroom drama *Night of January 16th*. His friend, Franklyn Gimbel, played the prosecutor. The play is staged as a murder trial, with the two lead lawyers choosing audience members to act as the jury. The plot is written with different endings, depending on the jury's verdict of guilty or not guilty.

Out of three performances, Habush won the first two verdicts. "Then Frank won the third," he recalls. "To this day, I think the drama coach instructed the jury to vote for Frank because he was feeling terrible about losing."

The competitive spirit between Habush and Gimbel also led them to vie for the attention of the same girls. "Frank was clearly the most handsome guy in high school," Habush says. "When I first started dating Mimi, I kept her away from him as much as possible because I was certain he would steal her away from me."

The play also foretold each of their careers as trial lawyers. Habush became a preeminent plaintiff's attorney, and Gimbel went on to become a federal prosecutor and then a criminal defense attorney, prominent in the trials of organized crime figures and corrupt politicians.

Although they may not have realized it at the time, the two classmates had developed skills and personalities at a young age that would befit them years later in the courtroom. They both were confident and outspoken, the only Jewish boys in their schools who played competitive sports. And they both competed on the forensics team, fine-tuning their talents as extemporaneous speakers.

Still friends today, Habush and Gimbel like to needle each other about *Night of January 16th*. "Bob always holds that play over my head, that he's a better lawyer than I am because he won two of those cases," Gimbel says. "To this day, the two things that he continues to have are a very keen sense of competition and intensity. Bob has always wanted to win. He's a consummate preparer, and he's persuasive. Those things compelled him to be as successful as he is."

Ironically, Habush had no particular ambition to become a lawyer after graduating from high school. Nor did his father ever encourage him to practice law and follow in his footsteps. In fact, when Habush entered the University of Wisconsin, he was a business student with a major in accounting.

He briefly considered going to medical school but ultimately leaned toward law school because he thought a CPA with a law degree would draw attention to his résumé. He planned to practice business law.

"When I graduated from law school in 1961, I was in the top 10 percent of my class, and I had written for the law review. So I was a pretty good candidate for a law firm," he says. "I sent my résumé around to all the big Milwaukee law firms. I never got a response. Back then, in the early 1960s, it was a policy among the business firms not to hire Jews unless they were bringing an extraordinary amount of business or they were number one in their class. Of the ten guys who were in the top 10 percent of my class, seven of us were Jewish. Only one got a job offer."

In the 1960s, a large number of bright young lawyers who, like Habush, ordinarily would have become business lawyers became personal injury lawyers instead. "Many of them were Jews who couldn't get jobs at business firms, so they were almost forced into the personal injury profession," he says. "It was only way they could make a living. They couldn't get jobs in the silk-stocking firms. So if you would have taken a poll of personal injury lawyers in the United States in 1960, maybe 90 percent of them would be Jews."

Over time, lawyers of all religions and ethnicities and skills saw personal injury law as lucrative and challenging. "These were guys who could have gotten jobs anywhere else," Habush says. "So we became really good, and we educated each other. We had seminars, and the entire bar became a terrific force. Our mentors were the Melvin Bellis and the Jack Fuchsbergs and all these other icons. A whole generation of lawyers my age became really good, taking on these big cases and winning and winning and winning. The ambulance chaser label just kind of died."

Habush did get offers from Chicago firms. Although Bob and Mimi didn't have much money, living mostly on the wages he made as manager of their Madison apartment building, they didn't want to move away from their families, who helped them out while Mimi cared for Sherri.

One day, Habush received an alarming call from his mother in Milwaukee. "Your father had a heart attack," she said. "You need to come home right away."

Gathered in a recovery room were his mother and sisters. His father lay quietly, attached to IV lines. As Habush pulled a chair up to the bed, his father whispered a demand. "I need you to run the law firm while I'm recovering."

Habush's heart sank. He and his father had never been close. Jesse Habush hadn't shown up for a single high school sports event. "It made me feel that maybe I was doing something wrong," Habush says. "He was a powerful figure, and he was a corporal punisher. He would slap me across the face without hesitation. My sisters and I would fight over the dining room chair that wasn't next to his. At dinner we were not allowed to talk. Just silence. It wasn't until shortly before his death in 1983 that he ever told me 'I love you.' By comparison, I had such a loving, embracing mother. She filled the void, so I never felt unloved. Still, my relationship with my father fed into that feeling of growing up different."

The hard feelings between father and son hadn't softened over the years. "The volcano that started to boil during my youth started to flame up the older I got. It further estranged me from him. Never was I planning to join my father's firm. I was aiming for business law. The last person I wanted to practice law with was my father. The last person."

Nevertheless, the choices for the young couple were few at the time. "Mimi and I were both emotional train wrecks over our daughter's health condition. I had no job offers in Milwaukee, and we didn't want to live in Chicago and be isolated," Habush explains. "We needed money; we were in debt. And we needed a support group. As young parents, we needed *our* parents. So I decided, 'I'm not going to become a tax lawyer for a while. I'm going to go back and do his bidding in his firm.'"

The Habushes moved to Milwaukee, and Bob went to work at his father's personal injury law firm, Habush, Gillick & Frinzi. The three lawyers were not partners. They shared an office suite on the fourth floor of the Caswell Building on West Wisconsin Avenue in Milwaukee. Larry Gillick specialized in workers' compensation cases, and Dominic Frinzi specialized in criminal defense. All three were very good at what they did. In their office hung a sign: "Sue the Bastards!"

"My father basically was a general practitioner," Habush says. "Along with divorce, real estate, tax returns, wills, and some criminal defense, he did hundreds of automobile accidents. Thousands. That's where he made most of his money. But auto accident lawyers were then considered the rump of the legal profession."

With a bachelor of business administration in accounting and a JD degree, Bob Habush came aboard fresh out of law school, smart, and ready to conquer the world. He just wasn't sure what world he would be conquering. "I never shied away from work—any kind of work," he says. "But my future was very uncertain. I didn't know where life was taking me. Work became an escape hatch. I had a sick kid at home, and the job provided financial resources and some level of emotional support. So I reconciled with my position at the time."

Instead of giving him complex, intellectually challenging cases to try, his father dumped fifty automobile accident cases on his desk on his first day of work. Bob Habush's law career had begun.

"I called those cases my cadavers," he says. "They were like the dead bodies that medical students dissect when they're training. I didn't have a single client who had the right of way. They were blowing stop signs, running red lights, making left turns without yielding. Every conceivable offense. But they had been hurt in the accidents and they wanted a lawyer."

Jesse Habush never turned down a case. According to his business plan, it was all about volume. "His theory was 'If I represent all these people, they'll go out and tell people that I'm their lawyer,'" Habush says. "This was long before TV advertising and marketing. For my father's firm, 'marketing' was having a jillion people out on the street saying,

'I've got Habush as a lawyer.' So he took every damn case, and none of them were any good."

Knowing they were bargain-basement cases, insurance companies seldom offered to settle, and if they did, they would lowball the younger Habush. "I ended up trying one or two cases a month for an entire year in front a jury and never winning one—not one."

Slowly, finally, after a year of "cadavers," Habush began getting clients with cases that had a little life to them. As he polished his courtroom demeanor and honed his art of persuasion, juries started to side with him. His efforts began producing awards for his clients. "The cases weren't worth a lot of money," he admits. "There was a while when I thought I'd never get a verdict over $10,000. I'd be offered $2,500 from an insurance company, and I'd turn it down, try the case, and win. Maybe I'd end up with $4,000. That's how I measured my victories in those days: if I could beat the offer, that was a victory." His incentive, though, was not always the slim margin between the defense's offer and the jury's verdict. Rather, he was propelled by his ingrained combativeness.

"In law school, I thought I was going to be a tax lawyer, not a litigator," he says. "When I started, I didn't know if I was going to be able to handle my anger in a courtroom. But I found it to be a natural way to channel this festering. It made me feel so damn good. I was angry with the insurance companies for making me try these shit cases, beating my head in, and now I was going to pay them back. Whenever I had a good liability case, no matter what they offered me, I would try it. That was my game: Beat the Offer. Once in a while I didn't beat it. But I didn't care, because the insurance companies started to say, 'Hey, this kid's crazy. He'll try anything at the drop of a hat.'"

From his boyhood on, he was out to get even. As a trial lawyer, that never faded. "I remember I had a crappy case that Larry Gillick, our workers' comp attorney, gave me. It was a guy who was in a union. His name was Norm Baylow. He worked at U.S. Rubber in Eau Claire, Wisconsin. One night, in the middle of winter, he was coming home from a bar. He'd had a couple of schnapps, and he's walking past a department store. Along the sidewalk was a steel trapdoor where they delivered produce to the store. It was covered with ice. Norm slips and goes down, boom. Breaks his arm and dislocates his shoulder. The insurance company's trial lawyer is named Mike Carroll. He's out of a firm in Eau Claire. No offer. 'Your guy was drunk, and he should have watched where he was going,' Carroll says. 'This is Wisconsin. People slip on ice all the time.'"

Habush spent a week in frosty Eau Claire prepping for the trial. The judge declared a mistrial, and Habush returned to Milwaukee empty-handed. When the trial was reset, again in the subarctic temperatures of Eau Claire, Habush was ready to deal. The defense attorney, however, was not. Travelers Insurance wanted to try the case, Carroll said. So it went to trial, and the jury returned with a fifty–fifty verdict: 50 percent negligence on the part of the department store and 50 percent negligence on the hapless Norm for not looking where he was going. "At that time, 50 percent on the plaintiff was a loss," Habush says. "I was really pissed!"

Fast-forward ten years. "I have an explosion case in Black River Falls, Wisconsin, against International Harvester. Injuries to my client from an engine fire, terrible burns to the guy. A strong case, perfect liability. Guess who the lawyer is on the other side? Mike Carroll. It's February and twenty-five below zero. He wants to settle the case, and I say no. Don't want to settle. So we start the trial.

"'Judge, I'd like to settle this case, but Mr. Habush won't,' says Carroll.

"'Why won't you settle?' the judge asks me.

"'Don't want to,' I tell him. Judges used to pressure me all the time when I wouldn't settle, and I just would ignore them. I didn't have to settle."

As the trial proceeded, Carroll increased the offer: $75,000; $125,000; $150,000. Habush refused each time, and each time, Carroll complained to the judge, to no avail.

The jury came back with a verdict of $175,000 for the plaintiff. Once again, Habush had beaten the offer.

"I'm sitting in the bar at Holiday Inn waiting for the verdict," he recalls. "Mike Carroll's at another table, knocking down martinis. He comes over to my table.

"'Bob, why wouldn't you settle this case?' he asks me. He's puzzled.

"'Mike,' I say, 'do you remember ten years ago, that young lawyer from Milwaukee with the client named Norm Baylow who slipped on the ice in front of the department store? You wouldn't settle the case.'

"Carroll is stunned—visibly stunned. 'Oh, my God. That was you?' he says, and staggers back to his table."

One more example of getting even.

One weekend, the Habushes went to Chicago to visit their friends, Howard and Sandy Davis. Bob Habush and Howard Davis had known each other since college; they had taken the same accounting classes in business school, had gone to law school together, and had gotten married around the same time. Walking along Michigan Avenue with their wives, the two friends began talking about their jobs. Davis was working as a tax attorney at Sonnenschein Nath & Rosenthal, a huge Chicago firm, the very type of work that Habush had once dreamed of doing. But he was not satisfied.

"Bob, I want to come to work for you," he said.

Habush couldn't believe it. "Are you nuts? Do you know what I do? I defend drunk drivers. I do divorces. I do collection work. I do crappy automobile cases. I mean, you are a tax lawyer. You're in one of the finest law firms in the country. This is what you've always wanted to do."

"I don't like it," said Davis. "It's boring. What you do sounds like fun."

Habush could see his friend was serious. Maybe he could help. "All right. Let me talk to my father. Maybe he'll hire you as my assistant. Let's see what he says."

Jesse Habush was less than enthusiastic about the idea. "I've been practicing for thirty-five years, and I never had an assistant," he said. "You've been here for two years, and now you need an assistant?"

"You know, Howard could do all the trial workup for me," said the younger Habush. "I'd have an inside guy. I could enhance my skills in the courtroom and have time to take on more cases."

Without a doubt, Jesse's son could be persuasive. "All right, but you pay him out of your salary," Jesse said. Habush, however, slyly figured out a way to beat the system, eventually doubling the amount he requested for his own pay and dishing off the extra money to his friend.

It wasn't the first time Habush had helped out Howard Davis. While at the University of Wisconsin, he and Davis joined the Army ROTC. They went through six weeks of basic training together at Fort Riley, Kansas. Davis was a large man, six foot four and about 225 pounds. He golfed and bowled but never played contact sports. In basic training, the two friends were required to maneuver what was called an infiltration course: a hundred yards of coiled barbed wire with exploding ordnance buried on either side of the route. As the grunts crawled along, live machine-gun fire ripped through the air three feet above their heads. "The incentive to stay down was pretty strong," notes Habush. He made it through the course and looked around for Davis.

"Your buddy is still out there," the sergeant told him.

"So maybe he's just slow," Habush said.

"No, he's back in the first strand of the course. And he's not moving," said the sergeant. "If he stays there, he flunks; he's out of the ROTC program. We submit it to the draft board and he gets drafted."

"Won't somebody go and help him?" said Habush.

"He's your friend. You go get him."

Habush gulped hard. "Oh shit," he thought. "What did I get myself into?"

He returned to the start of the course, dropped to all fours, and began crawling toward his friend. Davis was petrified, frozen in place.

"Howard, here's the deal," Habush said, machine-gun fire three feet above their business-school brains. "Choice number one: you stay here, they stop firing the machine guns, you flunk, you're kicked out, you get drafted, you're a private. Choice number two: you stand up and you get killed. Choice number three: you come through the course with me. I'll help you out and we finish this."

Davis thought for a long moment, then he started crawling. Habush lifted the barbed wire to help the larger man slide underneath, talking him along all the way.

Both made it through without a scratch, though Davis suffered a seriously wounded ego. After completing basic training in one piece, they both went on to military police school at Fort Gordon, Georgia.

After a couple of years working at the Habush firm, Davis was placed on salary. When Bob Habush took over the firm, Davis became a named partner. "For thirty years, Howard was the inside guy and I was the outside guy," Habush says. "I tried cases, he worked them up for me. Sometimes he would do the discovery and depositions, and he handled a lot of the administration because my dad was sick. Howard, being a CPA, was good with numbers, good with finances. We were a good team, and certainly he contributed to my success."

In early 1969, after years of toiling in the lower-level trenches, Bob Habush got a case that would mark a milestone in his career and change his life. Jesse walked over to his son one day and dropped a file on his desk. It was not an especially thick file, yet clearly something Jesse had no interest in taking on himself.

"I just got this referral from a Chicago lawyer I know," Jesse said. "He sent me the case to see if I would handle it. It looks like shit, but it'd be a nice training case for you. Oh, and by the way, the trial's in six weeks. Federal court in La Crosse."

Habush picked up the file and started to read.

In 1965, John "Jack" McPhee Jr. had been hired to work at the Erickson Hardwoods sawmill in Onalaska, Wisconsin, just outside of La Crosse, on the Mississippi River. McPhee's job involved feeding giant fresh-cut logs into a buzz saw five feet in diameter by means of a hydraulic carriage, or conveyor, that ran along a metal track. The logs eventually would be milled into planks: two-by-fours, four-by-fours, and the like. The hydraulic carriage was controlled by a stick lever, which operated the gears—forward, backward, and neutral. Occasionally wood chips and slivers would jam between the buzz saw and cutting shelf. The sawyer would reverse the carriage, stop it by shifting into neutral, and then step into a pit in front of the spinning buzz saw and clear the jam with a stick.

The twenty-four-year-old McPhee and his wife, Sheri, had a two-year-old child; Sheri was eight months pregnant with their second. He had been on the job at Erickson Hardwoods for just a few weeks, earning a weekly wage of $51, when one day the buzz saw jammed. Doing what he had done several times before—and what he had been instructed to do—McPhee reversed the conveyor, shifted it into neutral, and jumped into the pit to unjam the whirring saw.

This time, however, something went terribly wrong. As McPhee cleared the saw, with his back to the carriage, the gear lever on the control box suddenly fell out of neutral due to vibration. The carriage lurched forward, striking him in the back and feeding him through the buzz saw. Both of his legs were severed, the right leg just below the knee and the left all the way to the hip.

"Somehow the trauma to his body prevented him from bleeding out,"

Habush says. "His coworkers applied a tourniquet to the remaining leg and constant pressure to his hip, and miraculously Jack didn't die."

McPhee received workers' compensation benefits minus 20 percent, a penalty for his own negligence for going into the carriage pit to clear the jammed saw. Seven attorneys turned down his case. "Those seven lawyers thought McPhee's negligence was overwhelming," Habush says. "But they hadn't considered a product liability case against the manufacturer of the carriage control panel. The manufacturer was Corinth Machinery Company, the only company in Corinth, Mississippi." Corinth and its faulty design became his target.

"The first thing I did was meet with Jack and his wife. He's a handsome young man—black curly hair, big blue eyes, right out of a Hollywood set. Jack had gone through fifteen surgeries and a ton of rehab. And as we sat and talked about the accident, he explained that he was never trained in plant safety: 'Each employee used a different method of safety when running the machinery. And that is what they told me to do: put the carriage in neutral, go into the pit, and clear out the jam with a stick.' I asked him, 'Did the carriage vibrate?' And he said it vibrated a lot. It was obvious to me what had happened: the vibration of the control box and shaft had knocked it out of neutral. So I told him, 'Give me the names of your co-employees and I'll be in touch.'"

Habush moved into La Crosse's Stoddard Hotel and began visiting McPhee's former coworkers, one by one. "Sure enough, they confirmed that Jack wasn't doing anything out of the ordinary. 'This is what we were told to do,' they told me. 'Our supervisors said, "Don't shut down the machine. You go down there into the pit, you try to unplug the jam, get back up and go to work."'" Typical story. Don't stop the entire line, don't stop production.

"Next I visited with the workers' comp insurance carrier, Employers of Wausau, and, wouldn't you know, they had an investigator who specialized in sawmills. They were on the hook for $300,000 for this kid's claim, so I said to the investigator, 'I'm going to help you get your money back. And you are going to help me find other sawmills you've inspected that have safety devices that lock the carriage into neutral.' Sure enough, he came up with a key piece of evidence: a National Safety Council data sheet on logging operations. What do you think the council said in that document? Runaway carriages. It described a locking device on the control panel shaft that would prevent inadvertent movement from neutral to forward, thus stopping 'runaway carriages.'

"I'm pleading negligent design against the manufacturer, I'd never had a products liability case before, and now I've got to find an expert witness. I don't know any engineers at this point but was given the recommendation of a guy in Whitefish Bay who was a general engineer. Well, I gave him the story, asked him would he feel comfortable in criticizing the design, and he said, yeah, sure, he could do it. At the time, you didn't have judges throwing experts out of court, scrutinizing their expertise. I could have someone talk about what the moon is made of, he didn't have to be an astronaut. All I needed was a voice to get me past the judge and get me to the jury so I could make my case."

Before the start of the trial, Habush had gotten no offers from Corinth Machinery's defense lawyers, the father-son team of Tom Skemp and his son, Bill. "Bill was a big guy, six four—basketball player at the University of Wisconsin before he became a lawyer," Habush says. "They were a powerful duo, tried a lot of cases together—and two of the biggest jerks I'd ever met up to that point. They had no fear of losing. They were going to hand this kid from Milwaukee his head in a basket.

"The case was in federal court before the U.S. district judge James Doyle, the father of former Wisconsin governor Jim Doyle. The first thing I do is bring a motion for adjournment. 'No way,' the judge says. 'You've got six weeks, you can get ready.' So that's it. Six weeks later, we start the trial. As luck would have it, I've got twelve women on the jury because this was early spring in farm country and the men were out working the fields. An all-women jury, that was very unusual and a big advantage. Jack McPhee was good-looking, and his wife was beautiful, and their children were adorable. I needed all the sympathy I could get because I had very little else going for me."

During this trial, Mimi took the train to La Crosse from Milwaukee. At night the couple would sit in Habush's hotel room and play gin rummy. But he couldn't concentrate, consumed with doubt, second-guessing his every move: *I'm gonna lose. . . . I shouldn't have said that today. . . . The jury doesn't like me.* "I used every excuse in the world until Mimi finally told me to knock it off," he says.

Yet in court he was a dynamo, the picture of confidence, taking the offensive right out of the snap. He went after Corinth Machinery, and in one cross-examination, he made a witness hired by Corinth's defense team as a safety expert look uninformed and foolish:

Q: Mr. Morris, you have given a lot of opinions about the safety of this piece of sawmill equipment, haven't you?
A: I believe so, yes.
Q: The fact is that until this case you have never even been in a sawmill, isn't that true.
A: That is true.
Q: You had never worked for a sawmill equipment manufacturer?
A: No.
Q: You had never even consulted for one.
A: That's correct.
Q: You have never designed a piece of equipment similar to this one, had you?
A: No.

In cross-examination, Habush ingeniously turned the tables on another Corinth expert. He had gotten hold of the company's marketing material, which described in print how the sawmill conveyor moved "lickety-split." As a witness, Corinth called its sales engineer, who serviced the sawmill machinery. "Well," Habush says, "I lickety-split him to death."

Q: You stated on direct examination that you believed that the conveyor on which our client was injured was designed to move very slowly?
A: Yes, I stated that.
Q: Well, wasn't it designed to move "lickety split" along the track?
A: Lickety split? I can't agree to that.
Q: Mr. Nathan, let me familiarize you with your company's Customer Guide, and turn to page 98 and look at the second paragraph from the top.

A: Okay, I've got it.

Q: Read the description to the court and jury of how the operation of the unit is described.

A: "This unit will increase your production since it moves lickety split along the track."

Q: Is that the first time you've seen that?

A: I don't recall seeing that.

Q: Do you disagree with your own marketing department?

A: I don't agree with that characterization.

Q: Are you telling us that is fraudulent advertising?

A: No, it is not fraudulent, I just don't like it.

Q: Well, maybe you better tell someone in marketing and advertising.

And in another cross-examination, Habush cleverly established "foreseeability of risk" by obliterating a onetime sales and service engineer for Corinth.

Q: You sold to sawmills, didn't you?

A: Yes.

Q: Now, would it be a fair statement to say, sir, that in order to be able to do your job effectively you had to know and appreciate how sawmills were run and operated?

A: Yes, sir, that's correct.

Q: Is it a fair statement to say that you were aware of occasional catching of a wood sliver beneath a saw blade or in a saw blade as being one of the things that happened in the running of a sawmill?

A: I was aware of it, I have seen it happen, sure.

Q: Is it also a fact that you are aware that it is the custom too, if the saw is not overheating or wobbling, for the sawyer to leave his chair and remove that sliver often with the saw running? And come in close proximity to a moving saw blade?

A: I don't deny that I have seen it.

Q: You have seen it frequently, haven't you?

A: I wouldn't say frequently; I have seen sawyers do it.

Q: In the course of your work with Corinth and the sawmill machinery company that you [are] working for now, have you had occasion to see neutral carriage control levers with locking devices on them?

A: Yes, sir.

Q: And this carriage lock device that you saw on the sticks at these other mills prevented that stick from falling out of neutral, didn't they?

A: Yes.

Habush's cross-examinations were so effective it infuriated the defense lawyers to the point that Tom Skemp not-so-accidentally shoved Habush into the jury box rail as he passed him. A juror noticed the bump and whispered to Habush, "I hope your life insurance is paid up."

"The Skemps were not happy anymore," Habush recalls, "because the insurance company they represented, Kemper Insurance, only had $100,000 on the insurance policy, and they were looking at $300,000 in medical and God knows what else for the loss of two legs. By the end of the first week, the judge said to the Skemps, 'You're getting killed and you don't know it. You better make an offer.' They said to him, 'We'll get back to you.' They came back and made no offer. On the second week, we finished the trial and I prepared my final argument before the jury."

On the day of final arguments, Judge Doyle threw Habush a curveball. He ordered all the attorneys into his chambers and said, "Mr. Habush, I am going to find the plaintiff negligent as a matter of law."

"Judge, how can you do this to me?" Habush pleaded. "I have this whole section in my final argument on why my client is not negligent at all, that he was only doing what he was taught."

"I'm sorry," said Doyle, "but I will instruct the jury that this is my decision."

"Judge, can you at least give me some more time to redo my final argument?"

"I'll give you half an hour."

Habush was shell-shocked. As he walked out of the judge's chambers, he could hear the Skemps snickering.

"What happened? Why are they laughing?" asked Mimi, who was sitting nearby in the courtroom.

"The judge just killed me," Habush said.

"Well, are you going to lose?"

"Just wait," he said, scowling. "Just wait."

The kid from Milwaukee wasn't done yet. He tore up three pages of his prepared oratory and, in rapid, furious handwritten strokes on a legal pad, began to write the most important final argument of his young life, explaining with eloquence and passion why the jury should find Corinth Machinery Company at fault for the horrible injuries suffered by the twenty-four-year-old sawmill worker named Jack McPhee.

He stood from his chair, walked around the plaintiff's table, and stood three feet away from the jury box. Speaking quietly and slowly, meeting the eyes of each juror, he stated his case:

> It doesn't make a darn bit of difference that everyone in the industry does it one way. If it's wrong, they're all wrong! And, the court will so instruct you that that is the law. The fact that it might be commonly done in this way in the industry, and that they think this is a terrific way to do it, this doesn't conclude the issue here. Manufacturers and distributors are not entitled to continue in a practice, which is unsafe, and just hide behind that practice for protection with a statement, "Well, we are all doing it."
>
> If we show, ladies and gentlemen, that they should have known of hazards. If we show they had other means and resources to design against the hazards. If we convince you that it was reasonable for them to do so, that's enough. That's good old common sense.
>
> And you, ladies and gentlemen, you can evaluate this defendant. You can evaluate this industry, you can evaluate the practices. You have the right. You have the duty to sit in judgment of them and say whether they were doing it right or wrong, however small they are, however big they are, and however big the industry is. That's the purpose of this courtroom. That's the purpose of this jury. This is your right. This is your privilege. This is your duty.
>
> Sure, operating this machine can be dangerous. Sure it can cut you like it cut Jack McPhee. Sure, that carriage can run over you. Does this mean, ladies and gentlemen, that it's so hazardous the manufacturer just throws up his hands and says, "well, anyone that's crazy enough to work in a sawmill, we don't have to take care of them"? Of course not.

The fact of the matter is, if we take this argument to be true, that this was an ultra-hazardous occupation, that you have to watch every minute of the day, then isn't the responsibility increased to assure that safeguards are on the machinery? Of course. And it is.

The defendant's answer in these cases is always, "shut off the machine," "turn off the machine." Well, ladies and gentlemen, why do you think the National Safety Council required locking devices on the operating levers if they didn't contemplate the machines being a potential hazard while they are being operated? Wouldn't it be simple for them just to say in big print, "turn off the machine"?

The fact of the matter is that the National Safety Council's regulations and rules are created by people in the sawmill industry. They know that these units are not shut off during their operations. And, they know that there is a definite hazard to the sawyer if the stick falls out of neutral when the unit is running. If the unit is turned off, there is no danger to anybody. You wouldn't even need that requirement.

They have got to provide the safeguards, and the National Safety Council regulations tell them what they have got to do. If they don't do it, it is negligence. And it's a failure to exercise ordinary care on their part.

Pausing, Habush pivoted slightly to his left and walked the length of the jury box. Behind him, in the sight line of the jurors, sat the defense attorney.

Jack McPhee was fed into the saw blade, ladies and gentlemen, by a runaway carriage, which threw him into the revolving saw. The runaway carriage was caused by a drive stick disengaging itself. And this drive stick disengaged itself because of no locking device, which should have been on there. Corinth chose not to put it on.

Now, what about Jack McPhee's conduct? There are two questions in the Special Verdict concerning Jack McPhee's conduct. One concerns whether or not he was negligent in going down in the pit area in the manner he did. The other one concerns as to whether he was negligent in activating the control lever after proceeding into the carriage area.

The court has answered the first part, "Yes," as a matter of law.

That is, the court has made a determination that Mr. McPhee was negligent in going into the carriage pit area and that this was a cause of the accident.

But this is not the ball game. This does not affect Corinth's duty to anticipate this. This is not to be taken into consideration by you in determining the relative responsibility. You have to compare the responsibilities here, and you are still able to evaluate and character-ize Mr. McPhee's conduct as compared to the defendant's.

Jack McPhee came to work at Erickson's. He noticed sawyers get out of their chairs to remove chips. This is an assembly line. This is one man working that machine. He has got an edger down the line. He has got a trimmer down the line. He has got loggers putting the logs on the log loader. He sees a sliver, and what does he do? Does he do as he had seen others do, or does he say, "I don't think this is a safe practice"? Do you know how long he would last there? Or, he could say "I would like to call a meeting of all the sawmill operators and say this is really an unsafe practice."

Come on now! You go to work in a place and you learn how to do your job. There isn't one scintilla of evidence that Jack McPhee has done anything other than what he has seen others do.

Judge Doyle sat fixated on Habush's final argument. As Habush paced, all eyes in the courtroom followed.

Let's go back, knowing what he knew, what he appreciated about it then. Did he anticipate that the carriage would run him over then? Was he doing what other sawyers did then? That's how you have got to judge Jack McPhee—not as a designer, not as a safety expert, not as a teacher, not as an employer, but as a kid who went to work, who wanted to be a sawyer, who went to school and did what he saw others do.

Ladies and gentlemen, in connection with the comparing of the respon-sibility of this accident, don't indict Jack McPhee because of the way the sawmill industry allowed their people to operate in connection with their work. This is not fair. This is not reasonable. The law doesn't expect you to do that. You evaluate him based upon what he saw, what he knew at the time, and not in light of what happened, but rather, in light of what you would think was known before the accident happened.

Compare, ladies and gentlemen, the responsibility of a manufacturer and distributor who distributes all over the United States. Compare, if you will, a manufacturer who has a research department, who has engineers on the stand, who has trouble-shooters that go out to their prospects. Compare, if you will, the manufacturer who knows his product, knows the value, knows its tendency. Compare, if you will, this organization, the sawmill industry.

Compare these people and their responsibility for this accident to Jack McPhee, twenty-four years old, twenty-six weeks of sawyer's school, doing what he saw others do.

Sure, he was there. Sure, he went into the carriage area. If he hadn't come to work that day, the accident wouldn't have happened. But, he was performing his job and nobody has proven to the contrary that this is not the way it's performed. And, he was injured by an unknown, unforeseeable event, a runaway carriage. That's what he was injured by.

Did he know when he stepped off that stool that the carriage would engage itself and feed him into that saw? No. No.

Don't put Jack McPhee in the same category as Corinth Machinery Company as to the total cause of this accident. Don't say that he was equally to blame or that he was more to blame for this accident, for that is wrong. That is unjust and it's contrary to the evidence. Don't compare him to the manufacturers. They know the score, they know the hazards and they chose not to do a darn thing about it.

Next, in his argument for damages, Habush forcefully and persuasively impressed upon the jury the loss that McPhee and his family had suffered. Again, he drew close to the jury box, positioning himself so when each juror focused on him, that juror would also see the broken Jack McPhee sitting at the plaintiff's table.

The law allows you to give money damages for the injuries that Jack and Sheri McPhee have sustained. There is no magic formula here. I have no ready answer for you. But I can tell you that there are certain things that you can consider in awarding money damages.

It's not just pain and suffering. Pain and suffering certainly is a big factor, and, goodness knows, he had enough of that. The pain of the accident, the pain of subsequent operations. But I am also talking about Jack lying in the hospital wondering: What am I doing to do? Who's going to take care of my family? Where am I going to work? What do I look like? How is my wife going to react to me? How are my kids going to react to me? What's happened to my body? What's happened to me?

The humiliation, the anxiety. Oh, the pain he can take, and he took it like a champ. I am now suggesting to you this kid is going to continue to live. He is going to continue to have as happy a life with Sheri as he is going to have. He is going to rehabilitate himself. He has more guts than anyone can imagine, and that's good.

But we can evaluate for him what he has lost. He has lost, in some respect, the ability to enjoy life, to run with his kids, to play with his kids, to do things that you and I take for granted.

He has lost the right leg below the knee. He has lost the left leg and his left buttocks. You saw what is left. And he is not asking that he can hire someone to take care of him. He is asking you to some-how measure what is lost in terms of, not just his limbs, but in terms of his whole life, how it's going to affect his ability to earn a living, to go places, to do activities that you and I take for granted, to be a father, to be a husband, to be a lover.

There is no formula. You have got to feel it right here, ladies and gentlemen, and you have got to feel the enormity of this injury. And, you have got to know the importance of this.

May 28, 1965, Jack McPhee was a healthy and whole human being. He went into a situation with optimism, with hope for the future. He wanted to be a sawyer, maybe even a sawmill operator. He did what he was told, and he got his legs cut off for it. And all they had to do was put an inexpensive locking device on the lever.

They had the know-how, the money, the power, everything. Jack McPhee didn't. He had no way of knowing this would happen, no way of anticipating this could happen. It happened because they were negligent, because they didn't follow recommendations and it caused this disaster. And now, we are here today.

This is not revenge; this is not vindictiveness. That is not going to do Jack any good. He doesn't feel that way. This is the law. This is a courtroom. This is a dignified way of doing it.

You should tell them, "Corinth Machinery Company, it would have [been] so easy for you to do this. Why didn't you do it? And now the law [says] you must respond in money damages, and you should so respond. And we shan't let you off the hook." That's what we ask you to do. Nothing more, nothing less.

Habush returned to the plaintiff's table, pumped up and boiling inside, his face grim, his jaw set, his mind racing. It was a tough case, a tough trial, but he felt confident. Despite the judge's ruling against him, he was sure he had gotten through to the jurors. He was satisfied he had given his client all that he could give.

Less than three hours later, the jury came back with a verdict: finding the Corinth Machinery Company 80 percent negligent and McPhee 20 percent negligent, they awarded McPhee $650,000 in damages.

Corinth Machinery appealed to the Seventh U.S. Circuit Court of Appeals, and the verdict was sustained. Bob Habush and Jack McPhee had won, and they had won big.

For three and a half years, up until the trial, McPhee had suffered from post-traumatic stress disorder and "phantom limb" pain. He believed he was somehow at fault for the accident and condemned himself for depriving his wife of a "full-bodied man" and for being unable to support his children. The verdict had erased all that. While the sawmill worker could never be made "full-bodied," he could now live a comfortable life with his family, free from guilt and shame.

"Bob was totally aware that I was blaming myself—subconsciously, not consciously," McPhee said, just months before his death from cancer in October 2012. "So he said to me, 'Would you rather have all the money in the world, or would you rather be pain-free?' And I said, 'Oh, hell, that's not even fair. I'll take pain-free.' So he said, 'This is what the jury gave you,

Jack. It gave you *not guilty.*' And as a result of the not-guilty verdict, that was the end of the PTSD and the phantom pain."

After the trial, McPhee went on to live a productive life into his seventies. He bought a farm and bought and sold land and cattle. And in 1976, he was elected mayor of Prairie du Chien, a river town in southwestern Wisconsin. He served for three years.

"Truth is, the accident gave me more than it took away, and I don't mean in monetary value," he said, looking back. "The status of winning for the right reason—you couldn't take that away. All in all, I personally received a hell of an education out of it. I was represented by an up-front, top-of-the-line attorney, and I understood quickly the difference between offense and defense. For the first time in my life, I was given the opportunity to see how to analyze any given situation and go on the offense, to really kick ass. And that's what Bob did in the trial."

The McPhee trial was featured on the front page of the *Wall Street Journal,* and word of it got around Wisconsin legal circles like a brush fire. From that point on, the cases came in to Habush by the dozens. "It was the trigger to my career," he says.

He claims the case is his favorite. "It always was and always will be," he says. "Why? Because I was young, inexperienced, and it seemed like an impossible case to win. I didn't have a paralegal. I didn't have an investigator. I didn't have support from anyone. Nobody. I did it all myself—my own research, my own paralegaling, my own investigating—and I argued the shit out of the case. I won it on pure talent. It was at that time that I realized I had found my true calling."

CHAPTER THREE

A Fire in the Belly

By 1970, Bob Habush was running the law firm that his father had started. Jesse Habush, following his heart attack, suffered from progressive heart disease and eventually was sidelined from practicing law. Nonetheless, the son made room for his father at the firm, paying him a salary of $150,000—a symbolic and dutiful gesture.

"He would come into the office and read the *Wall Street Journal*; that's about all he would do," says Habush. "Despite our lack of a relationship and my lingering anger toward him, I felt morally obliged to take care of him until he died in 1983. I took care of my mother for ten years as well, while she had Alzheimer's."

Curiously, he also decided to keep his father's name in the firm's title, which in 1970 was changed to Habush, Gillick, Habush, Davis & Murphy to include Larry Gillick from the original firm and two lawyers who were made partners by Habush: Jim Murphy, a former prosecutor, and Howard Davis, Habush's old friend.

"It's inexplicable," Habush admits. "But my father did provide for my law school education. He did help support me financially. It was kind of like a debt. I didn't have to be in love with my creditor, but he was, in my mind, a creditor that I owed. To some extent I thought the name was catchy. Habush Habush had a certain marketing appeal."

Frank Daily, a prominent Milwaukee attorney and longtime friend of Habush, remembers the renaming of the firm. "I think he was driven, in part, by the desire to put his daddy on a pedestal or to provide a different legacy of his father," Daily says. "That's why he maintains Jesse's name in the firm:

Habush Habush. I once said to him, 'Bob, you only need one Habush.' And he said, 'No, my father started the firm.' In his conference room he has a great portrait of Jesse. So he's kept the faith, if you will."

Removing the name would have disgraced his father, something he did not want to do. Yet he consciously and persistently made every effort to surpass his father's professional standing.

"I just wanted to beat him," Habush insists. "From the time I first started at that office, to his death, even to this day, I have never wavered. I have always wanted to be much better than he was so that people would never remember Jesse Habush when they talked about lawyers, they'd remember me. I didn't want to be just a little bit better, I wanted to be a whole lot better. As a result, part of who I am is this competition with my father. Though I can't pinpoint it, it was a great relief to me when I knew I had succeeded."

Propelling his ascent as a rising star was his masterful work on a series of victories in the 1970s, some of which produced record financial awards for his clients and considerable revenue for his firm. Beginning with the successful verdict for injured sawmill worker Jack McPhee, the cases signaled to the legal community that the son of Jesse Habush had arrived.

"In those early years, I instinctively knew that I wasn't going to be able to establish my reputation as the go-to guy unless I took on tough cases," says Habush. "So I wasn't looking for the easy cases."

* * *

On the heels of the McPhee case, Habush sunk his teeth into a civil action against Firestone Tire and Rubber Company, a corporation with deep pockets for legal defense. Referred by a lawyer in Oshkosh, Wisconsin, the case centered on an explosion in a Firestone service shop that sold tires and other automotive goods. One day, a couple of employees at the shop decided to take a break. Clifford Bvocik, twenty-seven, and Jon LeClaire, nineteen, walked into a back storage room that was used as a break room. Bvocik went into an adjacent bathroom while LeClaire pulled out a pack of cigarettes.

In the break room sat a fifty-five-gallon drum that contained methanol, which was sold under the brand name Frigitol and used as an antifreeze.

Figure 1
Father and son
As a young attorney, Bob Habush worked at Jesse Habush's law firm.
Photo credit: Robert Habush

Neither of the two workers had ever handled the Frigitol in the course of their employment. Yet someone at the shop had failed to close the octagon-shaped cap on the top of the drum.

"LeClaire had been smoking a cigarette," Habush says, "and apparently, when he was done smoking, he flicked his cigarette onto the floor near the chemical drum. As bad luck would have it, vapors from the methanol had been seeping out of the drum's open cap."

The cigarette ignited the vapors and the drum exploded, spraying plumes of flaming methanol onto LeClaire and also Bvocik, who was sitting on the bathroom toilet. Rushed to Milwaukee County Hospital, both young men suffered severe third-degree burns, LeClaire on 85 percent of his body, Bvocik on 55 percent. Neither was expected to live.

Among the doctors who treated the burn victims were a plastic surgeon named Sidney Wynn, a clinical professor of plastic and reconstructive surgery at Marquette University, and an internist named Burton Waisbren. At the time, Waisbren was the medical director of the fledgling St. Mary's Regional Burn Center in Milwaukee.

"They developed a procedure that was quite novel," Habush recalls. "They debrided all the destroyed skin so that the victims essentially were without skin over the burned areas. Then they immediately grafted skin from cadavers, which prevented infection to the open tissue. The cadaver skin would last just so long, so the doctors would debride that skin and cover it again and again. In the meantime, they placed the victims in a tank of nitrous oxide, which also prevented infection and soothed the flesh. They went through dozens and dozens of debridement procedures and nitrous oxide washings, making slides and photographs of the whole process. [Bvocik and LeClaire] were in the hospital for three months, and they survived, even though the medical experts didn't think they had any chance. The treatment was written up in medical journals as one of the most exceptional cases of saving burn victims in medical history. It became part of the genesis of St. Mary's Regional Burn Center, which today is one of the top burn units in the country."

Habush studied the case file. It was a workplace accident. Bvocik and LeClaire were covered by workers' compensation insurance and had had a substantial amount of their medical expenses paid. They had received compensation for about 70 percent of their lost income, along with permanent disability awards. The lawyer who had originally handled the workers' comp case wondered whether there were third-party defendants that could be sued to provide reimbursement to the workers' compensation insurance carrier.

Habush had the cooperation of Hardware Mutual Insurance Company, the predecessor to Sentry Insurance, which had paid out several hundred thousand dollars in medical expenses to Bvocik and LeClaire. The insurance carrier's representatives wanted to recover expenses but hadn't filed a lawsuit. Instead, they were betting on Habush to come through for them. This was typical of workers' comp carriers. An insurer would not bring an action for judgment against another insurer.

"I'm looking at the case and thinking the owner of that particular store is probably negligent for placing that container in a break room," Habash recalls. "But I can't sue the employer because a plaintiff's only recourse against his employer is workers' comp. There probably was a coworker who didn't put the cap on the drum, but I can't sue the coworker either. The only thing I can think of is, there should have been a warning label—'Danger! Keep container closed' and 'Use only with adequate ventilation'—especially where it was placed, in a break room. At that time, you had lots of warnings on gasoline cans, for instance, but there weren't any on this methanol drum. I decided the potential damages warranted taking a flyer, so I sued Firestone on the basis of failure to warn."

Habush began amassing reports by public service organizations and trade groups, such as the National Safety Council and the Manufacturing Chemists' Association (now the American Chemistry Council), about classifications of certain substances, including methanol. For example, the Safety Council and the Chemists' Association both classified methanol as a flammable liquid, exceeded in severity of hazard by just 70 other substances out of 1,100.

He then set out to find experts to testify about the uses and combustibility of methanol. A Chicago trial lawyer he knew recommended Phoenix Chemical, a father-and-son company in the South Side area of Chicago. The son, Arthur Krawetz, agreed to work as Habush's expert. "Arthur was a brainy, nerdy guy and very interested in getting involved in forensic stuff,"

Habush says. "He was a chemist, so he could describe methanol and its flammable characteristics."

Habush next contacted Bill Blakey, an expert he had used before. "He was a clone for Orson Welles, an enormous man with a triple chin, but just brilliant. He had once worked for Phillips Petroleum. His basic education was in chemical engineering, but he could criticize the design of any product imaginable. He had a curriculum vitae that had interchangeable parts, and he was magnificent in court, totally untouchable on cross-examination. He would sit in the witness stand, his stomach hanging over the chair, and rest his papers on his stomach. He talked in a very slow and measured pace, almost like he was talking while sleepwalking. It would drive the defense lawyers nuts."

A trial was set in federal court in front of the U.S. district judge Myron Gordon. Habush was up against two of the best defense lawyers in Milwaukee. David Beckwith, the top trial lawyer at Foley & Lardner, represented Firestone. Clifford Kasdorf, another excellent lawyer, represented Olin Mathieson Chemical Corporation, the methanol manufacturer. The jury had to consider liability first; if it found liability, the same jury would be presented the case for damages.

The defense team brought in troops of expert witnesses. Yet throughout the trial, Habush capitalized on blunders made by the defense.

"One of the defense witnesses was very evasive," he recalls. "He'd listen to my question, which usually was worded to require a 'yes' or a 'no' answer in order to keep a tight rein on the witness. But this witness would ignore my question and go off and give a speech. So I'd have the court reporter repeat the question. And then I'd say, 'Do you understand the question?' He'd give me the same answer, the speech. I let it pass and go on to another question. He'd give me the same nonresponsive answer. I'd ask, 'Is there anything wrong with your hearing?' And he'd say, 'No.' I'd say, 'Am I speaking loudly enough for you?' He'd say, 'Yes.' I'd ask the court reporter to read back the question again. He'd behave himself for a couple questions and then another question and the same nonresponsive answer."

Habush finally complained to the judge, asking him to instruct the witness to answer the question, which required only "yes" or "no."

Judge Gordon, who had the temperament of a rattlesnake, looked down at the witness. "Answer the question," he snapped.

But despite the judge's displeasure, the witness continued to duck and dodge.

Judge Gordon had had enough. Following Habush's cross-examination, he glared at the recalcitrant witness. "Sir," he said, "you are the worst witness I've ever had on the stand." This reprimand doubtless scored points for Habush among the jurors.

In the rebuttal of the final argument, Habush tangled with a lawyer representing Olin Mathieson Chemical. A defense attorney named Al Clack came in as a substitute for Clifford Kasdorf, who had to travel outside of the country.

In his final argument, Clack pointed to Clifford Bvocik while speaking to the jury. "You know, Mr. Bvocik was sitting on the toilet when he got burned," he said, a slight grin forming on his face. "The situation he found himself in does have a humorous element."

Habush ripped into him. "Humorous, Mr. Clack? Humorous? Burned over his entire body, including his testicles and penis? Mr. Clack thinks this is funny."

The jury was not amused, and Habush scored another point.

To a large part, the case hinged on the range of combustibility of methanol. Habush used his experts to build the case that methanol vapors had escaped through the open cap of the fifty-five-gallon drum and collected at floor level near the drum's base. "Flammable liquids do not ignite unless there is a proper proportion of oxygen and liquid," Habush explained. "If there's more liquid than oxygen, it's too rich. It will not ignite. If it's too lean—too much air and not enough vapor—it will not ignite. It has to be proportionately perfect. In the Firestone shop, there was vapor leaking out of the top of the drum and into the room, and the proportion was perfect. When the spent cigarette hit the vapor, the vapor ignited, sending flames back into the top of the fifty-five-gallon drum, and kaboom!"

In the trial, Habush referred to classifications by the National Safety Council and the Manufacturing Chemists' Association. "They both recognize that methanol can evaporate in a flammable mixture, that the flammable mixture can be ignited outside of its container, that it will not diffuse immediately upon it. They both recognize that it can go to floor level and that ventilation is required in connection with the fire hazard. They both recognize that the container should be kept closed as to the fire hazard."

Firestone's defense attorney, Dave Beckwith, created a contrary theory, claiming that a cigarette tossed on the floor could not have ignited the methanol vapors. Rather than flicking the cigarette onto the floor, LeClaire must have dropped a match or cigarette directly into the drum, Beckwith argued. In fact, he suggested, the drum seemed to have been used as a giant ashtray by employees of the Firestone store.

To bolster his theory, Beckwith called on Stratton Hammon, a nationally known fire and explosion expert. Hammon replicated an earlier out-of-court experiment he had devised to show that methanol was not as combustible as Habush claimed. Sitting before the judge and jury, he poured three teaspoons of methanol into a small dish. He then lit a cigarette and slowly lowered his face toward the dish. "He bent down with the cigarette in his mouth," Habush remembers. "The jury, of course, is backing up, and the judge says, 'Are you sure you know what you're doing?' And I'm thinking to myself, 'Blow up, blow up, blow up!' Well, he leans down and douses the cigarette in the liquid, and nothing happens. Why? Because the proportion was too rich. Too much liquid in the dish and not enough air to create a combustible vapor."

In his cross-examination, Habush tore into Hammon's experiment, snuffing out the defense team's argument that LeClaire caused the explosion by dropping a match or cigarette into the methanol drum.

Q: As I understand your testimony, in your experiment you were trying to disprove the assertion that the methanol could be ignited by a cigarette?
A: Yes, that is so.
Q: Did you duplicate the temperature of the methanol that existed at the time of the accident ignition?
A: Since I don't know what it was, I couldn't duplicate it.
Q: So, the answer to my question is "no."
A: It's no.
Q: Do you know whether the mixture of methanol vapor and air was the same mixture in your test as on the day of the accident?
A: No, I can't tell you that.

Q: You can't even assure us that the temperature of the ignition source in your test was identical to that on the day of the fire, can you?

A: It was close enough.

Q: My question, sir, was can you tell us if the ignition temperatures were identical, yes or no?

A: No, I can't.

Q: And this test was conducted by you as a hired expert for the defense, isn't that right?

A: Yes, I am consulting for the defense.

Q: And you knew when you started the test that what you wanted to prove was that a cigarette wasn't an adequate ignition source to start methanol, am I correct?

A: Yes.

Q: On the day of the fire, the employee who was smoking didn't know that he might be in contact with escaping methanol vapors, did he?

A: I believe that is his testimony.

Q: The bottom line, sir, is that it's impossible in any test like this to substantially duplicate the conditions of the fire of that night?

A: Yes, that's true.

As Habush expected, the defense made no offer to settle. Near the end of the trial, however, Beckwith indicated that Firestone might be willing to bend. Habush told him he wasn't interested. Kurt Frauen, the attorney representing the workers' compensation carrier, was looking for reimbursement for the victims' claims. He negotiated with Beckwith on an amount and leaned heavily on Habush to settle.

"We came up with a figure of $100,000," Frauen told Habush. "The plaintiffs will get a third, you'll get a third, and the comp carrier will get a third."

"I don't like it. It's not enough." Habush said.

"Bob, you're never going to win this case. It's impossible."

Habush felt good about how the case was proceeding. He didn't like settling after the start of a trial. But he reconsidered the $100,000 offer and agreed to settle.

The next day, Frauen came back to Habush. Inexplicably, Firestone had authorized Beckwith to give no more than $90,000.

"No deal," Habush said. "Stick it up your ass. Let's finish the trial."

In deciding who was liable for the accident, the jury found Firestone to be 90 percent negligent for its failure to warn and found Olin Mathieson 10 percent at fault. Habush had proved that Bvocik and LeClaire had been put in harm's way. It was a satisfying victory. Next up: the trial for damages.

Shortly after the jury found liability, Habush got an unexpected call from Beckwith.

"Hello, Bob," he said. "How much do you want?"

"I don't want anything," said Habush.

"What do you mean? We're prepared to talk settlement."

"I'm not prepared to talk settlement."

"Why not?"

"Because you guys wouldn't make me a decent offer last time. You could have settled it for $100,000. You got cute and tried to screw me, and I resent it. Now you're going to see me try the damages. End of conversation."

The trial was bifurcated, and Habush tried the liability component first. Because the jury issued a guilty verdict, the trial moved into the damages portion. But before the damages trial resumed, Habush wanted to present as evidence dozens of color slides of photographs that had been taken of LeClaire and Bvocik as they endured more than six months of burn treatment. The images were disturbing: blackened skin, charred bones, disfigured limbs. To show the horrific photos, he needed approval from the judge.

"I'd like to show this to the jury," Habush told Judge Gordon.

"Objection," said Beckwith. "They're inflammatory. They're gruesome and they're playing to the passion of the jury."

But the judge allowed the slides as exhibits. "Overruled," he said. "I have smelling salts for the jurors in case they faint."

Standing before the jury box in his final argument in the four-week trial, Habush painted a compelling word picture of his clients' pain and suffering—and an equally compelling picture of a callous Firestone Tire and Rubber Company.

I represent not a large corporation, but people of personal injuries, not businesses. Mr. Beckwith wants you to believe that these two men made a marvelous recovery. They have not. The prognosis is permanent. It is like the brick in this courthouse. But because they had made something out of themselves, Mr. Beckwith asks you now to reward Firestone by diminishing damages. . . .

I'm so proud to represent these men I could bust, because they are two of the gutsiest guys you'll ever see in your lives while sitting on a jury. These injuries are incomparable. One of them is the most seriously burned survivor in history. The other suffered a burn where 60 to 70 percent of victims have died. Mr. Beckwith didn't want to talk about pain and suffering on his closing argument. I don't blame him.

And so, Firestone sends up Mr. Beckwith to try to undo what it has brought upon these two people the rest of their lives. It's your job, however you can do it, to compensate them for it.

The jury came back with a verdict of $642,000 for Bvocik and LeClaire, a monetary award that gave each of the burn victims hope for an improved life.

The win was a huge ego boost for Habush and a high-stakes defeat for Firestone. Following the verdict, Beckwith confided in Habush: "During the trial, I talked to the representative of Firestone's insurer, Lloyd's of London. He was sitting in the back of the courtroom, watching. He said to me, 'Offer that punk lawyer $90,000. He'll jump at it.' And I said, 'I don't think he will.' He said, 'Do it.'"

In the end, the case was lost for Firestone because of an ill-advised $10,000 gamble against Habush.

For Habush himself, it was one of the highest fees he had ever earned, $214,000, far surpassing his father's largest career fee of $40,000. Moreover, coming after the $450,000 award to Jack McPhee, it helped quell the skeptics and further established Bob Habush as a trial lawyer with talent, brains, and a lot of nerve.

"Maybe I got lucky on *McPhee*, but two in a row?" he says. "We got a lot of lawyers talking about it. And again it was a case we were not supposed to win. But we got one across."

❋ ❋ ❋

Habush was on top of the world. With his ability to win big cases fully established, his confidence soared. "Partners today at the firm say to me, 'You wouldn't take that case today, would you?' I say, 'Hell, no!' But back then, I was Marco Polo, I was Christopher Columbus, I was an explorer. Nothing frightened me."

Not long after the victory over Firestone, another high-risk case found its way to his office. A man named Larry Totsky, twenty-four, had been critically injured when his Volkswagen crashed on a freeway in Milwaukee. "I get the case from another lawyer," recalls Habush, "and I look at the facts of the case: He's driving home around midnight. He had been to a tavern. He had too much to drink and had a fight with his wife. He's coming around a curve near the Milwaukee County Zoo interchange and loses control of his Volkswagen Beetle. His car hits the curb, rolls two or three times, and he's ejected from the vehicle because, according to the police, he wasn't wearing his seat belt. He's paralyzed, a quadriplegic.

"I'm thinking, 'Come on, why should I take this? It's a loser on a number of levels.' Larry Totsky, to be charitable, was scraggly. He liked to go out at night and drink. He and his wife, Patty, didn't have a great marriage. Why in the world would I even think there was a case here?"

Habush recalls visiting Totsky at the rehabilitation hospital where he was staying. "He's in rough shape. The roof of his car had collapsed, breaking his neck. I sit down, and we talk for a while. 'I couldn't steer, I couldn't steer,' he tells me. 'The last thing I remember was the snapping of my neck.' I looked at the police report and, wouldn't you know, he had told the police officers at the scene and in the ER the same thing: he couldn't steer the car. I decide to take the case, thinking maybe there's something here after all."

Habush got permission from the court to examine what was left of the 1970 Volkswagen Beetle, which had ended up at a salvage yard in Iowa. Because Totsky claimed he couldn't steer the car, Habush started with its gearbox. He called on several experts, including Archie Easton, an expert on auto crashes and a professor of mechanical engineering at the University of Wisconsin; the design engineer, Bill Blakey, whom he had used in the Firestone case; and Stan Weiss, a metallurgist from the University of Wisconsin–Milwaukee.

Removing the metal cover to the gearbox, Easton, Blakey, and Weiss made a remarkable discovery. Mixed in with the grease and muck, they found a chunk of solid material about the size of a cherry and hard as a rock. When placed under an electron microscope, the chunk exhibited the same elements as concrete, including magnesium and calcium.

"Bob, there's concrete in this steering gearbox," Blakey said.

Habush was incredulous. "Come on. Is there any way it could have gotten lodged in the gears?"

The engineers examined the gears under the same electron microscope. They saw cracks in the surface of the gears, and inside the cracks were tiny particles of the same elements of concrete found in the cherry-size chunk.

"Our theory was this: when Totsky couldn't steer his car, it was because bits of concrete that had been dormant in the gearbox suddenly impeded the gears and locked the steering wheel in place," Habush explains. "So my case was, somewhere in Volkswagen's manufacturing plant, concrete got into the steering gearbox and jammed the steering mechanism while Totsky was going around that freeway curve."

But how could he prove it?

Habush figured he needed to learn everything he could about the assembly plant in Germany where the car had been built. He subpoenaed key witnesses from the factory and deposed them in his Milwaukee office, including the engineer from the assembly line where the gearbox was built. "The depositions showed that the gearboxes were open on the line until the very last step," Habush says. "The gears were installed, the grease was put in, and along it went down the line until lastly the cover was put on."

In the depositions, Habush questioned the German witnesses about the assembly facility itself: When was it built? What was its square footage? How was the assembly line laid out?

"What about the ceiling?" he asked. "Do you know what the ceiling was made of?"

"Yes. Concrete," one of the witnesses replied.

And suddenly Habush had the smoking gun.

"I had no idea what the hell was on that ceiling," Habush recalls. "If the guy would have said it was made out of wood, I would have been screwed. So there was a big gamble there. But from that moment on, my argument was there was an opportune time for a piece of concrete to drop from the

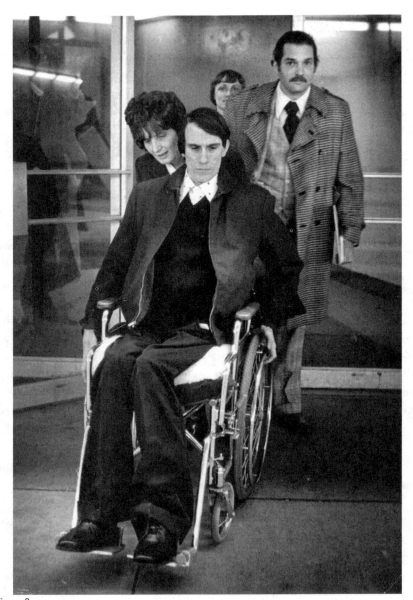

Figure 2
Crash victim
Larry Totsky was left paralyzed when the gearbox in his Volkswagen froze up and he lost control of his car.
Photo credit: *Milwaukee Journal*, with permission

ceiling into the uncovered steering box. When he answered, 'concrete,' my case was made."

The German automaker, though, had no plans to roll over. "Volkswagen went nuts," Habush says. "They couldn't accept my 'preposterous' theory. There was no way they were going to pay on this case. Totsky's a quadriplegic. He's got a few hundred thousand dollars of medicals and big damages. He can't work anymore. He's got to have full-time help to take care of him. So Volkswagen threw everything in the world at me. They brought in the best experts on automobile crashworthiness—Donald Huelke from the University of Michigan, Derwin Severy from the University of California—expert witnesses who had testified in hundreds of cases for car manufacturers and were schooled in testimony."

Both sides prepared for trial before the Milwaukee County judge David Jennings. Volkswagen dispatched its general counsel from New York and hired the Milwaukee attorney Edmund "Ned" Powell for its defense.

Among Habush's legal team, there were doubts about how the plaintiff would be viewed by jurors. "You can't go to trial with this guy," said his associates as they evaluated Totsky one day. "He's homely; he dropped out of high school in the tenth grade. He's just not a very likable character. The jury will hate him."

"Hold on, folks," Habush said, fending off a mutiny. "Just because *we* don't like him, don't assume the average gal and guy on the street is going to dislike him. They're not going to a party with Larry Totsky. They're not going to engage with him one-on-one. He'll do fine."

Reflecting today on how lawyers relate to jurors, Habush looks through a lens of fifty years of trial work. "Lawyers approach things much more critically, more cynically. Trial lawyers can make the terrible mistake of thinking jurors are going to evaluate their clients in the same way they've evaluated them. Jurors come from a whole different mind-set. They don't know the plaintiff as well as his or her lawyer."

Early on, he developed a subtle yet compelling style of persuasion before juries, based unwittingly on his experiences relating to the "everyman" mind-set of people he knew when he was young.

"In my youth, I worked on construction every summer. I was a mason laborer. I dug ditches. I worked with some pretty tough guys. These were not piano players, and I loved being around them. I could go out and have a beer with these guys. We could sit and have lunch.

"One summer I worked in a factory, the Continental Can Company. I would feed sheets of metal into a machine, and they would be rolled into cans. I had hundreds of cuts on my hands from lifting the metal sheets.

"When I wasn't working in the summer, I had a job selling shoes. I always worked, and that made me feel good. I was surrounded by people not of my economic status and education level, who did not have the opportunities I had. But I never felt it was demeaning. I never felt I was better than them. If anything, it gave me the foundation for dealing with juries and clients. This was part of my development, where I developed an empathy for the average guy."

To this end, he also learned how to approach jurors in a way that would demand their attention and win their confidence. "When I try a case, I get close to the jury—real close," he explains. "I stand at the rail and zero in on each of them, making eye contact one-by-one. Defense attorneys can't stand it. It drives them crazy. I remember during one trial, the defense attorney asked the judge to reprimand me because he said I was looking at the jury too often. Ridiculous. It's so ingrained in me that I can't *not* do it. So I kept on looking at the jury. The judge exploded. 'Mr. Habush!' he hollered. 'If you persist at staring at the jurors, I will cite you for contempt of court.'

"I was outraged. There are rules prohibiting counsel from talking, winking, or waving at jurors. But there is *no* prohibition against staring. Nevertheless, I smiled to the judge and obliged. I spun my chair around and, with my back to the jury, proceeded with my representation. The jury sided with my client in that case, by the way."

Susan Steingass, a former Dane County judge and onetime partner at Habush's Madison office, says jurors are influenced by his genuine and down-to-earth manner. "He can talk to a jury because he's a real person inside and he can communicate in a way that is clear and understandable," she says. "A lot of lawyers seem to communicate as if they were in a room of other lawyers. He's a real person who can really communicate in a straightforward and direct way. That's in addition to his excellent trial skills. The Bob Habush cross-examinations are pretty famous. You don't want to be on the other side of one if you can help it."

During the Totsky trial, more than five hundred exhibits were presented, including the front end and gearbox of Totsky's 1970 Beetle. A total of forty-eight witnesses were called by the two sides. In his cross-examinations of Volkswagen's witnesses, Habush frequently had the upper hand, systematically dismantling their conclusions and undermining their expertise. In one cross-examination, he tore into the credibility of a VW expert who had previously testified about the properties of concrete.

> Q: Had you ever done any testing on concrete before this case?
> A: Not concrete as such, but I have identified it in particular matter.
> Q: My question is, have you ever done any testing on concrete before this case?
> A: No.
> Q: Am I correct, sir, do you remember that you had never looked at trihydrate or magnesium carbonate [two elements found in concrete] in your entire career?
> A: Yes.

At another point, he exposed Derwyn Severy as a hired gun for Volkswagen. Severy betrayed his obvious pro-automaker bias in the courtroom exchange:

> Q: I believe you stated on direct examination that when asked by Mr. Powell [the defense counsel] the number of cases that you have been consulted on by automobile manufacturers, the answer was several hundred. Am I correct?
> A: Yes, I believe so, within the last 24 years.
> Q: And of that several hundred cases that you have worked for automobile manufacturers, for how many of those would you say you worked for Volkswagen?
> A: I have been contacted on about 80 cases and have worked about 40.
> Q: In addition to the other cases that you have worked for Volkswagen, did that involve cases in which they were being sued?
> A: Yes.
> Q: How many times have you appeared in court testifying on behalf of Volkswagen prior to this case?

A: I think probably 15 times is an estimate.

Q: How many times have you appeared before a court commissioner giving depositions on cases, in addition to that number where you testified in court on behalf of Volkswagen?

A: I would think probably between 20 and 30 as an estimate, sir.

Q: How many cases do you have presently pending currently where you're consulting for Volkswagen.

A: I estimate between 6 and 10 cases, sir.

Q: Between 1950 and 1970, while you were still at the University of California, Mr. Severy, did you receive a grant from the Domestic Auto Industry for approximately $200,000?

A: I don't think so, sir. I can think of a $50,000 grant, plus cars.

Q: Do you remember the deposition that you gave before a court commissioner on the 22nd day of November?

A: Yes, but you're talking about a single grant.

Q: My question was, do you remember the deposition?

A: Sure I remember, sir.

Q: Your Honor, I will read my question to Mr. Severy and his answer from the November 22 deposition:

"Q: During the period of 1950 to 1970, how much money was provided by the Domestic Automobile Manufacturers for your study?

"A: It wasn't very much. It was probably $200,000."

When he stood to deliver the first portion of his final argument, Habush took to task the "caravan" of witnesses who had testified on behalf of Volkswagen, excoriating them for losing evidence and for blatantly taking tens of thousands of dollars in fees from the auto industry for conducting faulty experiments and giving impeachable testimony. Then, without pretense or bluster, he explained to the jury why lawsuits such as Totsky's preserve the safety of consumers:

The history of product liability is a very interesting one. It started off with the theory "let the buyer beware." The buyer assumed the risk. And we then moved into a state of law where if you could prove negligence—that the product was defective and you could show that the manufacturer failed to exercise ordinary care or was at fault—you then could recover against a manufacturer. This was often times a very difficult task. So the ultimate consumer protection was passed and that is the law that we're applying to this case. It is called "strict liability." In strict liability, a manufacturer has a duty not to place into the market a defective product that is unreasonably dangerous to the user. Even though this manufacturer may have exercised all possible care in the manufacture of this product, if it's found to be defective when it left the plant, if it's found not to have received alterations, if it is being used as it was intended to be used, the manufacturer is deemed by the law to be negligent. And this is the ultimate in consumer protection.

What this law says to you, the public, is, it recognizes the products you get into your hands that are in a defective condition, even though it never happened before. If the circumstances are such that at one point in time one person is hurt by one defective product, the responsibility must rest at the feet of the manufacturer who put their product into the marketplace. They must bear the cost to the consumer.

When persuading the jury to award monetary damages to his client, Habush put a fine edge on how Larry Totsky had been brought back from the brink of death only to suffer physical and emotional trauma and the prospect of living the remainder of his life as an invalid. The closing argument epitomized the power and passion of courtroom oration, and it was later highlighted in Russ Herman's law school text *Courtroom Persuasion: Winning with Art, Drama, and Science.*

Larry Totsky is a quadriplegic. He cannot walk nor will he ever walk. He cannot sit erect because his trunk muscles do not function nor will he ever sit erect. He can use his arms but he has lost the dexterity in his hands. He has lost his bladder control and function. He will always have no bowel control. It will always be necessary to make a bowel movement by either the use of a suppository or a stimulation of a finger. He will always have the inability to sense pain. This may seem like a blessing, except that there's one problem—he will never be able to feel when he has to go to the bathroom. He never will be able to feel when he has an infection in his bladder or in his kidneys. He will never be able to feel when he knocks his legs up against a door and causes an injury. He will never be able to feel when he has developed an ulceration. He constantly has the threat of infection in his kidneys and a common ordinary cold will be a threat to him because of his lack of breathing ability due to the lack of trunk muscles.

He has lost, ladies and gentlemen, normal sexual gratification. That means different things to men and to women. But he has lost the ability to have an erection in the normal way other than just muscle and involuntary contraction. He has lost the ability to have a climax or ejaculation. He has lost the ability to assume a role in the sex act other than a submissive one. He has lost, in all probability, the ability to father another child.

Psychologically, he is now a totally dependent man as compared to what he was before. He has lost his economic importance, at least up to this date. He is uncertain about his future. He has lost his ability to stand like a man, like he had been, and I think he worries about his loss of manhood.

What does it mean to a man to have your wife put your clothes on for you?

What does it mean to a man who has trouble tying his shoes?

What does it mean to have that tube attached to your bladder and cleaned every day by your wife?

What does it mean, the simple hygienic task like washing, when it becomes a major physical exertion?

What does it mean not to be able to make a bowel movement, and what does it mean and how humiliating is it to have your wife with a rubber glove clean your rectum when the bowel gets stuck?

What does it mean to be confronted with episodes of dizziness, nausea, and sweating?

What does it mean to have to change positions every two hours for the rest of your life?

He can't stand and he can't even sit. What does it mean to look at your lifeless legs and see them jumping up and down in spasms and not being able to control them?

But more than that, what does it mean to him as a man, what does it mean not to be able to provide for your wife and your children economically? Is he no longer the man of the house? Is he no longer his wife's lover? Is that something that he is to concern himself with the rest of his life? And I'm sure Larry wonders will he ever work? Who will hire him? Can he keep a job? And, finally, will that angel always be there to take care of him?

We take so much for granted. What does it mean just to stand up and stretch? What does it mean to walk, to run, to take pride in a job, to be able to roll on the floor with a little child? To take a walk with your wife? To walk down the aisle in the future with your daughter? To hug and dance and enjoy yourself?

Ladies and gentlemen, this man has lost all of these things that you and I just don't even think about. He is a prisoner in that wheelchair for the rest of his life.

You have to evaluate human suffering in dollars and cents. It is a difficult task. But it is one you are compelled to render. Unsuspecting to him and to his family, this man—in Volkswagen's defective product—was cut down in the prime of life. It is up to you to speak to the truth, whatever that may be.

On January 17, 1975, the jury handed down a verdict of $1,860,995 to the plaintiff Larry Totsky, the largest personal injury award in the history of Wisconsin's state courts. It found Totsky 25 percent negligent, siding with the defense's argument that he had not been wearing his seat belt, and reduced the verdict to $1,328,246 for Totsky and $90,000 for his wife, Patricia.

If Habush's peers had been seeing him as just a flash in the pan or some "punk lawyer," this case quickly corrected that misperception. It catapulted him into the big leagues. From that point on, he was regarded by plaintiff and defense attorneys alike as one of the top trial lawyers in Wisconsin.

"Bob remains the best plaintiffs trial lawyer that I've ever tried a case against," says Frank Daily, who, as founder of the product liability defense practice at Milwaukee's Quarles and Brady, has represented manufacturers of chemicals, pharmaceuticals, construction equipment, automobiles, forklifts, motorcycles, and various other consumer products across the country. "And I've faced some of the best plaintiff's lawyers in the United States. He's clearly in the top echelon. I don't think you could say anybody's more tenacious than Bob."

But Volkswagen was not going down easy. Months after the trial, the automaker's attorney filed a motion to reopen the case. Volkswagen believed Larry Totsky had lied during testimony.

"I was on vacation in Hawaii and my partner, Howie Davis, wakes me up at two o'clock in the morning. 'Bob, I got bad news,' he tells me. 'The Supreme Court just ordered the Totsky case back for a rehearing.' 'What? On what basis?' I ask him. 'On the basis of Totsky committing perjury when he testified.'"

Volkswagen's defense lawyer had filed an affidavit from a friend of Totsky's who claimed Totsky had told him he had trouble steering the vehicle a year or so prior to the accident. Habush cut short his vacation and returned to Milwaukee to read the affidavit and talk to Totsky.

"Yes, he's a friend of mine," Totsky told him. "After the verdict, he came and asked me to give him money or he was going to overturn the lawsuit. I told him no."

The friend evidently then contacted the defense lawyer, telling him he had information that could help reverse the verdict. The lawyer had the friend sign an affidavit and put him up at a local hotel.

"Well, what to do?" says Habush. "We're scheduled to have a rehearing in front of Judge Jennings on whether to set aside the verdict on the grounds of perjury, and, of course, it stinks me up, too, because whenever a lawyer puts a witness on the stand and the witness is accused of perjury, the lawyer is suspected [of putting] him up to it."

Habush had an idea. He would outflank the defense attorney. He hired a private investigator to rent a room in the hotel where Totsky's so-called friend lived. "Make friends with him," he told the investigator. "See if we can find anything that would impeach him."

The investigator soon ingratiated himself with Totsky's friend, and they became drinking buddies. On one night out, the friend tipped his hand, saying he had contacted the defense attorney and made up a story about Totsky. He told the investigator that the attorney had offered to pay him $500, along with room and board, if he would sign an affidavit. The investigator was wearing a wire and recording the entire conversation.

"We now have the hearing before Judge Jennings," Habush says. "I put the lawyer on the stand and just impeached the shit out of him with that tape-recorded statement. The perjury claim went down in flames. I could never prove that the attorney *knew* the friend of Totsky's was making it up, but he didn't do anything to ascertain whether it was true or not. He was so excited about overturning this verdict that he didn't do the due diligence that other lawyers might have done. Jennings threw out the claim, and Volkswagen ultimately paid the verdict. But it was another reason for the attorney to hate me." The ill will would haunt Habush years later.

The mid-1970s was a time of growth for Habush professionally and for his law firm. He hired three additional attorneys and an investigator. But in the midst of tallying up two substantial victories, he found his personal life had become complicated. "It was a very difficult period of time," he says. "My wife and I had separated. I also was attempting to run a business venture, an auto insurance company that was struggling during the Carter inflation years. How I was able to keep a clear head and successfully try those two big cases is still amazing to me."

Habush overcame what he calls his "midlife crisis."

"Thankfully, my wife and I reconciled and have lived happily ever after. I was able to sell the insurance company but took a sizable loss financially and kick in the ass ego-wise. But it taught me to stick with what you're good at and what you know, and not venture into areas where you have no business experience."

Another high-profile case would come his way in 1977, a case that would unleash his signature skills and talents—his unbending tenacity, his meticulous preparation, and his practiced art of persuasion.

* * *

On a December night in 1972, newlyweds Leonard (Len) and Julie Retzloff were driving down a county highway near Menomonie, Wisconsin, a small college town an hour east of the Minnesota border. Len, 19, was at the wheel of their 1962 Plymouth Belvedere. Julie, his 18-year-old bride of three months, sat at his side, her body leaning into his.

The road was icy and a light mist fell. As Len slowed to make a turn, an oncoming car veered over the centerline and struck the Belvedere head-on.

Sitting in the middle of the wide bench seat, Julie had no seat belt around her waist to hold her in place. Upon impact, her chin struck the vinyl dashboard and then her head bounced into the metal rearview mirror above. The mirror, fixed rigidly to the top of the windshield frame, conformed around her head, and the small ball on which it pivoted fractured her skull, causing brain damage. She lapsed into a semi-comatose condition.

Three years and $58,000 in medical expenses later, a Madison attorney asked Habush to consider a lawsuit against the maker of the Retzloffs' car, the Chrysler Corporation. "I was asked to investigate whether there was a product liability case," Habush remembers. "This was following the verdict against Volkswagen, during this era that I was considered an expert in product liability cases. So I read the file and thought, 'This is a simple auto accident.' It wouldn't be worth suing the [other] driver, because he didn't have the resources to cover Julie's pain and suffering, much less the care she would require for the rest of her life. But how would I make a case against Chrysler? Where's the case?"

He pondered the question, and it occurred to him that since the mirror was the instrument that had caused Julie Retzloff's injury, perhaps it was somehow defective. Following his hunch, he called in his recently hired investigator, Terry Tadysak, a former police officer and investigator with the Milwaukee County DA's office. Tadysak had worked only one previous case with Habush, but his skills would become a cornerstone of the firm's exceptional discovery work.

"I told Terry I wanted him to go to the junkyards around Wisconsin. 'Find me as many Plymouth Belvederes and other Chryslers as you can of that vintage, OK? See if you come up with a rearview mirror that was made with a flex to it so it would push away if anything struck it.' Well, he came up with at least a dozen various cars of that same vintage that had a mirror with a double ball joint that moved inward when struck."

The assignment was a memorable one for the new employee. "Bob had me collect these mirrors from all over creation," recalls Tadysak. "I'll tell you, I got stung by more yellow jackets, wasps, and hornets, crawling in and out of vehicles, taking out rearview mirrors. But he refused to accept

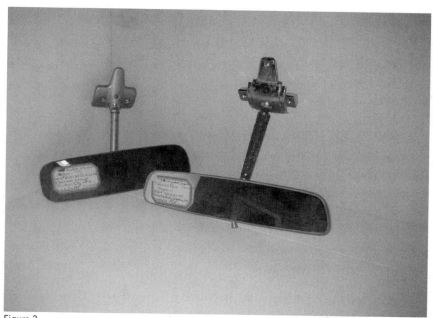

Figure 3
A better mirror
Use of these safer double-ball jointed mirrors would have prevented Julie Retzloff's injuries.
Photo credit: Robert Habush

that nobody was making these things safer. It was unimaginable to him that Chrysler would make this car unsafe. He was a strong proponent of things such as padded dashboards and recessed buttons. Even as a lawyer, he was thinking in terms of technology and safety improvement, much like Ralph Nader advocated for seat belts and air bags.

"So Bob had me go through junkyards all over half the state of Wisconsin, collecting rearview mirrors. And he was right. I found a host of vehicles that had double ball joint mirrors. The gold mine was that the expensive Chryslers—New Yorkers, Imperials, the top-of-the-line Chryslers that only very wealthy people could afford—all had double ball joint mirrors."

Habush filed a lawsuit on Julie Retzloff's behalf, claiming that Chrysler was negligent in designing an interior rearview mirror that did not flex or break away upon impact. In his civil action, he would show not only that it was possible to develop a safer rearview mirror but that Chrysler had, in fact, made one for its high-end, expensive automobiles. Essentially, safety was commensurate with economic status and income level. Rich people would buy safety, but the average person on the street got shortchanged.

Habush instructed Tadysak to assemble a giant display board to exhibit each double ball joint mirror along with the manufacturer's name, year of the vehicle, and VIN (vehicle identification number).

"Bob challenged Chrysler," says Tadysak, now the chief investigator at Habush's firm. "He contended that Chrysler, at the time they made that car, should have known that an unyielding mirror served as a hazard to occupants in a vehicle. This is at a time when product liability claims were essentially unheard of. It was almost unspeakable that a lawyer would even have the audacity to file a lawsuit against a major manufacturer and claim that they were negligent in making a product that caused injury. So here's Bob, a Milwaukee, Wisconsin, lawyer, trying this case in the town of Menomonie, Wisconsin, against this major manufacturer, Chrysler."

The trial was scheduled to be heard by the Dunn County judge John Bartholomew. Media coverage was extensive. "Julie Retzloff had been a cheerleader, a very beautiful young woman, very popular," Habush says. "When the case hit the newspapers, it became a subject of great interest to the townspeople. When the trial started, the courtroom was filled every day, and the local radio station broadcast from the courtroom."

Jury selection was out of the ordinary. Fifteen prospective jurors were excused by Judge Bartholomew, and another eight were preempted by the attorneys. Nearly all were men, many of them farmers who said they were harvesting their crops. As a result, an all-female jury was picked, made up of housewives, nurses' aides, a tavern owner, and a secretary. "With few exceptions, I will always prefer women jurors over men," says Habush. "Women are inherently more empathetic, sympathetic, and they view themselves as a minority, as not having pure equal rights."

The defense would argue that the driver of the striking vehicle was negligent and cast blame as well on Julie Retzloff for not wearing a seat belt. Habush would go after Chrysler for making a defective and dangerous product.

"I took depositions of Chrysler engineers," says Habush, "and of course they denied that there was anything wrong, claiming their rearview mirrors were state-of-the-art and that they were what every other car manufacturer had installed in their cars."

Habush knocked down the argument by calling his own experts, who criticized Chrysler for not installing safer mirrors. "Inexcusable," said one, an accident reconstruction engineer. "There's no reason why the Retzloff vehicle did not have the [double ball joint] mirror."

Armed with the impressive exhibit board and a trove of revealing depositions, Habush went to work, deftly impeaching the expertise of the defense's witnesses through cross-examinations and gutting Chrysler's insistence that its rearview mirror was not unsafe.

As in past cases he had tried, the trial once or twice took on the appearance of a contact sport, played out for the benefit of the jury. "Chrysler was represented by a lawyer named John Wilcox. He was from a well-known lawyer family in Eau Claire and one of the preeminent defense lawyers in Wisconsin. He graduated from Harvard Law School and wore a vest and a Phi Beta Kappa key under his pocket. Not exactly warm and huggable.

"I remember one time I was presenting evidence to the jury, very close-up. What I'd do is take an exhibit and stand in front of the jury. And then I'd have the expert come off the witness stand, with the permission of the court, and he and I would hold the exhibit, and I'd have him testify. I'd have him move from one end of the jury to the opposite end so all the jurors could see it. So I got two shots at presenting the evidence. I've done that my entire career. It's a great technique.

"I was standing right in front of the jury. Wilcox couldn't see what I was up to, so he sat down on the floor in front of the jury railing with his yellow pad, between the jury box and me. It really irritated me. I wanted to get him the hell away from my jury. So as I made one of my sweeps toward the other end of the jury box, I not-so-inadvertently stepped on his hand and his fountain pen. He yelped. Screamed out loud. 'Judge, he stepped on my hand!' And the judge said to him, 'Well, get off the floor, John.'"

Habush was primed for battle. In one particularly dexterous cross-examination, he destroyed the credibility of a Chrysler engineer, a liaison expert who fed information to the defense counsel. The engineer was asked to clarify the answers he had given to interrogatories that Habush had prepared—answers that in many respects were untrue and impeachable.

(Using interrogatories to produce and verify company information is no small task, due to the veil of secrecy that often surrounds corporations.) On the witness stand during the trial, the engineer did his level best to circumvent Habush's questions. But Habush never let him off the hook, referring back to the engineer's previous answers to lay bare damning inconsistencies and contradictions.

Habush earlier had questioned whether Chrysler manufactured or sold vehicles with a rearview mirror that "yielded in two directions"; in other words, a mirror with a double ball joint. Chrysler's engineer had responded in an interrogatory that all 1957 and in 1967 passenger car models included double ball joint mirrors. He later retracted that statement when deposed, saying his original response was based on "bad information." No such mirrors were installed prior to 1962, although some models installed double ball mirrors on the dashboard, he said, revising his answer.

In a cross-examination, the engineer clung stubbornly to the claim that the double ball joint in the mirror was not to provide passenger safety but to provide greater flexibility when adjusting the mirror for visibility. Habush took issue with this.

Q: That is not true, is it?
A: Yes, it is true.
Q: The fact of the matter is, sir, you didn't give us every reason that a double ball-joint mirror is installed on a Chrysler car, did you?
A: We gave you every reason that it was installed and those were used in those years, yes.
Q: Let me show you, sir, something from your own document, 1960, the Consumer's Guide to Safety Features in Chrysler cars.
A: Yes.
Q: Does that show a picture in the middle here of a double ball-joint mirror mounted on the dash?
A: Yes, it does.
Q: And under it, it gives two reasons there, doesn't it, sir, why it's installed. Does that not say "The rearview mirror moves aside for safety." Is that right?

A: That's what it says.

Q: It goes on to say, upon passenger impact it allows the mirror and the mounting to squirm out of the way. Now would you consider that a safety reason, sir?

A: I would say it's not necessarily a safety feature under all conditions.

Q: Maybe we better tell the people who put out this guide. Look right down here on the last page of that document. Why don't you read to the jury what it says.

A: "Safety features standard on most Chrysler cars."

Q: What does it describe as one of the safety features standard on most Chrysler cars?

A: "Double ball-joint mirror mount."

Q: Yes. Read that to the jury.

A: "On the inside, mirror reduces likelihood of any injury in an accident because of its flexible nature."

Habush went in for the kill, reminding the engineer again of questions he had answered in a recent deposition and producing inculpating evidence that the engineer did not know Habush had in his possession:

Q: There have been other occasions where you kept information from us too, has there not?

A: Never intentionally.

Q: Is that right? Let me read you a question from your deposition that was taken on September 23, 1977.

"Q. Are you able to tell me which models of car produced by Chrysler in 1962 had double ball mirrors?"

"A. No, not without records."

Q: Do you remember those questions and answers?

A: Do I remember that? Yes.

Q: That wasn't true, was it? As a matter of fact, on that very day you sat at that very deposition, you sat with this piece of paper in your pocket, didn't you?

A: Yes. I did.

Q: Why don't you describe to the jury what that is?

A: I made this sheet for myself to indicate those times when we had double ball-joint mirrors on different models of cars.

Q: Well, you made it for yourself, but your lawyer told us that on the way to the airport you discovered you had made an error in your testimony when you indicated the first mounting of a double ball-joint mirror into the header in a Chrysler car was a 1961 Chrysler sedan. You will see from the enclosed chart, which you had prepared but didn't refer [to] in the course of your testimony, that the Chrysler Imperial started to use a double ball-joint mirror in 1960. . . . Is that correct?

A: That's right.

Q: So when you were asked at the time of the Deposition, "What was the first year that you had double ball-joint mirrors?" you could have just pulled this piece of paper out of your pocket and answered right from there, couldn't you?

A: I could have, yes.

Q: But you didn't, did you? Did you?

A: I didn't, no.

Damaged by the impeachment of its witnesses, Chrysler's defense counsel had also made an issue of Julie Retzloff's physical and neurological condition. They produced experts who maintained she was unaware of any activity around her. The intent was to show that her life expectancy was short, and thus the award for damages should be minimal.

Retzloff's family, on the other hand, claimed she was in a "locked-in" state and could respond to outside stimuli with tears, facial movements, and the like.

"I had a neurosurgeon who I had used before on a couple malpractice cases," Habush says. "He agreed to examine Julie, and he testified that inside this comatose young woman was a live person who knew what was going on. We had nurses testify that she cried when her mother didn't show up and she cried when her mother left and she showed some degree of following movement with her eyes."

In the trial, Habush likened Retzloff to a woman locked in a coffin. "Julie Retzloff is not being kept alive on a machine," he told the jury. "She senses, she knows, she feels, she tries to communicate. . . . Can you imagine the torture?"

The defense, meanwhile, brought in its own neurologist. In testimony, says Habush, "the doctor described Julie as totally and permanently brain damaged, nothing more than 'a primitive animal.' I wasn't going to let that stand."

At a deposition, the doctor said he had determined that Julie was in a deep coma and didn't know what was going on around her. He purported to be an expert on comatose patients, and claimed he had written a scientific article on comas. Habush was unconvinced. "I had an associate go to the UW medical school library in Madison to get a copy of the neurologist's article on comas," he says. "In what's called the *Index Medicus*, he looked for a listing of this article. No article. He never wrote the article. So we're at trial and I have a stack of *Index Medicus* volumes in front of me, along with affidavits from librarians."

With the neurologist on the witness stand, Habush set the trap.

"Doctor," he said, "how often do you treat people in comas?"

"You don't treat them, you basically put them away."

"And what are your qualifications for treating someone who is in a coma?"

"I've treated people in coma states and have written an article about comatose patients."

"Let's talk about this article. Was it published in a medical journal?"

"Absolutely."

"Now, Doctor, have you heard of a book called the *Index Medicus*?" said Habush, holding up a volume.

The doctor's eyes narrowed. "Yes . . . I've heard of it."

"Am I correct that this book contains all the scientific articles written by doctors, whether in their residency or not?"

"Yes, that's so," the neurologist answered haltingly.

"Well," Habush said, dropping the book on the table in front of the doctor. "We've looked through all the volumes of the index, and I can't find your article anywhere."

"It must be a mistake."

"It isn't in there, Doctor, because you never wrote it."

Habush marked the *Index Medicus* as an exhibit. "Doctor, I have no further questions."

Disgraced, the neurologist stepped down from the witness stand and looked around the crowded room for an open seat. He saw one in the center of a row and asked the spectators if he could sit. "Excuse me," he said. "Excuse me, I'd like that seat." But everyone ignored him and stared straight ahead. No one would stand to let him in. Finally, with the jury watching, he shrugged his shoulders and walked out of the courtroom.

The neurologist's credibility had vanished. "I do not deal well with people that lie," says Habush. "Fortunately, I have the tools with which to expose them. Cross-examination exposes lies."

Habush had Chrysler on the ropes. "Chrysler started getting worried and started making offers to me, but the offer was a structured settlement annuity where Chrysler would pay so much for life. For life? When her life expectancy was, like, five minutes? So it meant nothing. It sounded great: $4,000 a week, $16,000 a month—but for life? It had no guarantee in it."

The guardian *ad litem* appointed by the court to protect Julie Retzloff's interests urged Habush to accept the offer.

"You've got to take it, Bob, take the settlement," he said, sitting at the plaintiff's table.

"Don't be ridiculous; it's for life," Habush replied. "I'm not going to even consider it."

Chrysler increased the amount, day by day, from $2,000 a week to $3,000 and then to $4,000. With each offer, the guardian hounded Habush to make the deal.

One day in the courtroom Habush finally lost his patience.

"Bob, take the settlement, take the settlement," the guardian said.

"Listen," Habush growled, just out of range of the jury. "If you say that to me once more, I'm gonna break your goddamn jaw!"

The guardian was stunned and asked to see the judge in chambers.

Judge Bartholomew directed the two men into his office. "All right, what's the problem?" he asked the guardian.

"I've been trying to get Mr. Habush to accept this settlement from Chrysler, and he told me that if I said it once more he'd break my jaw."

The judge looked at Habush. "Well, Mr. Habush, did you say that to him?"

"Yes, sir, I did."

The judge returned his gaze to the guardian. "Then don't say that to him anymore."

In his final argument, Habush aimed squarely at the Chrysler Corporation, undeterred by the company's might and influence as one of the largest manufacturers in the world. In fact, as he addressed the jury, he framed Julie Retzloff's lawsuit as something of a David versus Goliath battle—an innocent and vulnerable plaintiff against a gargantuan and seemingly unassailable corporation:

This is a products liability case, a consumer liability case. You twelve jurors are consumers and as consumers you can hold a manufacturer accountable, if you find from the evidence that they have not designed a product for your use that should have been designed safely. It isn't necessary, in other words, that you all be engineers. It's only necessary that you, as lay jurors, have been presented evidence, understandable evidence, which will allow you to hold a manufacturer accountable in this courtroom. Members of the jury, the greatest and smallest are the same. The greatest corporations in the land and the smallest and poorest person are the same in this courtroom, and you can judge them both equally.

On December 17, 1972, a bright, effervescent young girl of 18 years old, while riding with her husband, was involved in an automobile accident that she should have been able to walk away from. And she didn't, because of the negligence of the Chrysler Corporation.

What caused the brain damage to this girl? We contend quite simply it was this mirror, the inflexible mirror that couldn't move on impact, that was attached to the top of the windshield, like a weapon sticking out of that car in an area that Chrysler invited people to sit, in an area that provided no seat belts for those people.

I suggest to you that the automobile manufacturers—Ford, American Motors, Packard, Studebaker, and even the Chrysler cars, the 1961 Dodge Lancer, the 1961 Plymouth Valiant, the 1961 Chrysler Imperial—had the deflecting mirror in them. What was so good about the Imperial that the poor little Belvedere couldn't have a mirror like Chrysler put in their Imperial?

The all-female jury came back with a verdict of $1.5 million, one of the largest ever at the time in western Wisconsin. It found Chrysler 89 percent negligent for Retzloff's injuries, the driver of the oncoming car 10 percent negligent, and Julie Retzloff 1 percent negligent, apparently for not wearing the seat belt that was installed on the far right side of the car's bench seat.

The Retzloff family hailed the award as a dream come true. "This means I can do for Julie what I never could have done otherwise," said her mother, Bernice Rice, after hearing the verdict. "It's overwhelming. Maybe we can put a little happiness in her life."

Julie Retzloff lived another fifteen years. She died of pneumonia in 1994 while in the loving care of her mother, who fed her home-cooked food through a gastric tube every four hours, gave her medications, washed her hair, changed her diapers, brushed her teeth, and wiped away her tears. "It was never a burden," Bernice Rice said. To the end, she believed her daughter communicated with her from her "locked-in" state every day.

The verdict had a broad impact. The *Retzloff* case tightened the screw one more turn on automakers, pressuring them to rectify the hazardous designs of their cars. As Terry Tadysak says, "It helped shape and change the safety and integrity of automobiles that are manufactured even today."

CHAPTER FOUR

Civil Justice

The Inner Circle of Advocates held its inaugural meeting on June 26, 1972, in San Francisco. The original members were eleven trial lawyers from around the country with a mission to promote "the highest standards of courtroom competence and the exchange of knowledge." The threshold for membership into this exclusive club was at least one million-dollar verdict and the completion of fifty personal injury cases.

Bob Habush was invited into the Inner Circle of Advocates in March 1975. He was one of only fifty attorneys in the country who had achieved a seven-figure verdict—the $1.86 million award in the Totsky case. Habush remains an emeritus member.

Today, this group of trial lawyer "superstars," as *The National Law Review* describes them, has one hundred members. "It's probably the most elite group of plaintiff's lawyers in the country," says Dan Rottier, the president and CEO of Habush Habush & Rottier. "I'm a member also, so I hear from those people, all sorts of heads of law firms. They marvel at Bob's ability to be so successful in our legal climate over the years. His reputation is up there."

The objectives of the Inner Circle extend beyond monetary awards. As a legal brain trust of exceptionally qualified advocates, its aims are to give a voice to those who often have none and to challenge the deep-pocketed Goliaths that dominate the civil justice system. "Many times, people who have been injured and families who have lost loved ones find themselves facing big corporations or insurance companies with unlimited resources to deny just compensation to those they harmed," says Michael Koskoff, president of the organization. "Through the work and skill of our members, cover-ups can be exposed and those at fault held accountable. By punishing the guilty for their wrongs, we make America a safer place."

In his fifty-plus years as a trial lawyer, Habush has had a sizable role in making America a safer place. His success in hundreds of product liability cases in particular has compelled industries to recall or improve the designs of products that have caused harm or fatal injuries to users. In that sense, Habush and a limited group of top-notch plaintiff's lawyers have acted as consumer protectors, helping bring about appreciable changes in product design.

It's worth noting a few of those changes:

- High chairs were equipped with improved restraints to prevent children from slipping out of the seat and strangling in the seat strap.
- The venerable Coleman camp stove was redesigned to prevent the igniting of fumes that seeped from the fuel tank.
- Childproof plastic guards were added to extension cord sockets to prevent electrical shocks and burns. In only the second case of its kind in the country, Habush represented a three-year-old boy who suffered extensive burns after placing a cord in his mouth. He received a $900,000 settlement from Leviton Manufacturing Company.
- Threads of aluminum bottle caps were redesigned to relieve the pressure of carbonated drinks and prevent caps from shooting off the bottles. In 1983, a Milwaukee woman, a Habush client, won a $750,000 settlement against PepsiCo after losing vision in her left eye when a bottle she opened exploded.
- Representing a sixteen-year-old Milwaukee girl who died of toxic shock syndrome, Habush played a part in settling a succession of federal lawsuits against the nation's largest makers of tampons.
- The U.S. Food and Drug Administration ordered manufacturers to attach warning labels to their latex products, and eventually allergenic latex gloves were banned altogether from some health-care facilities, replaced by synthetic gloves.
- Pharmaceutical drug safety was upgraded significantly.
- A retailer stopped importing bicycles with weak, defective front forks after one was involved in a brain-damaging accident.

- Child seats in autos were redesigned to include shoulder restraints, greatly reducing spine and internal injuries to children.
- Front seat backs in American automobiles were redesigned and reinforced to prevent collapse during collisions.
- Pressured in large measure by Habush's case against Chrysler, U.S. automakers redesigned all rearview mirrors so they would break away upon impact.
- Automakers included three-point seat belts as standard equipment in middle and rear seat positions. Habush and his firm, among other plaintiff's attorneys, brought numerous lawsuits against the major auto manufacturers on behalf of passengers who were permanently disabled due to inadequate seat belt designs.
- The American Motors Company redesigned vehicles that had gas tanks too close to the rear, which had caused explosions and fires.
- Automobile door latches were redesigned with safety devices.
- Protective guards were added to auger delivery systems and rotating shafts on machinery, particularly farm machinery, such as manure spreaders, forage blowers, and corn pickers.
- Guards were added on various woodworking and metalworking machines, such as table saws, lumber mill saws, lathes, drill presses, and press brakes.
- Safety interlocks were added as standard equipment on a variety of machines.
- Designs and testing procedures for grinding wheels were upgraded for safety.
- Forklifts and front-end loaders were manufactured with overhead guards and rear guards to protect the operator.
- Boom cranes were designed to prevent overloading.
- Alarms were added to trucks and other service vehicles to warn people when the vehicles were in reverse.
- Snowmobile design was improved for greater safety.
- Excessively potent air bags in autos were improved.
- Garage door openers were made with safety devices that reverse the direction of the doors if they come in contact with objects, such as people or pets.

- Wooden ladder designs were changed to prevent accidents.
- Wiring practices for mobile homes were vastly improved.
- Grain elevator door design was revamped.
- Defectively designed water slides were recalled and redesigned.
- Toys with the potential for causing choking accidents were recalled.
- The design of the auto antitheft device called the Club was made safer.
- Metal porch railing design was improved.
- Space heaters and furnaces were redesigned to include automatic shut-off valves in case of leaks.
- A warning was added on tanks of methanol advising to keep the cap closed to prevent fire hazards.
- A warning was added on fumigants, advising the use of gas masks with special filters to curtail penetrating fumes.
- A warning was added to aspirin products to restrict giving them to children with the flu, which can cause Reye's syndrome, a deadly disease.

Most, if not all, of these changes have become standardized among products sold daily in the U.S. marketplace. Seat belts for back seats, extension cords with childproof guards—certainly they're taken for granted by the general public. Yet never by Habush's clients.

Here is one example of the kind of effect Habush's representation has had on the lives of his clients and their families, as related by his law partner Rottier:

> About three weeks ago, I had occasion to speak to the district attorney in a small county in Wisconsin. He asked me if I would pass a message on to Bob. He said Bob had represented his mother twenty-five years ago. The case involved a furniture store named American TV and Appliance that sometimes gave away free bicycles to its customers. These bicycles were imported from China and had defective front forks. This DA's mother had received one of the bikes. She was riding one day and the fork collapsed. She struck the pavement and suffered a brain injury.
>
> He asked me to pass on his appreciation to Bob because his mother had been living in her own home for the last twenty-five years with

twenty-four-hour care. As he put it, "Without the settlement, she would have died in a nursing home years ago." He was a child at the time of the accident. Money was set aside for his college education and law school, and now he's a district attorney. So it struck me that there's sometimes a ripple effect we don't often think about.

In this case, it turned out the Chinese manufacturer of the bicycle had falsified the quality of the components that had gone into the bike. The bicycles were recalled, I believe, and Bob ended up recovering for the lady.

Following are some of the cases that Bob Habush handled—cases that have had far-reaching impact in the workplace, on the highway, in the home; cases where human tragedy is ameliorated and injustice corrected through the aid of a strong legal advocate.

Lucija and Aleksander Jirgens v. A.M.F. Inc.

"Lucy Jirgens was a grandmother," recalls Habush. "No movie star, just a sixty-one-year-old grandma. She and her husband, Aleksander, were born in Latvia. During World War II, they were confined to a Russian labor camp.

"After the couple immigrated to the United States, Lucy worked in a Milwaukee baking company that made bread and hamburger buns. The hamburger buns were baked, cut in half, and carried along a conveyor to a metal tray at Lucy's station. Lucy was a racker on a machine called a 410 Pan-O-Mat, made by A.M.F. Incorporated in Richmond, Virginia. Her job was to reject the buns that were not cut or were cut incorrectly, and stack the good buns on a rack. Because the conveyor was constantly moving, some of the buns would fall into a catch pan under the conveyor. Lucy also was responsible for cleaning the area on the catch pan and floor under the Pan-O-Mat. Beneath the surface of the machine was a rotating shaft that propelled the conveyor. It was a very slow rotating shaft, but it was unguarded.

"At the time, women in the factory were required to wear hairnets on the job. One day, Lucy bent under the table to clean while the rotating shaft was moving, and her hairnet and hair became entangled in the rotating shaft. The force was so great it tore her scalp off from her eyelids, around each of her ears, to the back of her head. It was horribly painful, horrible looking.

"When the case came to my office, I had had a number of other cases—many of them involving machinery—where people were injured by rotating shafts without guards. Their clothing gets caught when they get too close, and they're crushed against the shaft, either killed or paralyzed by a spinal injury. I had a lawsuit against John Deere where a farmer had his hand ripped off by a combine with a rotating device. The rotating shafts are deceptively benign. They're just slowly rotating. There are no sharp blades, just plain, constant force."

Beginning work on the case, Habush gathered information from the National Safety Council and engineering texts that identified rotating shafts as hazardous if unguarded. He also had his investigator, Terry Tadysak, look into comparable machinery used by manufacturers in Europe. "Terry came up with a similar machine in a bakery in England that had a guard over the rotating shaft," Habush says. "It was produced by—guess who?—A.M.F. Incorporated, the same company that made the machine at the factory where Lucy worked. Same company. So in England it had a guard, and the United States didn't have a guard."

Habush tried the case against his nemesis from the *Totsky* trial, Edmund "Ned" Powell, a defense attorney who was considered one of the most successful at that time. Powell argued that the rotating shaft was "guarded by location . . . by remoteness from the working area."

Habush found an expert, a design engineer at Marquette University named Bobbie Richardson, who described how a guard could be designed. "He prepared a guard for me—just a plain hollow plastic tube that could be fit over the rotating shaft. It was a perfect guard. You could take it off to clean, and it cost five bucks to install material. Five bucks."

For the trial, Habush asked Richardson to craft a mock-up of the machine with the plastic tubular guard covering the shaft. The guard could be fastened with a handful of machine screws and nuts.

"We're presenting this in front of the jury," says Habush. "I wanted Bobbie to attach the guard. But he forgot his pliers and screwdriver, he forgot his toolbox. So he reached into his pocket for a coin and removed the guard with a quarter. It took him less than a minute."

It was an embarrassment to the defense—an inexpensive, easily attachable guard could have prevented the woman's injuries.

Lucy Jirgens had undergone six excruciating surgeries to replace her lost scalp with skin grafts. The surgeries failed. Jirgens remained permanently bald, resigned to wear a wig to cover her repulsive scars. In his closing argument, Habush fixed on the psychological and emotional scars that Jirgens endured.

> You know where her big scar is? It's in here, in her heart. There's plenty of scars on her head, but her real scar is in the heart. She's got to live with that.
>
> This lady has come a long way away from being in a slave labor camp during World War II. She is presenting herself here today to a jury of her peers, and this is an important case.
>
> Let the message ring out loud and clear, ladies and gentlemen, so they can hear it all the way to Richmond, what you people feel. That when they sell a piece of equipment, they should make it safe. Let everyone hear what you think the loss of human dignity to a fellow human being really is, what the scars in the heart are worth, what the scars in her head and face are worth.

The jury awarded Lucy Jirgens $625,872 for her medical expenses, wage loss, loss of companionship, and pain and suffering, past and future.

MacKensie Haupt v. Medical Protective Company, Jean Todd M.D., and Obstetrical and Gynecological Associates of Appleton

Habush didn't see his first medical malpractice case until he had been practicing law for fifteen years or so. "They were really rare," he says. "Not that malpractice didn't occur. There were just very few lawyers that would have the courage to take them on. Historically, doctors protect doctors. That's been true throughout the ages and it's true today. The only time there's an exception is if there's a really bad doctor who the other doctors hate and are continually bailing out of trouble. Then they'll assist you to get that doctor out of practice."

Determining whether malpractice has been committed is an expensive process. Credentialed medical experts—usually other MDs—must be hired to critique the case. "Over the years, we have identified people like that, usually younger doctors," says Habush. "They usually have an altruistic reason. They feel they need to do it because no one else will.

"We get a tremendous amount of calls from all over the state. We screen hundreds of cases a month. We turn away 90 percent of them. Most of them are not cases. Some of them are negligence cases but you can't prove that the doctor's negligence made a difference. In other words, when you're dealing with a person that has a disease like cancer and there was a failure to diagnose it, you'd have to get oncologists to say that if the doctor caught it, the outcome would have been different—the patient would have avoided surgery or chemotherapy. They would have avoided death. So the real boogeyman in all these malpractice cases is, even if there's a departure from the standard of care, did it affect the outcome? Because you're always dealing with the disease that has its own progression, whether there's good care or bad care.

"Moreover, when I do a malpractice case, I have to learn the science. In a trial, I'll cross-examine a doctor who went to med school and went through residency and then went through an internship and then was practicing for X number of years. They know everything about the body and how it reacts to procedures and medicines and the studies that have been done. A plaintiff lawyer has to get up to speed to even have a chance at criticizing the technique. You have to use your own experts to teach. You have to be very smart and very adaptable to learning the medicine. If you're unwilling to invest in that kind of intellectual learning process, forget it.

"We still do malpractice cases, and we still get good settlements," he adds, "because there is a fear on the part of the defense attorney that every once in a while, if we get the right jury and the doctor makes a bad impression on the witness stand, we can win the case. Juries, though, will always believe the doctor. They forgive their misses, their absences of notes, unlike other kinds of cases. So these cases are just fraught with problems. If by chance you get a case [where] there appears to be negligence, then you have to face a built-in bias by jurors. Simply put, people need doctors more than they need lawyers, especially older people. So jurors tend to want to protect doctors."

Nevertheless, medical malpractice remains a worthy part of Habush's firm's repertoire. "Every medical malpractice that I've won alerted hospitals and doctors to better peer-review safety practices. They all bitched about it, and they all wanted legislative protection against it. But every time a doctor got hit with a malpractice verdict or settlement, it improved patient safety. That's just a general proposition."

One of his most gratifying cases involved the birth of MacKensie Haupt of Appleton, Wisconsin. The delivery was difficult and soon escalated to an emergency. The baby's right shoulder was hooked on the mother's pelvis, a condition known as shoulder dystocia.

The obstetrician was Dr. Jean Todd. "My regular doctor was out of town, and she was the one on call," says MacKensie's mother, Clementine Haupt. "I never had seen her before in my life."

Typically, an obstetrician uses a certain technique to maneuver the shoulder and dislodge the infant. But countless children have been born brain damaged because the physician could not get the infant out soon enough and the baby became hypoxic (deprived of oxygen).

MacKensie's father, Bruce Haupt, recalls his daughter's birth. "I actually think the doctor got frustrated because she wasn't coming out. She pulled on the head, pulling and twisting it. Then she felt something happen." After a twelve-hour labor and delivery, MacKensie finally was born, but severely agitated. "I'll never forget the face on the baby," Haupt says.

"The obstetrician just blew it," recalls Habush. "She had to break the baby's collarbone and shoulder in order to get her out. Right below that is an area called the brachial plexus, which is an intersection of nerves. The baby suffered nerve damage and was born with a deformed, useless arm."

Another doctor privately confided in the Haupts. "He more or less told us he would never go against another doctor," says Bruce, "but said this was not right. There was a mistake here."

At first, the Haupts thought MacKensie's arm would heal and she would regain its normal use. But the deformed right arm did not grow as rapidly as her left arm.

"My mom had eleven children," Clementine Haupt says. "She said she had never seen anything like this in her life. She said MacKensie's arm would never work to full capacity, and she was right. That made me wonder why this really happened. I wanted to find out."

Clementine dialed what she thought was the phone number for the Habush firm. Instead, she got an ex-associate of Habush, Jim Murphy. "He did a good job," says Bruce Haupt. "But I don't think he was as polished or as good as Bob was."

Murphy represented the Haupts in a hearing before the Wisconsin Patient's Compensation Panel, which offered additional medical malpractice coverage to health-care providers and funds to compensate injured patients. When the panel dismissed the case in a 5–0 vote, Clementine Haupt decided to call Habush.

"I was pretty positive about pursing this," she says. "When I met Bob, I felt this was the lawyer I should have had in the first place. He cared more about me than any monetary payments. That was never brought up. He was eloquent with words, the way he talked to us. He made us feel comfortable, and he didn't give the case to an associate. He was in the courtroom every day."

Watching Habush in action gave the Haupts hope. Recalls Bruce: "The way he walked around the room during his cross-examinations, trying to read the jury, his glasses pulled down—it was like watching Perry Mason on TV. He knew exactly what to do."

Habush, in his signature style, painted a vivid and compelling image of MacKensie's pain and suffering when arguing for damages before the jury.

This baby is five years old. She is already tasting a little bit of the future. She is already realizing that she is different. . . . She is going to have difficulty with simple tasks like dressing, buttoning. Two-handed tasks, playing catch, jumping rope. There will be countless days, as this baby becomes older and a young woman, where she is going to feel rejected, sad, and depressed. "What did I do to deserve this?" she might say to herself, as she grows into adolescence, when boys notice girls for the first time and girls notice boys for the first time. Maybe because she's so darn pretty that people will look past that. I hope so.

I am not pleased to stand here and tell you that Dr. Todd was wrong. It gives me no pleasure to say that a professional did something wrong. And although I believe that she may feel bad, that is too little, too late. She may recall from time to time MacKensie Haupt and what happened that day, and what this trial was. But MacKensie and her parents will live every day, every day, with the effect of what happened. Every day will be a reminder.

Finding Dr. Todd and her clinic at fault, the jury awarded the Haupts $250,000. The award provided financial assistance for MacKensie's medical expenses and a sense of closure for her parents.

Shortly after the trial, Dr. Todd left Wisconsin and moved to Iowa to practice medicine. Today, MacKensie Haupt, at age thirty-three, is married and has three children. Though her right arm remains shorter than her left and the fingers don't function well and her right arm remains shorter than her left, "she has learned to live with her handicap," says her mother.

Clementine Haupt says she also felt a connection to Habush because he, too, had a daughter who suffered a handicap at the hands of a physician. "Bob made us feel like family, and for a long time after the trial we stayed in touch."

Roger Schulz v. Bituminous Casualty Corp.

Roger Schulz was a twenty-one-year employee of Kohl's Foods in Milwaukee. Loyal and hardworking, he drove a forklift at the company's grocery warehouse, unloading truckloads of packaged foods, meat, and produce.

Working overtime one day, he was asked to unload a few pallets of potatoes from a semitrailer truck parked at the loading dock. Schulz drove an Eaton-Yale forklift, a 1972–73 stand-up model with a small operator compartment that opened at the rear. As he had done many times before, he guided a hydraulic steel dock board into place to bridge the gap between the semitrailer and the loading dock. While he was backing out of the trailer and onto the steel dock board, the truck unexpectedly lurched forward. The forklift fell backward, its front wheels in the truck, its back wheels on the collapsing dock board.

Still standing aboard the forklift, Schulz was caught between a portion of the steel dock board and his forklift. The impact crushed his vertebrae and nearly severed his spinal cord, leaving him paralyzed.

"On that particular day, the delivery truck had not been secured properly," Habush explains. "The truck driver had not set the parking brake or blocked the tires of the truck. When Roger fell, there was no back protection on the forklift at all."

He looked for liability. The truck driver clearly erred by not preventing his truck from rolling. But the trucker carried limited insurance, not nearly enough to cover Roger Schulz's past and present medical expenses, loss of income, and pain and suffering. Schulz, now a paraplegic, would be in a wheelchair for the rest of his life.

Habush decided to take a flyer. Tearing a page out of his own playbook, he decided he could build a case against the forklift manufacturer, Eaton Corporation, based in Cleveland, for making a defective and unsafe product. Schulz's lawsuit named Eaton's insurance carrier, Bituminous Casualty Corporation, and the owner of the truck, Pre-Pac Corporation, as defendants.

Eaton claimed that it was not liable and blamed the truck driver for his incompetence. The defense argued that Schulz should have jumped off the forklift as it fell and that a rear guard would not have protected him.

"You want to have the operator be able to jump back," says Frank Daily, the Milwaukee defense attorney who represented Eaton. "If the back was obstructed, then he goes down every time with the truck." Daily says that Eaton did nothing wrong. "Our theory, which I still believe is the right one, was that [Schulz] landed on his butt and had the injury you see in snowmobile cases, where your spinal column is compressed, and if you damage your spinal column, you're a paraplegic."

Habush assembled a corps of witnesses. He deposed medical experts to dispel Daily's theory. He cited industry experts who maintained that forklift operators are advised to remain with the vehicle rather than "jumping ship" and exposing themselves to falling goods. And he called on Bobbie Richardson, his engineering expert from Marquette University, to come up with a rendering of the forklift with a rear protective guard. "It wasn't rocket science," says Habush, "but it would have prevented Roger from being injured."

Nevertheless, he knew it would be a difficult case to win. The truck driver was inexperienced and hadn't followed protocol, failing to chock the truck's tires and secure the brake. Frank Daily would surely have little trouble persuading a jury that the driver was at least partly responsible.

He searched for a viable theory. At the time, warehouses across North America had made major changes in how they stored goods. Shelving systems twenty-five feet tall or taller were built to efficiently hold layer upon layer of inventory. Stacked on pallets, goods were added and removed by forklifts. Many manufacturers of stand-up forklifts redesigned their machines to accommodate the updated shelving systems by simply adding a set of rear-side steel posts to protect the operators' backs should they accidentally slam backward into a metal shelf.

Responding to interrogatories and "requests for production" submitted by Habush, Eaton claimed it only made forklifts with two front posts. "Their experts all took the position of 'the forklifts don't need a rear guard,'" he says. "I mean, that was their whole defense."

Habush didn't buy it. Acting on a hunch (or sheer instinct), he instructed Terry Tadysak, his investigator, to search across the United States for any Eaton-Yale dealer who might have obtained or even seen an Eaton-Yale with additional posts in the rear that would function as an operator guard.

Tadysak began making phone calls. There were nearly two hundred Eaton-Yale dealerships in the country at the time. "Someplace after the seventy-fifth dealer, I found one in California who said he had serviced Eaton-Yale forklifts at a local warehouse," he says. "[The warehouse] had purchased three attachable rear guards from him." The dealer told Tadysak he had contacted Eaton's engineering department, who said Eaton could provide "nonadvertised" guard assemblies with two posts that mounted on the front and two additional posts that could be bolted on the back. "The dealer ordered them, received them, and put them on the forklifts," he says.

Taking the hunt a step further, Tadysak called the warehouse and asked for photographs of the Eaton-Yale guard assembly. The warehouse obliged.

Habush submitted the photos as discovery to the defense attorney Daily. "We wanted to see the blueprints of this guard," he says, "and they denied its existence, denied its existence, denied its existence throughout the entire discovery. 'We don't know what you're talking about,' they said. 'We've never seen this. It's not ours.'"

Habush again tried to break through the stonewall and subpoenaed the rear guard in California. But the warehouse said it no longer used the machines. The last forklift it had was gone. All Habush had were the photos.

The trial commenced, and to drive home their defense, Daily and Eaton's product safety engineer constructed an elaborate exhibit board, replete with reason after reason why the company never would have added the rear guard posts to its forklifts: *The posts would not have mounted on the back. The shape of the tubing was inconsistent with current models.*

Habush tried to knock down the defense's argument in his cross-examinations. He waved the photographs of the California rear guard in front of Eaton's product safety engineer. "Isn't it true, sir, that you made this very guard for a customer in California?" he asked.

The engineer strenuously denied it.

"Are you sure, sir?" asked Habush, his eyes fixed on the witness.

The engineer wouldn't budge.

Daily had tried other cases against Habush. Each time, he warned his witnesses not to fall prey to what he calls "the Habush stare." "Bob can catch somebody's eye and affix his stare on him and not blink. He'll put his glasses down on the end of his nose and stare. I'll say to my experts, 'You know, after you've finished your answer, if Bob doesn't like the answer, he will sit and glare at you.' Some people get very uncomfortable, and they'll start talking again and revise their answer. They've got to resist that."

Habush also applies his intimidating stare to jurors. "He stands in front of the courtroom, right at the door," Daily notes, "and as each one of them walks out of the jury box, he [stares] at each of them. Once I figured out what he was doing, I'd run up to the front and try to position myself in between him and the jury box. We looked like two guys trying to get a rebound or something."

Daily recalls another expert witness who was subjected to Habush's merciless cross-examination. "Bob would be grilling him, and the witness would answer by saying, 'I don't remember.' Again and again he'd say, 'I don't remember.' Finally Bob turns to the witness and, with his glasses on the end of his nose, says, 'Well, Mr. Expert, have you been in a serious car accident recently?' And the witness says no. Bob says, 'Well, do you have a brain injury?' And the witness says, 'How would I know?' Really pissed off Bob."

On the day before the trial was to end, Habush played another card. He sent Tadysak to an Eaton-Yale dealership in the Chicago area. Using his real name but posing as a consumer, Tadysak showed a salesman in the parts department a photo of Eaton's modified rear guard.

"I found a machine in California with a guard like this," he said. "Could Eaton-Yale make the same guard for me?"

"Let me find out," the man replied. As Tadysak waited, the parts rep faxed a copy of the photo directly to Eaton's engineering department, along with a message: "I've got a customer here who wants this part. Can you make it?"

Minutes later, there was a phone call, and the salesman told Tadysak, "Eaton says they have what they call a 'nonadvertised' guard assembly and they'll sell it to you for $325."

Tadysak thought it over. "Tell them I'd like the blueprint number," he said. "I want proof that I'm ordering this exact part so there's no screwups in case it doesn't fit or something."

The company replied by Teletype with a purchase agreement: "We have received the copy of the photograph. This is the blueprint number of the part you ordered. We agree to sell it for $325 plus shipping."

Tadysak paid for the order and, with the purchase agreement in hand, raced back to the Milwaukee County courthouse. During a recess in the trial, he passed the information to Habush. The blueprint could be the smoking gun.

"Terry, you damn well better be right," Habush said, fixing him with the infamous stare.

Habush immediately asked to see the circuit judge, Thomas Doherty, in his chambers, where he explained his discovery. "Judge," he said, "it's very important that I see that blueprint." Judge Doherty agreed and ordered Frank Daily to have the blueprint delivered to court the following day.

"That case," Daily says ruefully today, "was just one example of how relentless Bob Habush is."

On the final day of the trial, Habush played his last card, calling to the stand for one more round of questions Eaton's product safety engineer, the same witness who had presented the extravagant exhibit board showing why his company never would have manufactured rear guard posts—guard posts exactly like the one on the blueprint that Habush now held in his hand.

After successfully impeaching the engineer, he continued to unleash his outrage in a blistering final argument:

So now you know why they were so concerned that we wouldn't find rear post optional guards that would fit the 1972–73 machine. Because they knew, members of the jury, as their product safety expert said that, if those posts had been on this machine, they were strong enough to prevent this injury that Roger Schulz experienced.

The product safety engineer claims he knows all about dealer modification requests. He claims he knows about the "network" with respect to accidents. He's worked on 450 lawsuits. He's done extensive work in connection with this lawsuit, strategizing, preparing witnesses, working with the lawyers.

Now, having that in mind, let me remind you of what he told you under oath. "It would take a major modification of the forklift truck to put on rear guard posts prior to 1976." He never saw an overhead guard like the one which I just held up from California, he said. "There was," he said, "no type of guard in existence where an owner could put rear posts on the machine to make it safer." He said there was "no blueprint that would describe rear posts," and on the last day of the trial, before he knew that I had discovered the part number for this guard, he stood up in front of you in this court and proceeded to tell you it would not be safe. Why? Because, at that time, he wanted you to believe that this guard, which was known as the Evans guard, was no good, that it was some cockamamie scheme that some dealer dreamed up and made in his back shop, that it was dangerous. Because, he was worried that you folks would like their guard and this thing should have been on the machine. And so, he had to tell you that a straight guard was unsafe and proceeded to do so with this exhibit.

But, that afternoon he was given the part number and before the trial ended, up came the blueprints. And lo and behold, what do the blueprints show? A straight guard with two rear posts. Posts that go into not any machine, *our* accident machine. And blueprints that describe it as a "drive-in rack overheard guard."

Members of the jury, here's where the common sense comes in. You ask yourselves why, why would he be so concerned about that guard being discovered? Because, as I told you, he knew that it was available on our machine. It was an option. He knew it should have been standard. He knew that it would increase operator protection. He knew that it would have prevented this injury. He knows it.

And I ask you, use your common sense. Can you believe that this man, with all his experience, all his involvement, all his contact with Eaton, that he did not know this existed? That he was surprised? That a lawyer and investigator from Milwaukee, Wisconsin, had to find a blueprint *he couldn't find*, with all their technology and their computers in their parts department, when he knew I was looking for it? Come on! He knew it was there all along! And in this trial, day after day, question after question, he denied it! He denied it! He denied it!

This is their blueprint. It is Eaton's. It's there on the blueprint. They had it! They could have sold the guard as a standard or option. They could have put it on. This man would not be sitting in a wheelchair today if it had been on this machine.

In its verdict, the jury awarded Roger Schulz $1.5 million, finding Eaton and Pre-Pac equally negligent. From the Milwaukee courthouse, the verdict sent a resounding message to manufacturers that worker safety should be a paramount responsibility.

Mitchell Miller v. International Harvester Co.

Mitch Miller was the oldest of five brothers, a shade under six feet four, with a baby face and blue eyes. He was in his early twenties when he went to work at Hynite Corporation, a company in Oak Creek, Wisconsin, that processed leather scraps into fertilizer. Miller operated an International Harvester front-end loader, called the Payloader H-25B—a rubber-tired industrial truck with a large lift bucket on its front.

One day in March 1979, he was hauling two nine-hundred-pound bales of scrap leather from a utility yard into the Hynite warehouse. As he came to a stop and raised the lift bucket, the load suddenly shifted. One of the bales fell onto Miller's head and back, breaking his neck and paralyzing the young worker from the chest down.

"International Harvester in its promotional literature had touted the Payloader as a versatile machine capable of being used in small, tight places," Habush says. But International Harvester had designed these front-end loaders with an overhead guard that was too tall to fit through the doorways of some of the older industrial plants, including the aging warehouse at Hynite.

The overhead guard was shaped like a canopy and made of two-inch steel bars. With the guard in place, the Payloader stood seven feet five inches tall, five inches higher than industry standards. "Designing that guard that high made it inapplicable for use at many companies," Habush says.

At Hynite's request, the IH local dealer had supplied the Payloader H-25B without the protective overhead guard so it could be maneuvered more easily in Hynite's facility.

Habush had misgivings about the case at the outset. It seemed likely that Hynite was liable for a high degree of negligence by allowing the vehicle to be operated without the guard. Although under Wisconsin's workers' compensation law the employer was immune from liabilities, it was almost certain that International Harvester would claim contributory negligence, blaming Hynite and Miller for contributing to the cause of the accident.

Habush devised an alternate theory, placing International Harvester in the crosshairs: the company was negligent, he reasoned, by not designing the Payloader with an overhead guard that could be used safely inside all manufacturing plants. "That was my starting point in going after the manufacturer, International Harvester, for making a defectively designed product," he explains.

Habush filed a lawsuit claiming that IH was responsible for Miller's injuries because it negligently designed the Payloader H-25B. Looking back, he recounts how he made the decision to take on the giant manufacturer.

"I'm well on my way to going ahead, but I haven't started a lawsuit. I'm still evaluating it. I'm thinking it's going to be very difficult because the employer asked to have the overhead guard taken off. But I think I've got a chance of a case by arguing that the manufacturer can't require the employer to become a designer of machines, that the manufacturer should do it itself.

"Of course, in the back of my mind I know I've got a very sympathetic plaintiff that the jury is going to like, and that's going to give me an edge. I'm representing a kid who's living in this terrible world, [totally] dependent, and I certainly start to feel emotionally connected to him, which gives me more incentive—as if I needed it—to try to make this right for him.

"I've got other cases that I'm working on at the same time. And so I'm getting my associates to evaluate all the medical information and bringing reports to me. I always want to involve myself with my best expert witness, however—in this case, an engineer, because I want him to feel confident that I can protect him if he goes out on a limb by saying he could design a safer front-end loader.

"I push ahead. I never expected the case to get settled, and at that point I didn't care. That's something I've carried with me my entire career. I don't say, 'I'm going to take this because I think I can settle it.' I take it if I think I can win it. That may be the difference between me and some other plaintiff's lawyers. When I'm preparing the case, I'm not preparing it for settlement. I'm preparing it for trial."

The case went to trial, and from his arsenal Habush produced evidence that International Harvester had advertised the H-25B with an "optional" overhead guard. As he revealed in a vigorous cross-examination of the company's chief engineer of safety, only after four or five similar negligence lawsuits were filed against International Harvester—including a 1974 case in which a Milwaukee man using a similar unguarded vehicle had been killed—did the manufacturer change its brochures to promote the over-head guards as "standard" equipment. Yet IH still allowed dealers to sell the machines without the guard—at a discounted price of $546.

Habush showed the jury how he could remove the guard by unscrewing a few bolts with an ordinary wrench. He demonstrated how Hynite had jury-rigged its own guard on the Payloader: an open cage made of thin pieces of steel. Finally, he showed how other manufacturers had built front-end loaders with much shorter overhead guards and how the guards were welded on permanently or built into the frames.

Figure 4
Faulty design
Mitchell Miller (with his parents) was paralyzed when driving an International Harvester front-end loader without an overhead guard.
Photo credit: *Milwaukee Journal*, with permission

The trial was not without a few unpredictable twists and turns. "International Harvester was represented by a lawyer named Gilbert Church, with Foley & Lardner. A very smart guy," Habush remembers. "After maybe a week or two into the trial, as I'm leaving for the courthouse, an envelope is slid under my office door. I open it up, and it's a letter from Gil Church with an offer of $1 million. Of course, I thought it was ridiculous. I wasn't going to take $1 million. My guy's a quadriplegic, for God's sake, and the case was going good. So I put it inside my coat pocket.

"Over the lunch hour, as I'm having lunch with my next expert witness, I want to write something down, and I'm looking for a piece of paper. The expert has his files piled all over the table. So I reach in my pocket, and I pull out this letter with the million-dollar offer. On the back, I begin scribbling an outline for the direct examination of my expert.

"Back in court, Gil cross-examines my guy. 'Can I see your file, sir?' he says, and the expert hands him a file folder. He's rummaging through it, rummaging through it. He takes out a piece of paper, marks it as an exhibit, and gives it to me to inspect. I see it's in my handwriting. And suddenly it occurs to me that this is my outline, and Church was going to impeach the expert by showing I had coached him.

"I'm thinking, 'Where did this come from?' I flip it over, and there on the other side is Gil's letter from International Harvester offering me the $1 million. Now in milliseconds it's going through my brain: Do I let him introduce this into evidence? Do I let the jury know that the offer was $1 million, that the defense is lowballing me? Is that good? Is it bad? Is it a mistrial or not?

"Finally I make a decision. I call Gil over and give him the letter. 'Look at the other side.' He flips it over, and he sees his letter offering me $1 million and turns white as a sheet. He plops it back down on my desk and moves on, never entering it as evidence."

In an elaborate display of demonstrative evidence (and a brilliant piece of showmanship), Habush had an IH front-end loader and an IH forklift delivered to a lot outside the courthouse. He had a defense witness measure the height of each machine and the distance between the operator's seat and overhead guard. In the presentation, Habush showed how the witness's measurements contradicted those listed in International Harvester's own literature.

Habush also produced a videotape that described in vivid detail a typical day in the life of the accident victim, a tactic he would use routinely in dozens of other personal injury lawsuits. He solemnly reminded jurors that Mitch Miller had nearly been killed in the accident and that he would live the rest of his days as a high-level quadriplegic.

"Most people, jurors included, think about quadriplegics as just being paralyzed," he says. "But they have other severe health problems: severe threats of colds, infections, ulcers from sitting in the wheelchair, breathing problems, skin problems, spasms in legs that are paralyzed, pain, and of course the loss of dignity. They become totally dependent babies. It's a terrible injury. Some doctors will say that it's the worst injury that could happen to a person. Many brain-damaged victims don't realize what they lost; victims with spinal cord injuries do."

In his closing argument for deciding damages, Habush put the hammer down:

> You, ladies and gentlemen, are the community conscience. You can hold a manufacturer accountable no matter how small, if it's a local machine shop, no matter how big, if it's an international company. You, ladies and gentlemen, in a products liability case, are competent to tell a manufacturer, "Manufacturer, you blew it, you did wrong." Because you're the community. And let me tell you something, folks, what you do here today will be heard in the board rooms of International Harvester and everywhere else in this world, because you will be telling manufacturers what they can do and what they cannot do. And this is a very significant responsibility on your part.

The jury sided with Habush's argument that Mitch Miller was not to blame for his injuries. Instead, jurors found International Harvester 55 percent negligent, Hynite Corporation 30 percent negligent, and the front-end dealer 15 percent negligent. They awarded Miller $5.5 million, the largest jury award in the history of Wisconsin's state courts.

* * *

As Habush won verdict after verdict against some of the most powerful companies in the country, his reputation as a dragon slayer grew nationally.

"He never set being the best in Wisconsin as his goal. It was the best nationwide," says Dan Rottier, who started at the firm in 1979. "I can recall hearing that in the very early eighties as his reputation developed around the country."

While Habush had resisted negotiating settlements his entire career, it became increasingly difficult to avoid. CEOs, public relations executives, surgeons—all did their best to avoid bad publicity. If trials weren't going their way, clients would instruct their defense attorneys to bail out.

For Habush, a negotiated settlement is a bitter pill to swallow.

"Not having to go to court is sometimes better for the client than going to court," he says. "It's a traumatic experience. But it's almost always necessary, for the client and especially the public interest. One of the things I've worked for all these years is making things safer: products, automobiles, medical procedures, you name it. Each winning verdict adds incentive for manufacturers to improve product safety.

"That is gone with a settlement agreement. It's a private agreement, and many times the company insists on confidentiality. If there's no record of liability, the public never finds out that a product is defective or that a doctor is incompetent. Even when there is no confidentiality clause, no one is going to know about it unless the case is big enough to make the newspaper. Even then, the story is seen and forgotten the next day. I'm not that jaundiced to take the position that industries do not try to make their products safer. Many do, absolutely. But there are some who don't, and there are some who will retain a dangerous aspect of their product because it's cheaper than recalling and cheaper than fighting an occasional lawsuit.

"The famous Ford Pinto case is the best example of that," he says. "The Pinto was a subcompact produced in the 1970s. It was designed with its gas tank at the back end of the car. In a rear-end collision, the force of the impact would push the tank forward into the bolts of the differential. The tank would puncture, gas would pour out, and the car would explode. Some twenty-seven deaths resulted because of the poor design.

"In the course of an investigation and lawsuit, a Ford memo was discovered that said the automaker had evaluated how many deaths would occur from the exploding rear-end gas tank. In its cost-benefit analysis, Ford calculated how many payoffs they'd have for wrongful death cases from people who were killed versus the cost of recalling the entire fleet and replacing the gas tank with a new fuel system."

Many of Habush's cases involved products with dangerous aspects to them. "But it took the lawsuit for the manufacturer to decide that, what the hell, let's redesign it and make it safe. In the area of farm machinery in the seventies and eighties, I used to have twenty files in the office at one time. Most of them were failure to guard a farmer against a moving part, like a rotating shaft. I just beat the shit out of these machinery manufacturers in trial. Finally they asked me to address their engineers in a seminar, and I told them how stupid they were. Well, they put me out of business. I haven't had a farm machinery case in fifteen years. Not one. And I mean I had every kind you can imagine: manure spreaders, tractors, harvesters, wagons. None of them were guarded, because they didn't have OSHA inspecting them or insurance companies inspecting them. The farm workers had no union to push for safety standards. The accidents were terrible. They lost their arms, they lost their legs. It was like the coal miners, a very unsafe occupation. I changed that."

Michelle Stich v. Kmart Apparel of Wisconsin, S. S. Kresge Co., and Ganis Brothers Inc.

One such settlement negotiated by Habush came in the heart-wrenching case of Michelle Stich. At age four, while playing house with her sister, Michelle got her hands on a cigarette lighter. An accidental flick of the lighter ignited Michelle's 100-percent-cotton pajamas, causing second- and third-degree burns to 15 percent of her body.

Stich's family hired Habush and his law firm. Certain he could prove that the pajamas' all-cotton fabric was not treated with a flame retardant, as required by law, he set out to identify the retailer and manufacturer. "It was like a B movie," Habush says. Michelle's grandmother told him she had bought the PJs at a Milwaukee Kmart store as a Christmas present. She had paid cash and hadn't kept the receipt, however. With nothing but a remnant of the pajama fabric worn by Michelle, Habush began his quest.

First, he approached Kmart. But the retailer denied selling all-cotton pajamas of that particular brand with that particular pattern—a cartoon drawing of a yawning monkey. When Habush asked for the names of the companies who sold their pajama lines to Kmart, he was given the names of five companies. None used patterns that matched Michelle's pajamas.

"We took depositions from the five companies," Habush says. "They brought out their books of patterns and they said, 'I'm sorry. We don't have any pattern like that.'"

Undaunted, he pressed the companies for more information. "Some lawyers would have said, 'OK, I give up.' But I smelled a rat. I was sure Kmart was lying, and I was very suspicious that I was being conned."

From a deposition he had taken, Habush remembered one of the pajama manufacturers saying he had seen a fabric sample card from a textile mill in North Carolina that was the same type of fabric as Michelle Stich's pajamas. Habush tracked down the firm, Randall Mills, and discovered the pajama fabric was sold to a clothing manufacturer in New York, Ganis Brothers. Ganis denied making the pajamas, claiming the pattern, thread, and seams of the fabric were different.

Again, Habush wouldn't take no for an answer. He pored over Kmart's invoices and found records of numerous payments made by Kmart to Ganis Brothers. His eyes fell on another invoice that raised his suspicions even more: an invoice showing delivery of a shipment of pajamas to Kmart from Cookeville, Tennessee.

He played his hunch. "These assholes Ganis Brothers have got a plant in Tennessee, and nobody knows about it," he told his investigator, Terry Tadysak. "I want you to go down there and don't come back until you find something."

Tadysak flew to Cookeville, a small town in the foothills of the Appalachian Mountains. Within days he confirmed Habush's suspicions. Talking to the plant manager, he learned that the owners of Ganis Brothers were in fact operating a garment plant in Cookeville under the alias of "the Cannon brothers."

Tadysak recalls the long and winding investigation that ultimately led to the smoking gun: "Bob uncovered an underground manufacturing operation of very sophisticated, very bad people who were buying up material that

Figure 5
Flammable fabric
Habush and his investigator tracked down the manufacturer of pajamas made without fire retardant.
Photo credit: Robert Habush

hadn't been treated with flame retardant. All of these reams of fabric were basically worthless. The Ganis Brothers out of New York bought warehouses of these untreated fabrics and had it all delivered to Tennessee—fabrics with little elephants and pink bunnies and sleepy monkeys. They made the pajamas and had labels sewn into the garments claiming they were treated with flame retardant, but they were not. The pajamas were being distributed in Kmart and major retail chain stores throughout North America. And Bob was able to uncover what was taking place."

Habush brought suit against Kmart, its parent company, S. S. Kresge, and Ganis Brothers, linking the Cookeville plant through Ganis to the Milwaukee Kmart store, which, as he was able to prove, purchased the garments in 1973.

Habush began preparing for trial. Two weeks before the trial, Ganis Brothers approached him with an offer: a lump-sum payment of $125,000. Habush turned it down. When they made a second offer, a structured settlement of $3.7 million, he rejected that one, too. Finally, on the day of the trial, a settlement was reached. Michelle Stich would receive $1,000 a month, compounded at 4 percent annually, for life. With a life expectancy of seventy years for Michelle, the potential award would amount to $4,721,485, including medical expenses and a fee of $250,000 to Habush.

The settlement at the time was the largest ever in a Wisconsin product liability suit. "This case and compensation to the Stich family," Habush told the press, "is something good for all children."

Teresa Fuentes v. Cosco Inc.

On April 27, 1996, the Fuentes family was on their way to a gathering in Eugene, Oregon. Three-year-old Teresa Fuentes was sitting in a car seat in the back of the family's Ford Explorer. A car coming from the opposite direction crossed the centerline and crashed head-on with the Explorer. Teresa jackknifed over her car seat, severely tearing her spine. She was crippled for life, rendered a quadriplegic and unable to breathe without a ventilator and constant care.

Child car seats at the time were woefully inadequate, designed and manufactured without restraints that would hold fragile bodies in place and cushion them against impact. Teresa's seat, made by the Cosco Company of Indiana, was a low-shield booster without any restraints at all above the child's stomach.

The Fuenteses retained Habush in a product liability lawsuit against Cosco. Before the case went to trial, Cosco settled with the family for $4.3 million.

The case epitomizes the callous unwillingness of manufacturers to put consumer safety above profit, says Habush, looking back. "Children's car seats had originally been made by furniture companies and toy manufacturers," he notes. "They were not designed by engineers. The first ones had a groove in the back of the seat that would attach to the lap belt. That's it. There were no shoulder restraints, just a shield in front that was supposed to keep the kid in. But nothing prevented the kid from sliding under or getting catapulted over or even just slamming against it with his chest.

"Then the manufacturers put a belt underneath to prevent kids from sliding under. This was the type used by Teresa Fuentes. But a taller child could still flex over it. That injured a lot of kids. Their heads would slam against the front, or they would flex to a point where they suffered spinal cord injuries or brain damage or had eviscerated intestines.

"There were dozens, hundreds, of cases against the car seat manufacturers. The companies finally started adding shoulder restraints that would come from the back of the seat over the kids' shoulders and attach in the front, then down to their legs. They called them five-point belts. Those seats protected the kids."

Rarely did these car seat cases go to trial. Invariably the companies settled out of court to avoid negative publicity and legal fees. "Clearly, there's been an education of the manufacturers," Habush adds. "They dragged their feet for years. Yes, they had to redesign and recast the whole seat, and that was expensive. But the redesigns sure stopped the lawsuits. More importantly, it stopped the injuries to these kids."

The Fuentes case was one of a string of successful child seat lawsuits that Habush and his firm worked on. In another horrifying accident, a baby was ejected from her car seat when it failed to restrain her upper torso. Her

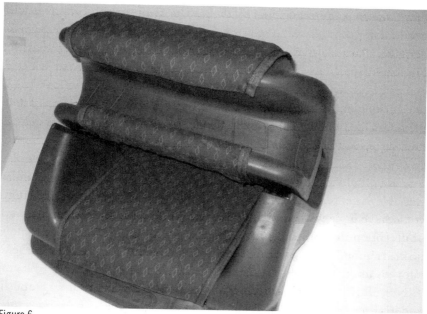

Figure 6

Inadequate restraint

This poorly designed child car seat did not provide protection in high-impact accidents.
Photo credit: Robert Habush

small body was crushed beneath the front passenger seat. Tim Trecek, a Habush partner who handles a large percentage of product liability lawsuits for the firm, remembers working on the case. "After the accident, the mother, who was also injured, was looking for her baby and couldn't find her in the car. She thought she was tossed into a cornfield. Police came on the scene, and they spent fifteen, twenty minutes looking for this little girl. It got to the point where the officers finally asked, 'Are you sure you really had your daughter in the car?' They ultimately found her underneath the seat."

The car seat manufacturer argued that it was not liable for the girl's death. But this case had an insidious twist. "This was a specific car seat that had been the subject of litigation for years," says Trecek. "There was a subsequent purchaser of the company that manufactured this seat. So what Bob did was ask for the purchase agreement between the seller and the buyer. In that document, which must have been close to 150 pages long, there was an acknowledgment by the purchaser of the company that they would not recall this seat.

"With that information, Bob amended the complaint to say that the original manufacturer and the subsequent purchaser had engaged in a civil conspiracy to keep this seat on the market so they could continue selling it and making profits. And by doing that, they endangered the safety of tens of thousands of children who were being put in this seat with the companies knowing how dangerous it was."

The case did not go to trial because of that one critical bit of information buried in the document. "It enabled Bob to increase the compensation he was able to get for his client," notes Trecek, "because of the fear of what he could have done with that information in front of a jury. This is the kind of deception that Bob has seen for decades and decades. The general public hears about things like this in the movies or on TV and don't believe it happens in the world. But it does."

Not every case, no matter how heartbreaking, is accepted by Habush and his firm. He is careful to make sure prospective clients have bona fide injuries, and he checks diligently for malingerers. "Legitimacy is a huge part of deciding to handle cases in this firm," says Terry Tadysak. "For my first ten years working with the firm, I had in my office the annual reports for the men's and women's bowling leagues in the greater Milwaukee area. When somebody came in and said they were hurt in an automobile accident, and they couldn't pick up the groceries, they couldn't carry their child, they were off of work for two or three months and were in pain every day, the attorneys had me go through bowling records to see whether or not the potential client continued to show up for their bowling league after the injury. If they were still bowling, we would disqualify them as clients. These are not the sorts of people Bob wants to represent. There's an expression, 'You take them as you get them.' There's some truth to that. But if there's any inkling that what these people are claiming is not legitimate, or not to the extent that they are suggesting, these are cases we would decline."

But when a prospective client is truly injured and in need of strong representation, Habush will take the case for all the right reasons. "We have a products team meeting every month where we discuss new cases that are coming in," says Ken Jarvis, a paralegal at Habush Habush & Rottier since 1989. "I remember this one case, a four-year-old girl who was injured in a car crash." The girl was sitting in the back seat of her mother's Ford Explorer, strapped into a conventional seat belt. Ford, at the time, did not install adjusters on seat belts in the back seat with shoulder straps that can be raised or lowered in accordance with a pssenger's height. They ensure a snug fit. So when the Explorer was struck by another car, the girl rolled out of the seat belt and suffered injuries that rendered her a paraplegic.

The products team turned down the case, says Jarvis. "I thought, 'Man, we're talking about a four-year-old paraplegic? I'm going to do some research.' and see if there are any other similar cases against Ford.'" He turned up several cases and presented his findings to Habush, who overturned the products team. "It was Bob being angry at what could have been a simple fix," Jarvis says. "All Ford had to do was put the strap adjuster in the back seat, and that would have prevented this four-year-old child from being a paraplegic." Ford settled with the girl's family for about $2 million, Jarvis recalls.

"Bob will be the last one, for the most part, to say no," he adds. "That's because he wants to say yes so bad, even in the face of some facts that might not look so good to us."

For example, contributory negligence is frequently used as a defense to a negligence case. "This is where our client contributed to some degree to his own injuries," Jarvis explains. "The level of that contributory negligence will dictate whether we take the case or not. A lot of times in our meetings, somebody will say, 'Look at how high the contrib is. I don't know how we can win this.' And Bob will say, 'You guys need to convince a jury that, yeah, he contributed to his own accident. But you know what? He wasn't the designer of the product. He doesn't know what the designer should have known. He's a poor guy at a factory who was trying to make a day's living.'

"Bob knows he can sway a jury. He knows he can lessen that percentage of contributory negligence on our client because of his talent, and he wants to instill that in the others. Of course, we have to look at it from a business perspective, but it's also a matter of right and wrong."

Wendy Kummer v. General Motors Corp.

Wendy Kummer was a typical, happy-go-lucky teenager from Sheboygan, Wisconsin. She went out for a drive one winter day with her girlfriends, buckling herself into the back seat of a friend's 1988 Oldsmobile Delta 88. No horseplay, no drinking, just a bunch of high school kids having fun.

As they drove along, a gust of snow blew across the asphalt, and suddenly the Oldsmobile was enshrouded in white. The driver applied the brakes but didn't see the snowplow in front of her in time and crashed. With no shoulder strap to hold her, Wendy jackknifed over her seat belt and broke her back.

"It was a horrible thing," remembers Terry Tadysak, the Habush investigator who worked the case. "She came into the office in a wheelchair, and her eyes swelled with tears. Her entire life had been turned upside down. Her father didn't know which way to turn, what to do next. He asked if there was something Mr. Habush could do to help. And that, I believe, was the beginning of Bob taking on these automakers with rear-seat lap belts in their vehicles. Every vehicle manufactured in the United States up until the late 1980s did not have three-point belts in the back seat. Bob was instrumental in bringing about those changes."

Habush went after General Motors on Wendy Kummer's behalf. He ultimately negotiated a settlement with the automobile giant for $6 million. Years later, Wendy won a beauty contest for young women who were paraplegics.

The advancement of seat belt design was ponderous. Manufacturers resisted making changes—until they were pushed. "First, the auto manufacturers put lap belts in the front seat," says Habush. "Then they put three-point belts in the front seat but not the back seat. The automakers fought that for years. 'The back seat is safer,' they said. 'Put your kids in back because if you get into a crash, the rear passengers are protected by the front seats,' blah, blah, blah.

"It took years of personal injury cases to get a shoulder strap on the rear seat system. But for the middle of the seat, they still maintained that a lap belt was enough. Like they weren't smart enough to figure out how to get a shoulder belt in the middle seat. I had cases of people getting paralyzed sitting in the middle. The force of the belt impacting the abdomen as the body moves forward would tear people's intestines and bowel. Most frequently, once the speeds got beyond twenty or twenty-five miles per hour on impact, people wound up being paralyzed from the waist down with vertebral fractures.

"Finally, Detroit figured out it was cheaper to put the goddamn three-point belt on all seat positions than to fight lawsuits. But there's a perfect example of stubbornness of manufacturers. They didn't want to be the first company to do it. The salespeople told them, 'People are going to think our car is dangerous because the competitors don't have three-point belts in theirs.' No one wanted to be a leader."

In another seat belt case, Habush went after Chrysler, a company he had gone up against years earlier when representing Julie Retzloff, the young woman who suffered brain damage when her skull was fractured by a non-flexing rearview mirror. This time, he represented a child injured in a Chrysler minivan. To demonstrate how manufacturers shortchanged the safety of American car owners, he sent Terry Tadysak to Europe, where automakers were required to install as standard equipment three-point seat belts that had shoulder restraints.

"He had me go to Europe to purchase a 1988 Chrysler minivan and ship that thing back to Milwaukee in a metal box," says Tadysak. "He brought it into the courtroom, the entire vehicle, to show the jury how Chrysler manufactured the minivan on the assembly line in North America—in Windsor, Canada—and then shipped it brand-new to Germany with three-point belts. Brand new. So the Germans got the three-point belt protection, and the Americans were driving around with Chrysler's family van unprotected for their children.

"Bob's ability to use demonstrative evidence is just phenomenal," he adds. "He has taken entire vehicles and reassembled them in courtrooms. When he tried the Larry Totsky case and assembled the transmission from the Volkswagen, lawyers came from all over the state to look at the exhibits. He's brought full motorcycles in. I even remember in one case we built a miniature airstrip in the courtroom to demonstrate how an airplane had crashed.

"But he is very careful about how he does it. He wants the attention to focus on his ability to persuade, as opposed to the physical demonstrations that he's presenting being more convincing than he is. Like with the Chrysler minivan, it was more important to Bob that the jurors believed what he was telling them, and his position on this product not being safe, than the actual piece of evidence. His art of persuasion ranks very high on his list of accomplishments."

Toni Newton v. General Motors Corp.

Habush's representation of Toni Newton was yet another product liability case against General Motors. However, as Habush tells it, this one proved to be a particular thorny case that turned scrappy and, at times, farcical.

Toni Newton was riding in the front seat of a 1978 Oldsmobile Cutlass Supreme, sandwiched between her boyfriend, who was driving, and a passenger to her right on a wide bucket seat. During a heavy rainstorm, the Oldsmobile hydroplaned and spun 180 degrees, crashing into an oncoming car.

Upon impact, the front seat of the Oldsmobile collapsed backward, and Newton and the other two occupants were thrown into the rear. Her head struck the back seat, breaking several vertebrae. At age twenty, she was a paraplegic. "When the police found her," Habush says, "she wasn't seat-belted because at that time there were no seat belts in that middle portion of front seats."

This was not a typical car crash case. "First of all, it was against General Motors," he says, "and at that time, my theory of how she was injured was on the cutting edge of crashworthiness—the seats collapsed and catapulted a passenger into the rear seat, creating a spinal cord injury. More than that, the car spun out of control so that it was traveling rearward on the highway. Worse than that, Toni wasn't even sitting in the passenger, driver, or back seat. She was sitting on the edge of the oversized bucket seat. So it was a peculiar rear-ender, to say the least."

The trial was scheduled in federal court in Shreveport, Louisiana. Habush had six weeks to prepare. To get the lay of the land, he consulted with a friend, Scotty Baldwin, a trial lawyer from eastern Texas who knew Louisiana.

"Oh, no," Baldwin told Habush. "You are going in front of the worst damn judge you could ever imagine, Federal Judge Thomas Stagg. He's a Nixon appointee, and he's just a bear. He's got a terrible temperament. On top of that, Shreveport is a hotbed of tort reform *and* a General Motors company town. There's a GM truck plant right in town. It's a huge employer."

As he listened, Habush started to fume. "How the hell did I get myself into this mess," he muttered.

He asked Baldwin for advice on winning over a southern jury. "I don't know how they're going to accept a Yankee down there," Habush said, "so give me a few local colloquialisms that I can use that would make me seem like one of the folks."

Baldwin rolled off a few idioms: All hat, no cattle . . . Don't buy a pig in a poke . . . That dog don't hunt.

The last expression caught Habush's attention. "That's a good one," he said. "It's like saying, 'That's bullshit.' In a case against General Motors, I'm sure I'll have a chance to use it."

(He waited for the opportunity to use the phrase through the entire trial but never got the chance. Until the final arguments. "The General Motors attorney, Burkholder, got up, gave his argument," Habush recalls. "I waited for my rebuttal, and then I tore into him for some nonsense he was spewing. 'That is the biggest bunch of baloney,' I said to the jury. 'If you buy that, go to the jury room and go home. You know, where I come from up in Wisconsin, we have an expression: 'That dog don't hunt.' I don't know if you have that down here. 'That dog don't hunt.' Well, the jury looked at me like 'What the hell is he talking about? What dog? Where is the dog in this case?' A total lack of response. And I'm thinking, 'I'm gonna kill Scotty Baldwin the next time I see him. I'm gonna kill him.'")

Habush was convinced he was walking into a losing case. "I tried to get the trial adjourned but wasn't successful. So we go down to Shreveport, and I put together my usual experts, a neurosurgeon and a biomechanical engineer. The neurosurgeon had worked with the U.S. Department of Transportation and had done a study on head and neck injuries caused by lack of proper design in automobiles. So he was not only a neurosurgeon but also a forensic neurosurgeon who was wily in the ways of courtroom. He was nationally known, just a treasure. The biomechanical engineer, interestingly enough, had filed a petition with the National Highway Traffic Safety Administration, pressing them to increase the strength of the seat backs. The car companies had never done it. Their position was that if you made the seat back too stiff, it would cause injury in a rear-ender because people's heads would crash into the roof lining or snap back and cause whiplash. So they said it was good to have seats that 'yielded.' Never once did they use the word 'collapsed,' despite the fact that there were dozens of photos showing that the seats in the Newton car had completely collapsed."

Through discovery, Habush and his team found that a General Motors engineer years earlier had written about the weakness of seat backs in connection with tests of other matters. GM had also made a video for the purpose of headrest analysis, showing crash-test dummies getting thrust into the rear and hitting the back seat. "Only one video, and after that they said they had never tested it again," Habush says. "So I had the engineer's article, and I had that one tape. Which was not very much."

For a "show-and-tell" before the jury, he had what he calls a cut-off buck constructed. "It's a portion of the car frame with the seats and seat belts in it," Habush explains. "The front end and rear of the car are cut off completely, so it looks like a skeleton car. That's what I used as an exhibit to demonstrate how the front seat back collapsed and Toni Newton was slung into the rear seat. I started to feel a little better about the case."

Habush went to the Shreveport courthouse one day to mark exhibits. There he met Judge Stagg. He was a formidable man, six feet tall with a full head of white hair and a booming voice, like he was talking from deep inside a well.

"You're from Milwaukee?" the judge said, eyeing Habush.

"Yes, sir, I am."

"Well, I want to tell you something, Mr. *Hay*bush. All your demonstrative evidence isn't going to do a damn thing down here. Forget about all that fancy stuff you do and all the tricks you've played on juries, because our jurors are as dumb as fence posts. None of it's going to work on them. I promise you that. And I am not going to let you get away with any kind of funny business. Do you understand that, Mr. *Hay*bush?"

The newly warned Bob "Haybush" couldn't believe what he was hearing. "I'm thinking to myself, 'Oh, God, it isn't bad enough I've got to be in

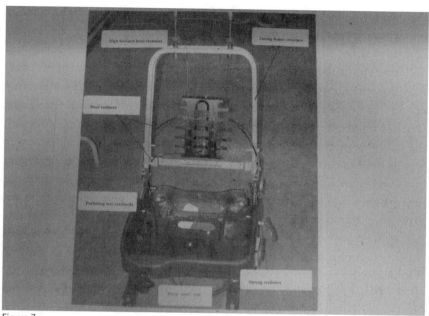

Figure 7
Automobile safety
Habush demonstrated how a reinforced seat back would prevent collapse in rear-end collisions.
Photo credit: Robert Habush

Shreveport, a city with a General Motors factory, with tort reform signs all over the place. But now I've got this judge who's up my ass before I even start. This isn't happening to me. This is a nightmare. I know I'm going to wake up and this will all be a big joke.'"

The trial started days later. Judge Stagg's courtroom was palatial, paneled wood with all the latest electronic equipment. "It was like a millionaire's house," recalls Habush. He was up against a defense attorney named Evan Burkholder, who was from a Virginia law firm that specialized in representing General Motors and other automakers.

The defense argued that Newton hit her head on the front door panel, not on the back seat, even though she had no bruises or cuts whatsoever. "Their whole specialty was defending crash-related cases against guys like me that are loony enough to take them," says Habush. "But Burkholder was uncharismatic. He was anal, more serious than an undertaker. He was the antithesis of someone with jury appeal. Apparently he must've been good, or they wouldn't have kept using him over and over again. But he and I got along like oil and water right from the get-go."

Throughout most of the trial, Toni Newton sat in a wheelchair only fifteen feet from the jurors. "Toni was just twenty years old, five feet two, young and beautiful. And vulnerable," Habush says. "The jury knew that she was rendered paraplegic by the accident. They had the dimensions of the calamity right there in front of them."

Most of Habush's expert witnesses held up well under oath. One witness was especially effective: a former design engineer for General Motors. He testified that GM had designed a stronger optional seat that would have prevented Newton from being flung into the back seat of the Oldsmobile. And he testified that the 1970 Volkswagen Beetle and 1973 American Motors Gremlin both had stronger seat backs than the GM Oldsmobile. If the older Beetle and Gremlin could have strong seat backs, why not the 1978 Oldsmobile Cutlass Supreme?

Habush got the upper hand on his cross-examinations of several defense witnesses. "One of them had testified a hundred times for General Motors," he says. "He hadn't testified for anyone else other than car companies. He was medical doctor who seldom practiced, and he had degrees in civil engineering and nuclear engineering. He testified on direct examination that he was more experienced and skilled than my expert neurosurgeon, Dr. Ayub Ommaya, who also was a biomechanical engineer and the chief medical adviser to the National Highway Traffic Safety Administration. Well, I wasn't going to let that stand. So on cross-examination, I had the GM witness's CV, his curriculum vitae, which was about a half inch thick. Next to it, I have a New York City phone book."

Q: You're aware that Dr. Ommaya [Habush's expert] has 177 papers that he's written?
A: In various medical dissipations, sure.
Q: Are you aware that he's made 128 lectures? [He taps the phone book.]
A: I didn't count them.
Q: How many lectures are listed on your CV?

A: I don't list every lecture on my CV.

Q: You must list the most important ones, wouldn't you?

A: No.

Q: Have you listed any?

A: Yes. I have listed one of the courses I taught in a seminar to the Association for the Advancement of Automotive Medicine.

Q: Have you ever been a medical advisor to the National Highway Traffic and Safety Administration, like Dr. Ommaya?

A: No.

Q: Have you ever been asked to consult, like Dr. Ommaya, for the Department of Transportation by the Secretary of Transportation?

A: No.

Q: Are you aware of the kind of work that Dr. Ommaya has done with head and neck injury mechanisms for the National Highway Traffic Safety Administration?

A: In his advisory capacity, yes.

Q: Are you aware of the extensiveness of his effort from 1980 to 1985 researching accidents and head and neck injuries from automobile accidents?

A: I'm not intimately familiar with it, but I know he's done considerable work.

Q: Don't you think you might want to become intimately familiar with it before you tell this court and jury that you're more qualified than he is?

A: No.

Q: By the way, I found your bill. . . . You budgeted how much for this case?

A: The total amount budgeted by my office is $43,400.

Q: Are you up to the budget yet of $43,400?

A: I don't know. Probably not.

Q: Pretty close?

A: Getting there.

In the verbal thrust and parry between attorney and witness, Habush clearly dominated, piercing the credibility of the defense team's prize witness.

During another witness's testimony, Habush was far more forgiving and gentlemanly, taking the high road yet managing to get in a dig against his adversary. Burkholder, the defense attorney, was questioning a GM expert witness when the witness began to cough, prompting this exchange:

WITNESS: Excuse me, I've got a cold. I've been taking this medicine and my mouth gets dry. And I need to go get a quick sip.
BURKHOLDER: Why don't you bring the cup over, sir.
HABUSH: Want one of my cough drops?
BURKHOLDER: Don't take it from him. Don't take a cough drop.
HABUSH: I'll swallow one first, then you wait five minutes and see if I die.
WITNESS: I'll try one, thank you.
HABUSH: You're welcome.
WITNESS: Is this an approved cough drop?
HABUSH: Yes, made by General Motors.

"These are the kind of things that happen in a trial that you can't anticipate but you've got to be ready for," says Habush, laughing. "And if you have a sense of humor and you're lighthearted, even in an otherwise tense situation you can take advantage of stuff like that. A cough drop."

With the trial nearly complete, all that remained were final arguments. Again, Judge Stagg came at him from out of left field.

"All right, I got a stopwatch on you guys," he said to the lawyers. "Mr. Haybush, I'll let you have thirty minutes for your opening and your rebuttal. You can use whatever you need for opening and save the rest for rebuttal, but if you use up the thirty minutes on the opening part, you can't do a rebuttal."

"This ought to be very interesting," Habush muttered to himself as he unstrapped his wristwatch and placed it in his hand. Dividing his gaze between his watch and the jurors, he delivered his closing argument in twenty minutes, saving ten short minutes for his rebuttal, picking apart the evidence given by each GM expert. As the plaintiff's attorney, Habush had the last word, although it was abbreviated, as with all rebuttals. He spoke at a rapid-fire pace, but convincingly, acknowledging that the Shreveport jurors lived in a GM town, yet reminding them that Toni Newton was one of their own, as revealed in this excerpt:

> You haven't heard one word said by Mr. Burkholder about something we talked about in the trial. What about pickup truck seats? All pickup trucks made in this town, millions of pickup trucks in the United States have completely inflexible stiff seats, do they not? Do they go back? They're stiff.
>
> You can judge the quality of a case by the quality of the evidence, and when lawyers make things up or tell you things that aren't the truth with respect to what's in that record, you judge it accordingly. This is a room where justice is done. It's not where games are played, not where professional witnesses are presented to you, not dazzling you with wonderful shows and demonstrations. Common sense, members of the jury, common sense! It's right from wrong. It's wrong that this seat should have collapsed like that. It's wrong this little girl got paralyzed by this. It's wrong.
>
> This wonderful corporation—and they do a lot of great things—they blew it this time. They made a mistake, so admit it. It's not so terrible. Once in a while they can be wrong. The seats in this particular car for the center seating position were unreasonably dangerous. It's not the end of the world for them. They can be wrong. So only you, her peers, members of the community, her neighbors, can answer that question for her. We hope, we hope and pray that you will see it the way we see it.

Habush barely made it to the finish line. "I'm saying my final word, taking my last breath, and *Bing! Bing! Bing!* the alarm goes off. 'You're through, Mr. Haybush,' said the judge. And I said to him, 'You bet I am.'"

The jury's verdict split liability: General Motors, 67 percent negligent; the driver of the car, 33 percent negligent.

Because the case was bifurcated, the attorneys were ordered to reconvene in a week with the same jury to argue damages. Habush returned to Milwaukee, satisfied and tremendously relieved by the verdict.

In the interim, one of his lawyers discovered, buried in medical records, that Toni Newton had had an abortion shortly before the accident. Habush

Figure 8
David v. Goliath
Habush won a jury verdict against GM for crash victim Toni Newton.
Photo credit: Robert Habush

would be required to inform the defense attorney of the discovery. He had no way of knowing whether the judge would allow it to be admitted as evidence. But because having an abortion is known to cause psychological trauma to some women, he knew this piece of information could play badly among the jurors and undermine his argument for damages. "In a redneck jurisdiction, who knows how many antiabortion evangelists and Southern Baptists would be on the jury," he says.

But fortune smiled on him. Before the trial reconvened, GM's chief negotiator, Michael Rezmerski, arrived in Milwaukee to offer a settlement. ("He looked like an identical twin to the actor Wilfred Brimley," Habush remembers. "A big guy with a drooping mustache.") Rezmerski wrote out a check for $3.5 million, and the case was over.

"From that point on, the *Newton* case was the gift that kept on giving," says Habush. "Rezmerski never again wanted me to go to trial against him. And every General Motors case I had thereafter—there must have been twenty of them—he settled for big bucks. As far as Rezmerski was concerned—and this is a quote from him—I was 'in the pantheon of trial lawyers in the United States.' He respected me greatly. Why? Because I beat him in a case that he thought I couldn't win. He never forgot that."

To cap off the victory, Habush and his legal team went to a Shreveport restaurant with Toni Newton and her family to celebrate. It was a happy occasion. As Habush and his investigator, Terry Tadysak, left the restaurant, they heard gunfire popping in the night. "Terry throws me down into a ditch to protect me," Habush says. Could it have been some local GM worker getting even with the northerner plaintiff's attorney? "Turns out Shreveport had the highest crime rate in the state of Louisiana. Gunfights were commonplace in that town."

CHAPTER FIVE

The Activist

Bob Habush was two years out of law school and working at his father's firm when a case came into the office one day of a little girl who was injured in a Milwaukee park. Three-year-old Janet Holytz was playing near a drinking fountain by a playground. A steel trapdoor covering an underground water meter had been left unlocked and open by a city employee. As the toddler was playing, the trapdoor, weighing fifty pounds, slammed shut, crushing her hand.

Janet's parents wanted the city to reimburse them for medical expenses, so they sued. Jesse Habush gave the case—*Holytz v. City of Milwaukee*—to his son.

"The case was demurred; the judge dismissed it," Bob Habush says. "As well he should have. The fact was the City of Milwaukee had immunity from negligence lawsuits." Under the doctrine of governmental tort immunity, a private citizen who is injured due to a local, state, or federal government's negligence has no cause of action against that government.

The concept of immunity to tort claims is based on England's "divine right of kings" and dates back to a 1788 English case: *Russell v. the Men Dwelling in the County of Devon*. When a citizen named "Russell" was injured leading his wagon over a worn-out public bridge, the County of Devon was ruled exempt from liability. In its decision, the English court said the community did not have the funds to pay damages. "It is better that an individual should sustain an injury than that the public should suffer an inconvenience," reasoned the court.

The municipal immunity doctrine was first adopted in the United States in 1812 and in Wisconsin in 1873.

Although municipal immunity was a long-standing common law, Habush's case against the City of Milwaukee was not quite finished. A brief writer at his father's firm wrote a legal brief for the Wisconsin Supreme Court, arguing that the immunity rule should be overturned, following the pattern in several other states at that time.

"My father gave me the brief and said, 'Here, you go argue it.' I wasn't following the Wisconsin Supreme Court at the time, and I remember thinking they were all old-timers, all men, including Justice Myron Gordon, who I had a significant history with afterwards. He was a trial judge in Milwaukee and then a federal judge. He had heard the case I tried against Firestone for the two employees who were nearly burned to death in a chemical fire."

The Milwaukee city attorney argued the case for the city. "Of course he had a lot of precedent going for him," Habush says. "I argued against the immunity law being wrongful and depriving people of their constitutional rights, and blah, blah, blah. I remember the city attorney came up to me after the argument and said, 'Nice job, kid, but no luck. You're not going to win.' Wouldn't you know, the Supreme Court overruled governmental immunity. I was twenty-six years old, this little pisser in his first Wisconsin Supreme Court argument who did away with governmental immunity in Wisconsin.

"As a side note, this case further estranged me from my father. He thought I did OK, but when it was written up in the national publications, he took credit for it. It became 'the Jesse Habush lawsuit that did away with governmental immunity in Wisconsin.'"

The state legislature was quick to react to the decision. It placed a $50,000 recovery cap on lawsuits that were brought against municipalities. "There also were certain notice requirements you had to meet, file a notice of claim, et cetera," Habush says. "And that has stayed in existence ever since. So the state took back its immunity. Not totally, but for all intents and purposes it made the cases have very limited value for victims and plaintiff's attorneys."

Tort law in general began to evolve with the passing in 1946 of the Federal Tort Claims Act, which allowed citizens to sue the U.S. government for monetary damages for "loss of property, or personal injury or death caused by the negligent or wrongful act or omission of any employee of the government." Yet common law in the United States contained rigid precedents that had been adopted from English law.

"For example, under the common law, if you were killed in an accident, your survivors could not sue for you," says Habush. "The only cases for injuries were for victims that survived. Death claims did not exist. There were no claims for people killed. There's a legendary story, which no doubt was made up, with respect to train crashes. The story goes, the railroad companies would position an employee in the caboose of every train. In the event of a wreck, he would run car by car and make sure that the seriously injured did not survive. The crowbar would finish them off so there wouldn't be any lawsuits."

States began to pass wrongful death statutes one by one, allowing survivors to make liability claims, but with caps to limit the amount of damages that could be awarded. "Wisconsin had a $22,500 limit on pecuniary loss; that is, loss of income," Habush says. "The loss of society claim—or the loss of love and affection—was limited to $2,500. Total $25,000, rich, poor, good, bad.

"Over the years, through the efforts of trial lawyers lobbying, and friendly governors and legislators, the limit on wrongful death would be increased, and eventually the cap on pecuniary loss would be eliminated. The cap on loss of society continued; it went to $5,000, $10,000, and so on, to where the cap on loss of society and wrongful death is now $300,000 for an adult, $500,000 for a child. That's the maximum."

As tort law progressed, the so-called tort reform movement had yet to be born. In the 1970s, though, things began to change. In more and more states, the business community—particularly the insurance industry—successfully pressured sympathetic lawmakers to push for additional limits on tort law.

One such attempt was "no-fault" auto insurance. Under this idea, insured motorists would receive reimbursement for losses without proof of fault in an accident. In return, unless they could prove permanent injury, policyholders were prohibited from seeking damages through the tort system for losses caused by others involved in the accident. The goal of no-fault was to lower premiums by reducing costly litigation.

"No-fault became very popular," Habush says. "It was adopted in multiple states and pretty much destroyed the automobile practice for lawyers, especially personal injury lawyers. In Wisconsin, however, the insurance companies were doing so well they didn't want to attach a type of health insurance provision. Accordingly, they didn't press for no-fault legislation."

Because the Wisconsin insurance industry did not back no-fault legislation, Habush and other trial attorneys handily turned back its proponents. "No-fault never passed; it was defeated," he says. "But that was the first ugly manifestation of what I would call tort reform, although it wasn't called tort reform at the time."

The legislative battle over no-fault insurance politicized Habush. He was twice elected president of the Wisconsin Academy of Trial Lawyers (now the Wisconsin Association of Justice)—the state's voluntary trial bar—and for ten years chaired its legislative committee, which was nicknamed the war council. By the 1980s, tort reform had become a full-fledged national offensive, and Habush was leading the fight in Washington, D.C., to stop it.

As the nation's largest trial bar, in 1985 the Association of Trial Lawyers of America was a powerful and robust force on Capitol Hill and in state chapters around the country. Now called the American Association for Justice, the group was formed in 1946 by a handful of plaintiff's lawyers who represented victims of industrial accidents in workers' compensation cases. The organization grew to sixty thousand members. Their aim: to use the American civil justice system as a regulatory solution to problems ill resolved by the legislative process, unchecked by governmental agencies, and ignored by the private sector.

In the 1970s, Habush had been elected to the ATLA's board of governors and, rising through the ranks, was elected as a parliamentarian and secretary of the association. In 1985, after having withdrawn for a few years from an active role in ATLA politics, he decided to get involved again and run for second vice president, the next level above secretary.

"It was customary for a small clique of past presidents to get together and anoint various people to run for office. They handpicked them," he explains. "And if they didn't handpick you, you couldn't do it. The group said to me, 'We already have someone else picked for second vice president, and it isn't you. You can run for parliamentarian again.' I said, 'I've already been parliamentarian.' And they told me, 'Too bad, run again.' Well, this was the wrong thing to say to me. I said, 'I'll tell you what. I'm going to run for president-elect against your chosen candidate.'"

Bucking the status quo, he challenged the candidacy of the presumed president-elect, an attorney from Detroit named Sheldon Miller. "I threw my name in the hat and traveled all over the United States at my own expense to visit with trial lawyers associations in California, Washington, Texas, Florida, Kentucky, New York, Illinois. I talked to all of them and got their commitment to vote for me. My opponent didn't know what was going on because he thought he had it locked."

With the ATLA convention to be held in Chicago, Habush zeroed in on securing the support of Leonard Ring, Illinois's top ATLA leader. Ring, with considerable assistance from one of Habush's best friends, the Chicago personal injury attorney Richard Fleisher, came through with more than four hundred votes from Illinois alone. Habush also marshaled the support of dozens of lawyers who bused in from Wisconsin to the north. "The Wisconsin lawyers might have been happy to get me out of the state for a couple years, maybe that was their incentive, I don't know," Habush says. "Sheldon Miller brought in people from Detroit, too, but I brought in more. He didn't have a chance."

Habush took office as ATLA president-elect in 1985 and became president in 1986. Topping his list of objectives: stopping tort reform. "Before I became president, tort reform had manifested itself in numerous ways. One, of course, was caps on monetary damages, caps on pain and suffering. Another manifestation was to do away with 'joint and several liability.' Under the existing common law, if you had two people at fault, say, and one was 90 percent at fault and one was 10 percent at fault, you could recover the entire judgment against the 10 percenter, which was very beneficial for plaintiffs and their lawyers when the 10 percent defendant had deep pockets and the 90 percent defendant had no insurance at all. That was at the top of the list of tort reformers, and it was eliminated in most states."

Russ Herman, an outstanding Louisiana trial attorney and longtime ATLA member, got to know Habush when he was campaigning for ATLA president-elect. Herman himself was elected president of the association for the 1989–90 term.

"During my first term on the board, I didn't really know any of the internal politics," Herman says. "I had met a lawyer from Detroit, a really likable guy, Sheldon Miller. And he recruited me to vote for him for ATLA president-elect. I didn't meet Bob Habush till much later, when he was Miller's opponent. I was really impressed with Bob, and I went up to him and I said, 'You know, I gave a commitment to Sheldon Miller, and I don't break my commitments, but I want to tell you I have a lot of respect for you, and I wish you well.' He nodded and just moved on.

"After he was elected, he sought me out, and he said, 'Look, I know you didn't vote for me, but your peers on the board really respect you, and I do too. They tell me you built an outstanding 'key-person' network in Louisiana, and I want you to be my key-person committee chairman.' I thought, 'He's looking to get the job done, and he's not concerned about whether I voted for him or not. Once I heard that, I said, "OK, this guy has got character. He's got depth, he's got class.' From that moment on, I was not just loyal to Bob, but I've had a very, very warm spot in my heart for Bob."

The same year Habush took office, the tort reform movement organized under the umbrella of the American Tort Reform Association, made up of the U.S. Chamber of Commerce, the American Medical Association, the American Insurance Association, and the American Council of Engineering Companies, along with various trade associations and corporations, including several that Habush had gone against in trial: Chrysler, Ford, Caterpillar, Farmers Insurance, State Farm, Merck, Pfizer, Coca Cola, Shell Oil.

"When I became ATLA's president, tort reform had sprung up all over the United States," Habush says. "It was a huge multimillion-dollar public relations onslaught against the tort system and an attack on the civil jury system. Some of the state offices had terrific lobbying organizations, and they were able to beat it back. But still we were vulnerable because it was almost impossible to fight a battle in all fifty states. So many of the bills at the state level did get passed.

"What I did was try to change ATLA from a primarily educational organization into a 'war machine.' I brought in leaders from all the states, and we organized a national battle against tort reform. We published white papers and briefs on the unconstitutionality of caps. I testified in Congress, both in the House and the Senate. And the tort reformers were never able to get any bills passed on the national level. This was true even though then–Wisconsin senator Bob Kasten had obsessively tried to pass a products liability bill that would restrict lawsuits against product manufacturers and sellers."

When Habush took over, ATLA's public relations effort was in disarray, Herman says. "Bob was instrumental in kick-starting the association. He is a very dynamic fella, very thoughtful, and very, very focused. Under his leadership we were able to institute a real public relations committee and get it funded. We founded a political 'key-persons' committee that became very active. And the first piece of legislation that ATLA had to fight on the floor of the Congress was defeated through his leadership and our key-person committee."

The legislation, a maritime bill, would have capped recoveries by seamen injured on navigable waters. Introduced in a Democrat-controlled House by Rep. Gerry Studds, a Democrat from Massachusetts, it was the first bill ever introduced in Congress that put caps on damages.

Habush looks back to the battle. "The bill had the backing of the maritime union. Our legislative director of ATLA, Allen Parker, said, 'We can't beat it. Let it go.' I said, 'Hell, no. I am not going to allow the first tort reform bill to pass on my watch in the first month of my presidency.' I got our lobbyists to agree to fight it, and I called into Washington a lawyer from each state to lobby their representatives. I put Russ Herman, a fabulous attorney, in charge of what was to become our first battle group that in later battles proved decisive. I personally met with all the legislative leaders and reminded them that trial lawyers were their loyal contributors and that they would be very unhappy if this bill passed, and that I was the leader of sixty thousand trial lawyers."

The bill was voted down by a substantial margin.

"After that victory," Herman recalls, "there was some news report that referred to ATLA as the strongest lobbying force of Congress. . . . The so-called lawsuit crisis—a myth created by the major corporations along with the Chamber of Commerce and the American Tort Reform Association—was counterattacked through Bob's emphasis on public relations."

In a chronicle of the fifty-year history of the Association of Trial Lawyers of America, titled *David v. Goliath: ATLA and the Fight for Everyday Justice*, authors Richard S. Jacobson and Jeffrey R. White single out Habush for taking action to repair the frayed reputation of trial lawyers, a goal of his since his days at his father's "bargain basement" law firm.

"ATLA's leaders were clearly concerned that incidents of blatant solicitation undermined their effectiveness in combatting tort reform," wrote the authors. "President Robert Habush stated that the conduct of lawyers who appeared at Bhopal [following the 1984 gas disaster] as well as at train derailments and airplane crashes 'was ghoulish. It was repugnant. It made everything easier for our enemies to push through what was then conveniently labeled anti-lawyer legislation.' Habush proposed, and the board adopted, resolutions against frivolous lawsuits, unlawful solicitations, frivolous defenses and excessive legal fees."

Jacobson and White praise Habush for championing the battle against those who sought to vilify civil law practitioners.

When Robert Habush assumed the presidency in 1986, he took command of a heavily embattled garrison. ATLA was facing a flood of "lawsuit crisis" propaganda, hundreds of tort reform proposals in state legislatures, and special interest legislation affecting products liability, admiralty and aviation cases in Congress.

In the past, most trial lawyers were content to stand back and let their skilled leaders and lobbyists wage their legislative battles. Those leaders and lobbyists, in fact, preferred that the rank and file not get too actively involved. Not this time. Habush issued a "call to arms" in *TRIAL* [magazine] and at every gathering he could address. This time, he stated, no trial lawyer could stand on the sidelines. All were needed, not only for their political action contributions, but also to devote their time and energy to ATLA's committees, communicate their views to their representatives, and take every opportunity to educate the public about what they stand to lose.

Habush knew he could not take for granted that all trial lawyers would answer the call enthusiastically. He had won the presidency after a hard fought and expensive election campaign, defeating the popular incumbent vice-president, Sheldon Miller. Habush needed to gain the respect and support of those who had wanted a different hand at the helm.

He earned that respect and support by giving ATLA what it most desperately needed: strong leadership. ATLA was battling for its very survival, he insisted. He worked ceaselessly through 18-hour days to bend every element of the association toward winning that battle.

Habush launched a "truth campaign" to respond to inaccurate media reports with facts and figures that exposed the fraudulent nature of the "lawsuit crisis."

He also pushed for repeal of the McCarran-Ferguson Act, to clear the way for federal regulation of the insurance industry. He pointed out that insurance had become as important to American business as water and electricity. "They have become a damn big utility," Habush told Congress. Yet they were wholly unregulated, except by ineffective state insurance commissioners. What was needed, he told lawmakers, was "direct regulations by the Federal Trade Commission. . . ."

Habush recognized that the insurance industry was now joined by a new and more dangerous alliance. They were small businesses, day care centers and ski resorts. They were professionals such as architects and accountants. They were city and county governments and charitable organizations.

"These people have now organized into a very effective political force that really doesn't give a damn anymore about insurance even though they were screwed by insurance companies. That's not their agenda," Habush explained. "They believe they should never be sued no matter what they do." In their view, the tort system serves no good or useful purpose. It was something that was run by lawyers for their own benefit, and it threatened their own good work. "This became a religion with them. It had nothing to do anymore with the cost of insurance," Habush declared. "It's become a cult."

And they were far more difficult to oppose. Unlike the insurance industry and big corporations, the small businesses, local governments, and charities were tort reformers with human faces. They received sympathetic portrayals in the media, and often touched people in lawmakers' home districts. Debunking the insurance industry's propaganda was no longer sufficient. "Legislators knew intellectually that there was no litigation explosion in their states," Habush said. "But they also wanted to be reelected."

Habush put his finger on a profound shift in legal thinking. The true believers in the tort reform cult reflected a broader movement driven by ideology, politics and money. It would be several more years before most trial lawyers recognized its full import. . . .

Generals often fail because they march on to a new battlefield with a strategy from the previous war. Bob Habush did not make this mistake. ATLA could not fight alone in defense of the civil-justice system, as it had in the 1970s. The onslaught was simply too well-organized and well-financed. Moreover, legislators and the public, unconcerned by the blatant self-interest of tort reformers seeking to avoid accountability, often dismissed the message from trial lawyers as self-serving.

Habush's first move was to forage the collection of consumer, senior, environmental, and labor organizations that his predecessor Peter Perlman had recruited into a politically effective grassroots organization. A new director of field operations was charged with organizing these groups at the local level. Major organizations included the Consumer Federation of America, Consumers Union, Public Citizen, Public Interest Research Groups, along with education and labor groups. They met frequently in Washington D.C. to exchange information and discuss common goals and strategies. Those organizations, in turn, worked with their local chapters and affiliates.

Soon coalition groups were active in 60 cities and 30 states. They attracted media attention and press conferences where defective products were put on display and had victims tell their stories. They appeared at legislative hearings, dispelling the myth that only self-interested trial lawyers opposed tort reform. . . .

Habush brought with him 15 years of state lobbying experience, and he wasn't shy about wielding whatever political clout he could bring to bear on legislators. He could speak to the fine points of joint and several liability. "But I wanted to talk political action money. I wanted to talk politics. I wanted to talk power—power represented by thousands of trial lawyers who in turn represented thousands of little people and millions of the public seeking their rights in courts."

The political straight talk was amplified by a network of politically savvy and connected trial lawyers around the country who could be counted on to deliver ATLA's message directly to their representatives. Habush tapped Russ Herman for the job of rejuvenating ATLA's neglected key-person network. Herman and his team of Louisiana volunteers burned up the phone lines tracking down and recruiting members with access to legislators. . . .

Habush worked to strengthen the state trial lawyer associations through State Development Fund grants to increase membership and augment political action activities. He also insisted that ATLA put its own house in order, supporting board resolutions that condemned lawyer solicitation at disaster sites, frivolous lawsuits, and excessive fees. His strategy was to remove the misconduct of some lawyers as a front-line issue and keep the focus on the loss of consumer and worker rights under tort reform.

By the end of his term, Habush committed every available ATLA resource to the defense of the civil justice system.

Today, in a political climate that has swung to the right, tort reform has seen a resurgence. In Habush's home state of Wisconsin, the first bill passed by a Republican legislature and signed into law by the Republican governor Scott Walker was an anti-tort law that limited punitive damages and damages for pain and suffering in medical malpractice cases.

"It's always been a Republican versus a Democrat fight," Habush says. "Republicans have always been against the tort system and the recovery of damages because they represent businesses, large and small. But the biggest culprit has been the U.S. Chamber of Commerce. They make personal injury lawyers out to be devils, parasites. The Chamber creates horror stories of burglars who get hurt during a burglary and are able to sue. They come up with these anecdotal stories, most of which are bullshit.

"Take the McDonald's story of the woman who spilled hot coffee in her lap. They claimed that was a frivolous case. It wasn't. McDonald's had been warned that their coffee was too hot, 180 degrees Fahrenheit. There had been hundreds of injuries. This 79-year-old woman suffered third-degree burns from the coffee, and they turned her into a laughingstock. As it turns out, it was a legitimate case.

"In the PR war against trial lawyers, we were convenient scapegoats, greedy bastards that contributed nothing to society. When I was president of ATLA, we had victims testify in front of congressional committees, people in wheelchairs who were injured by drunk drivers, and people who were horribly burned. It didn't make any difference to some Congress members. They were beholden to the special interests, and if they could do away with tort law and the jury system, they would."

Recovery through litigation, as unpopular as it is among the people who get sued, is the primary instigator of safety measures in this country, Habush says. "I was just one of the trial lawyers who was able to exact changes of various types of products. Would Habush Habush & Rottier be the firm it is today if the tort reformers had gotten their way? Absolutely not. I would have still been practicing law, but I don't know if I would have had the financial backing to take on these big rich defendants. Success allows you to have the resources to do that.

"The Industrial Revolution in this country made the United States the greatest industrial might in the history of the world. But most people forget that workers were dying and crippled left and right. They had no recourse against very negligent employers. All kinds of laws were established that in fact prevented workers from suing negligent employers. And finally, Wisconsin became the first state to adopt workers' compensation. Employees gave up the right to sue their employers, but they were given benefits— scheduled payments for permanent injuries, for example, so they could pay their medical bills."

Tort reform in the eighties coincided with tremendous anti–big government, pro-business sentiments that led to deregulation measures by the Reagan administration. Ironically, the deregulation surge produced an environment that was ripe for lawsuits.

Habush explains: "Deregulation allowed manufacturers to run amok and not worry about wings falling off of airplanes and working conditions that were hazardous, about products that were not properly designed and inspected and drugs that came into the marketplace that weren't safe. All this deregulation should have produced greater opportunities for personal injury lawyers, and in many respects it did. But at the same time you had this tension, this paradox, provoked by deregulation and tort reform: government was loosening protections and thus allowing people to get hurt, while at the same time laws were proposed that restricted people who got hurt from getting even."

In 1996, in recognition of Habush's work, the ATLA (today the American Association for Justice) created the AAJ Robert L. Habush Endowment. The multimillion-dollar endowment provides grants to projects that protect and promote a greater public understanding of the civil justice system. In addition, the association awarded him its highest honor: the Champion of Justice Award. And in 2000, AAJ's Wisconsin chapter, the Wisconsin Academy of Justice, named its annual award for trial lawyer of the year after Robert L. Habush.

* * *

In 1977, the U.S. Supreme Court ruled that lawyers had the right to advertise their services. Until then, ethics rules in states across the country had prohibited lawyers from promoting their services in print advertisements or television or radio commercials. Attorneys who violated the rules faced penalties.

The rules grew out of a traditional belief that lawyer ads were imprudent and demeaning to the profession. Lawyers would generate clients based on reputation and word of mouth, so went the theory.

The Supreme Court's decision stemmed from a case called *Bates v. State Bar of Arizona*. Arizona attorneys John Bates and Van O'Steen, just two years out of law school, started a legal clinic in Phoenix. To drum up business, they placed a newspaper ad in the *Arizona Republic*, offering their services at "reasonable rates" for clients with modest incomes. When the Arizona State Bar's disciplinary committee called for a six-month suspension from the bar for Bates and O'Steen, they sued.

The case went to the U.S. Supreme Court, which ruled that the ban violated the two lawyers' First Amendment rights and functioned "to perpetuate the market position of established attorneys." The decision swung open the door for lawyers to advertise and eventually led the way to advertisements among all professions: from doctors and dentists to pharmacists and veterinarians.

In Wisconsin, Bob Habush was one of the first—with reservations. "I read *Bates*," he says, "and I thought, 'Is it going to be open season now for anybody to do an ad and convince some gullible, unsophisticated people that they should come to that lawyer, regardless of ability?' So I mused about that for a while, and one day a TV ad popped up from some lawyer named Ken Hur in Madison. It had him emerging from a lake wearing scuba gear and [saying], 'If you're in over your head, we'll put you through bankruptcy for only $100.' It was totally gimmicky, really discrediting as far as lawyers are concerned. Everyone made fun of it."

TV ads began airing in other states. "In meetings I had attended with other personal injury lawyers, such as the Inner Circle of Advocates, lawyers were starting to worry about whether the ads were going to cut into their business," Habush recalls. "Personal injury law firms have basically two sources of business. If you've been established in a community, particularly a smaller one, you get a lot of direct business. People have heard of your reputation. Clients tell their friends and relatives, so you get repeat business. And then there's referrals from other lawyers who can't do the work themselves."

Habush began to wonder whether advertising would be a necessity to draw more cases to his firm, which he was expanding in smaller markets around the state. "Maybe this is the future," he reasoned. "Maybe in order to ensure that this firm I'm developing survives, I need to start advertising."

He struggled with the decision. "I had mixed feelings, because I had a sense this would piss off other lawyers. If a TV ad aired in their small towns, I would be soliciting business that would take food off of their tables. My referral sources would potentially dry up.

"I was sure I could be the number one advertiser in Wisconsin, because this guy Ken Hur wasn't going anywhere. So in terms of a legitimate high-profile lawyer advertising, I would be the first. But I was certain I would pay a price—perhaps a loss of reputation, perhaps criticism from the judiciary and other lawyers, and potentially a loss of business. Still, I just had a sense advertising was going to become epidemic and it was going to cut into our source of revenue unless we jumped on it."

Habush called Dick McDonald, head of the Milwaukee ad agency McDonald Davis & Associates. After several meetings, the two of them hatched the idea for what would become the Knowing the Law campaign, a series of thirty-second informational television commercials "hosted" by Habush.

"They were designed to be non-hustle, non-solicitation ads," Habush says. "I would teach various topics to anyone who might be involved in a personal injury case, whether it was the meaning of 'negligence,' understanding insurance coverage, or how a jury is picked." No jokes, no gimmicks.

McDonald and Habush taped several commercials at a Milwaukee television studio, WTMJ-TV. Each begins with the ringing sound of a gavel pounding three times. Habush then appears, standing in a mock-up of a wood-paneled office, with plants in the background and faux artwork on the wall. He is dressed in a three-piece pinstriped suit and holding a law book. He presents a question, such as "Do you know what injuries are compensable under workers' compensation law?" or "What are your rights if you are injured by a defective or unsafe product?" Then he delivers a brief lesson and signs off with "The more you know, the better you can protect your family. At Habush Habush & Davis law firm, we want you to know the law."

With a dozen or so ads taped, Habush still wasn't sure he wanted to pull the trigger. He delayed the decision to air them for months. "Here I was, risking a reputation that is very precious. I was almost certain to alienate a great many lawyers by appealing directly to their potential clientele."

Finally he gave the go-ahead. The first spot—a sixty-second introduction—aired on March 27, 1982; from then on, the infomercials ran every Sunday during WTMJ's 10 p.m. news show.

"We started the spots, and the silence from bar association members was thunderous," he says. "I didn't get any nasty letters or nasty phone calls. Just silence.

"Interesting enough, four months later, the *American Bar Association Journal* published an article with me on the cover and the headline 'The Right Way to Advertise on TV.' It was like a *Good Housekeeping* Seal of Approval. It emboldened me, but clearly I noticed a dwindling of the referral business. It just became less and less and less, and it happened at a time when my competition started increasing."

Some of his stiffest competitors were lawyers who had left the Habush firm under especially strained circumstances. Jim Murphy, for one, was a former assistant district attorney hired by Habush in the early 1970s. As a partner, Murphy worked mostly on product liability cases, and when he left the firm in 1979, he immediately became a competitor.

Bill Cannon and Pat Dunphy, two young and aggressive trial lawyers, had one of the more acrimonious departures. One evening, on July 3, 1985, a Milwaukee lawyer happened to be walking with his wife past the Habush offices. He spotted Pat Dunphy loading up a minivan with files. "I said to my wife, 'I can't believe how hard those Habush guys work,'" recalls Laurence Fehring, now a managing partner at the Habush firm. "'They're working on July third, right before the Independence Day holiday.' Little did I know then that Dunphy was taking files and leaving the Habush firm, literally in the evening hours after everyone else had left work." Within weeks, Cannon and Dunphy started a law firm together.

"The timing couldn't have been worse," Habush says. "Here I had a half-dozen lawyers emerging as potential competitors that I'd never had before. The referral work had other places to go, and it went."

His reputation also took a hit. The more he advertised, the more he was identified as "that lawyer on TV." Articles in the local magazines and newspapers implied that his reputation was made through his advertising. "I became known as a 'prominent TV advertiser' rather than a 'prominent trial lawyer.' That really bothered me," Habush admits. "It was one of the unintended consequences of being a TV advertiser and being the main spokesperson for the firm."

As time went on, other lawyers began appearing over the airwaves with their own commercials, usually flat-out hard-sell solicitations. The overly aggressive ads made Habush's look scholarly and genteel by comparison.

His spots had evolved into mini-performances on an upgraded stage. A leather wing chair and a wall of bookshelves were added to the mock office. He frequently appeared in an empty courtroom, explaining, as he slowly paced across the room, how a trial by jury is a constitutional right, or, seated in the witness stand, how witnesses are cross-examined in court.

In one of the courtroom commercials, Habush's political activism seems to bleed into the script, as he extols the virtues of trial lawyers and the civil justice system: "It is victories here in the courtroom that capture the attention of the corrupters and polluters of our air, water, ground, and bodies. It is right here and only here that the poor and the powerless can confront and prevail against the rich and the powerful. What then is the most important mission? It is to oppose unrelentingly those who would deprive the poor of their key to the courtroom by eliminating their access to competent attorneys. It is only through these courtrooms that trial lawyers everywhere, fighting injustice wherever found, will continue to get the attention of carriers of death and injury and of those who chose to ignore the powerless."

His on-camera persona had improved immensely. He smiled and moved in a natural and confident manner, gesturing toward the judge's bench or jury box as if he were trying a case. His suits were silk, stylish, and tailor-made to fit his slender frame.

Eric McDonald, Dick's son, took over the Habush account in 1986. With a background as a television photojournalist, Eric saw Habush as a trailblazer: "Bob Habush was one of these early adapters, those early pioneers in the industry that took the bull by the horns and decided to market himself and his firm, but he did it in a very, very innovative way. He did not do it as an ambulance chaser. He did it as a community service provider. He would break down the principles of law and make them very understandable to the layperson."

Habush, McDonald says, demonstrated an on-camera warmth that belied the image of trial lawyers as pugnacious bullies. "It's in the eyes," he explains. "It's all about the humanity, and that comes from the eyes. It comes from the expressiveness. It comes from the tone. It comes from the warmth. That is what differentiated him in that marketing mode. He had that magical ability to be able to smooth and soften a tough subject."

Habush's friend Franklyn Gimbel, a Milwaukee attorney, gives the ads high marks. "There was nothing schlocky about what he did," says Gimbel, who has known Habush since their high school days. "There was almost a public-service quality to his advertising, and so it wasn't just like a used-car ad. I think he set the tone for lawyer advertising on a high level. That's not to say that all lawyer advertising stayed at a high level. It doesn't, and it isn't OK."

The Knowing the Law series had a remarkable run. Hundreds of commercials were aired, and eventually the brand was licensed and franchised to law firms around the country. But after nine years, it finally ran its course.

"Bob is a great visioneer," Eric McDonald says. "He knew he couldn't beat this horse forever. Times were a-changing."

McDonald both guided and followed Habush into new territory, convincing him to highlight his impeccable credentials and extraordinary career—to beat his chest a little bit. "I didn't carve the man as far as an on-camera performer," McDonald says. "I joined him in midprogress. What I tried to do was elevate him up to a national-caliber personality. This guy is the past president of the Association of Trial Lawyers of America. He's got national credentials among lawyers in this field. I began to realize I was working with one of the top dogs around. So I began to start what we called the National Credentials campaign."

The new commercials spotlighted the recognition Habush had achieved, using the tagline "Recognition comes to those who excel. Robert Habush of Habush Habush & Davis, known and respected throughout Wisconsin and America."

"We took him to a new level," McDonald says. "We took him from a video clip in a TV station into studios with the big thirty-five-millimeter film cameras, film crews, lighting trucks, and everything else. We began to make him a star. We elevated him from this friendly guy with the informational series to this national champion of champions."

The National Credentials series boosted Habush's public visibility. "I remember, when I was picking a jury, I asked whether anyone had any objection to me advertising," he says. "Every once in a while I got someone who would raise his hand. Then, after it became more popular, the defense lawyers would ask the question, 'Does Mr. Habush have an advantage in your minds because you see him on television?'

"I started doing it because I was worried that jurors would be biased against me. And as time went on, the defense lawyers were worried that jurors would be biased *in favor* of me because I had some kind of celebrity."

In their next campaign, called One Thing in Common, McDonald and Habush targeted the everyman (and everywoman). One spot opens with images of kids on in-line skates; one shows a boy chasing his dog. In another, a man is raking leaves, a woman is waterskiing, and a farmer is operating a tractor. Over the images, a narrator sets the hook: "South central Wisconsin has all kinds of good people who get hurt in accidents through no fault of their own." The ad cuts to Habush in a conference room meeting with associates or to a Habush lawyer speaking about the firm's history and credentials.

"They were the antithesis of the carnival barker ads," McDonald says. "Soft-sell spots that played to the 'Chevy trucks and apple pie' lifestyle," conformed to reach potential clients in each of the state's four major media markets.

Now lawyer commercials trend back to the no-holds-barred days of Ken Hur's scuba-gear ad, gimmicky and ostentatious. To grab viewers' attention, lawyers rely on catchy slogans and implied and expressed endorsements by celebrities such as Green Bay Packers quarterback Aaron Rodgers and *Star Trek*'s William Shatner.

"I look upon them more as marketers than down-and-dirty trial lawyers," says Habush. "It's mostly marketing and less litigating. But that's the way it is." Meanwhile, he has gone digital. Billboard and TV ads simply direct prospective clients to his firm's website address.

"Before the *Bates* decision, I never thought about advertising," he says. "And when we got the legal right to do it, that didn't mean that it wasn't going to be frowned upon. It was revolutionary. Now, of course, you see ads from doctors, hospitals, accountants, and on and on. Professionals. So it's accepted.

"When I look back on *Bates*, it turns out that, in the perpetuation of my firm, it was the right decision. Would we ever stop it? We couldn't. You know, it's like riding the back of the tiger. You got to keep riding. Once you fall off, the tiger's gonna eat ya."

CHAPTER SIX

Landmarks

A lawyer's success can be measured in many ways: the number of cases won, the number of honors and awards, the monetary amount of verdicts. Another good gauge of success is the extent to which a legal case shapes law or influences policy and practices. In the two hundred cases he has tried and the hundreds he has settled, Bob Habush has left a lasting imprint on case law as well as government policies and industry practices.

Tim Trecek, a former civil defense attorney and a current partner at the Habush firm, has observed Habush's extraordinary impact from both sides of the bar: "Whether it deals with product liability law or governmental immunity or punitive damages, the landscape of Wisconsin law in a large part has been formed by Bob Habush, by his cases and his efforts."

Three cases in particular illustrate the agency of his actions in Wisconsin and far beyond.

John Carroll v. Blood Center of Southeastern Wisconsin et al

At age sixty, John Carroll seemed to have it all. Happily married to wife Sandy for nearly forty years, he had two grown children, a good income running an insurance agency, and an active lifestyle—swimming, bicycling, hiking, and fishing. Heart bypass surgery in 1985 slowed him down a little, but Carroll bounced back after just two weeks, resuming a forty-hour workweek and looking ahead to the day when he and Sandy could sell their home in suburban Milwaukee and retire to a cabin in the North-woods of Wisconsin.

Then, out of the blue, several months after his bypass, a phone call shook his world. Sitting at his office desk, Carroll listened in stunned silence as his doctor delivered the numbing news. During his surgery, Carroll had been given a blood product used to help stop postoperative bleeding. The blood product, cryoprecipitate, had contained blood from numerous donors, and it was discovered that one of the donors carried the AIDS virus. "I think it would best if you got tested for AIDS," the doctor told him.

Carroll was thunderstruck. How could this happen? Why wasn't the blood product screened for the virus? Who was to blame? Months passed, and finally he went in for the test. The results confirmed what his doctor had suspected: Carroll was infected with the human immunodeficiency virus, HIV, which causes AIDS.

In 1987, the Carrolls decided to hire an attorney to get answers to their growing list of questions. They called Bob Habush because of his reputation for winning tough cases.

Habush recalls his first meeting with John Carroll. "I remember being so struck by the man," he says. "He's sitting in front of me and telling me he has the AIDS virus. He's an insurance guy, World War II vet, long-term marriage, kids, just a straight shooter. I ask him, 'Well, how did you contract it?' And he tells me it was through a blood transfusion. I'm thinking, 'I always thought blood transfusions were safe.'"

Awareness of the AIDS epidemic was growing fast. Following his surgery, Carroll knew enough about the virus and its relentlessly damaging effects to insist that the blood he would receive in a transfusion was tested for it. However, he did not know that the blood derivative he got to induce clotting was not tested.

The Blood Center of Southeastern Wisconsin was responsible for monitoring and maintaining the area's blood supply for Milwaukee hospitals, including St. Joseph's, where Carroll's operation was performed. But how could Habush prove that the Blood Center, the largest blood bank in the state, or St. Joseph's, one of the top hospitals in the city, negligently allowed tainted blood to get into John Carroll's body?

"I didn't immediately see a product liability case. I had some misgivings,"

Habush says. "Just because he got bad blood didn't mean I was going to sue the hospital or the Blood Center. But I thought his case was serious enough. I was dealing with a guy with HIV, which at the time was a death sentence. So I took the case. John was such a wonderful man in a truly pathetic situation."

Complicating the case were "blood shield statutes" in state laws. "Practically every state has given blood centers almost immunity from lawsuits," Habush explained at the time. "They say that the delivery of blood is not a product but is a service." If the delivery of blood was in fact seen as a service, a lawsuit like Carroll's would have been similar to a medical malpractice suit—a much more difficult case to win.

The *Carroll* case was without precedent. There had been no other Wisconsin lawsuit brought against a blood bank that involved the AIDS virus. In fact, there were only two similar lawsuits nationwide: a jury trial in San Francisco that was ongoing at the time and a case in Atlanta, which would be reversed.

So Habush started digging, scheduling one deposition after the next and filing motion after motion for discovery, trying to find a link. Eventually, with hospital records of the surgery and a deposition of the Blood Center's president, he began to piece together an incriminating time line. He discovered that on March 2, 1985, the U.S. Food and Drug Administration approved a blood test to detect the AIDS antibody. Five days later, on March 7, 1985, the Blood Center of Southeastern Wisconsin began using the new test kits to screen blood donors. However, the infected person whose blood went into the cryoprecipitate given to Carroll had donated blood one day earlier, on March 6. The cryoprecipitate containing the contaminated blood had been shipped untested to St. Joseph's Hospital.

In court testimony, Blood Center executives claimed they were not confident that the tested blood would be safer than the untested blood. The center's president said he feared people who were at risk of contracting AIDS might donate blood solely to be tested for the virus.

The Blood Center did replace its inventory of untested blood and blood derivatives. But records obtained by Habush revealed that the center continued to ship untested blood to hospitals and did not replace untested blood products at St. Joseph's until the end of April—nearly two months after the FDA approved the test kits for use. Carroll's surgery was performed on April 23, 1985, before the cryoprecipitate was pulled from the shelves of the hospital.

Blood banks from other cities sided with the center. "They were fighting me," says Habush. "The Blood Center retained heads of blood banks in Sacramento, Minneapolis, and Michigan who testified that there was nothing improper with what happened. They weren't sure the new test was that perfect, they said. They thought it was still experimental. Getting AIDS from the tainted blood product was just John Carroll's bad luck, claimed the defense, not negligence. Of course, you know, the blood bank directors were blanketed with the cloak of 'They do good. They save people's lives. How can you sue a blood center?' I took all their depositions. And I thought they were a bunch of arrogant assholes and that there was no way they were going to sell the case to the jury. Meanwhile, John is getting sicker and sicker."

Habush searched the country for his own experts. He found three with renowned credentials: Dr. Ronald Kerman, an immunologist at the University of Texas; Dr. James Mosley, an epidemiologist from the University of California in Los Angeles; and Dr. Edgar Engleman, the founder and medical director of the Stanford Blood Center. Engleman's center was the first in the country to screen for AIDS-contaminated blood. That was in 1983, two years before the test was developed by the FDA and used by the Blood Center of Southeastern Wisconsin.

"In the beginning, shortly after the virus was discovered, scientists thought AIDS was only transferred sexually," Habush says. "It wasn't until a couple years into the epidemic that they found out it could be contracted through a blood transfusion. Engleman was one of the forerunners of that knowledge. I went out to visit him at Stanford, but he was not excited about testifying. First of all, most doctors don't want to testify against other doctors. It took me maybe four or five visits to Stanford, and finally I built a case for him to help. What convinced him was the attitude of these other blood bank directors. When he read the depositions of these highly recognized directors saying the test still was not proven, they were flying in the face of his work. They were saying, 'Well, we're not sure that you can get AIDS through blood transfusions, and we're not sure that this test was perfect.

You could have false positives.' And on and on. Every time I would feed him with their depositions, he'd get madder and madder. Finally he said, 'OK, damn it. I'll help you.'"

In court, Engleman gave the jury a lesson in AIDS 101, explaining how the virus was acquired and how a blood-banking system should be scrupulously designed and implemented to ensure the safety of local blood supplies. He told jurors he was puzzled by the Wisconsin Blood Center's decision to test donors while neglecting to test its blood inventory or label and remove untested blood products from hospitals. "It seems to me it was not only prudent but mandatory to test everything, to label everything, to recall or exchange," he said.

Other plaintiff experts buffeted Engleman's testimony. "They should have been more diligent in informing the hospitals of the hazards of untested materials," Mosley told the jury. Kerman, meanwhile, castigated the center for initially testing only incoming blood and not its on-hand inventory. "Their decision was scientifically unconscionable," he said.

The most emotionally charged testimony, though, came from John Carroll himself. When he first called Habush for help, Carroll had been reluctant to use his real name. Fearing he would be subjected to hate mail and threats, he used a pseudonym. "For many months, he was known as 'John Carpenter' in our office," Habush says. But when he took the stand to introduce himself to jurors, Carroll went by his real name, revealing a heart-wrenching story of what it was like to live with AIDS.

"I truly expect I will die within a year," he said, looking pale and gaunt. "I feel like I'm rolling down a hill and I can't stop myself." He had sold his insurance agency, stopped exercising, and abandoned his dream of retiring in northern Wisconsin; his life had become a constant battle against painful opportunistic diseases, like pneumocystis carinii pneumonia, and a daily regimen of medications. "I feel like I'm turning into a skeleton," he said, noting that he had been losing two pounds a week. "I'm ashamed of myself, I'm so weak."

Before leaving the witness stand, he recited for the jury a passage from the Bible, Psalm 38: "I am stooped and bowed down profoundly. All the day I go in mourning, for my loins are filled with burning pain. There is no health in my flesh. I am numbed and severely crushed, and I roar with anguish of heart."

It had taken Habush a year and a half to prepare the case. By the time it went to trial, he had witnessed his client's physical deterioration, from a healthy and vibrant man on the verge of his golden years to a man defeated, stooped over and barely able to feed himself.

"John's testimony was just heartbreaking and compelling," he says. "And his quotation from the Psalm of David was unbelievable. The whole trial was very emotional. I remember during final argument I had a hard time keeping from tearing up. You know, you get so caught up in the emotion of some of these cases. I do, at least. I'm not up there just being a mouthpiece."

Getting "caught up in the emotion" marks the essence of an exceptional plaintiff's attorney. "For some lawyers, it's just the money or the ego," says defense attorney Frank Daily. "But for Bob, it's the fact that he has compassion for people. He sees somebody who has been seriously injured and believes they should be provided for.

"If you don't have compassion for people—true compassion—you won't be a successful plaintiff's lawyer, and you should look for something else to do, something where there's no heartache and tears and sorrow. But if you're going to be a good plaintiff's lawyer, I think you have to feel that sense of loss and that sense of sorrow that attends those kinds of injuries."

Law partner Dan Rottier says Habush appreciates the struggles that people have in their lives. "There's no doubt he's had his own struggles, and I think he realizes everyone has a struggle of their own. He factors that in," Rottier says. "Is he impatient? Sure. He can be very impatient. But I am 100 percent sure he has never displayed anger in court, because it's counterproductive."

The emotional weight of the case was evident in Habush's closing arguments for liability and damages, as he described Carroll's grievous condition and slammed the blood banks for their smugness and irresponsibility:

What does it mean to a man who knows he's dying, an innocent man, an innocent victim, a victim of carelessness? He not only knows he's dying, but he knows how horrible his death is going to be. He knows what the final ordeal is going to be like. You know, there is an old saying, "People have asked for death, but no one asks for pain." But in this case, no one would ask for this death.

You know, members of the jury, last night I thought to myself, how am I going to be able to reach down and express to these people what these folks feel now, and I thought that nobody, nobody, if they had an envelope sitting on this table, and in the envelope it said when you were going to die and how you were going to die, I don't think anybody would go over there and open that envelope up, because I don't think the human mind wants to live with the knowledge of the date of your death or the probability of your death, in terms of within a year or so.

We all know we are going to die, but I'm talking about knowing soon and how, and that is an aspect of suffering that I think is so unique in this case. . . .

What kind of undeserved torture has been visited on this man? What can he look forward to? Slow, painful, horrible death. He can watch the pain in his beloved Sandy's eyes as she is watching him being ravaged, eaten up by this disease. "What will Sandy do when I'm gone?" he thinks.

Her loss is staggering. She has literally lost her husband and companion and friend of 40 years. She must feel his pain as if it were hers. And I bet she'd gladly trade places with him if she could. He's slipping away. It's all so stupid. It's all so unnecessary. She will wash him, she will medicate him, she will take care of him until he dies, but the despair for this woman is incalculable. She will live, forever, the memories of these last months and what he looks like when he dies. She has to witness what very few people ever have to witness in a lifetime, the man she loves, being tortured by a disease. . . .

As if by some perverse prophecy, when John Carroll was in the hospital, he asked the nurse, "Has this blood been tested for AIDS?" And until he was assured, he wouldn't take the blood. Now it wasn't that blood that affected him, ironically. It was cryoprecipitate, a blood coagulator that was given to him while he was unconscious. He didn't know he got that. He would have loved to have the choice, I can tell you that. He would have loved to have had the choice of not accepting that cryoprecipitate. Anyone with a whit of sense in the spring of 1985, if given a choice, would have asked for testing.

One wonders how the next crisis is going to be handled by these blood bankers. Maybe the biggest sin is not in their negligence as described above, but in not recognizing that they've been wrong, and in not admitting that they've been wrong. Members of the jury, you have a chance to set the standard. You have a chance to say, "We will not permit you to unnecessarily endanger the lives of men, women, and children by what you do." They will listen. The whole state will listen. The country will listen. And so I ask you to find that they were negligent. I ask you to find it was causal.

On December 9, 1988, the jury unanimously found the Blood Center of Southeastern Wisconsin negligent in causing damage to John Carroll. It awarded John and Sandy Carroll $3.9 million in compensation for medical expenses, loss of past and future earnings, and past and future pain, suffering, and disability.

The case completed a trilogy of AIDS-related lawsuits that had concluded within weeks of one another. A federal jury in Atlanta two months earlier had awarded $1.6 million to a man infected with HIV from a hemophilia drug. But a judge reversed that verdict two days before the *Carroll* verdict. And eight days before the Carroll verdict, a San Francisco jury voted 9–3 to award $750,000 to the family of a five-year-old who received AIDS-tainted blood through a local blood bank shortly after he was born. (The court later reduced that award to $416,307.)

The *Carroll* case was a landmark for Habush, in Wisconsin and nationally. Amid the flurry of AIDS transmission cases, the verdict was the largest. It made headlines across the country and put blood banks on notice for their mishandling of an increasingly vulnerable blood supply.

"There had been an attitude permeating the industry that they were immune to lawsuits and impervious to criticism," Habush told the *Chicago Tribune* at the time. "In some cases, now, I believe juries will find the industry took this cavalier attitude with some risk involved."

To Carroll, the verdict was an affirmation. "The most important point," he told the *Milwaukee Journal*, "is that the blood banks in Wisconsin and throughout the U.S. will in the future take greater precautionary measures to assure all blood product recipients that they are receiving the safest blood possible."

Carroll announced that he and his wife would donate much of their award to "help the sick and the poor elderly, and victims of disaster." As he had so somberly predicted, he died within a year of the trial.

Months after the verdict, Habush reflected on the national impact of John Carroll's case in a lengthy article in the *Saturday Evening Post*. "From this case," he said, "we've gotten the attention of the blood-banking industry in a way that nobody has gotten it before. Blood banks now feel vulnerable because a jury in the conservative Midwest has told them they were wrong. They threw the best and the brightest against us in the defense. They tried to whitewash what they did as being something 'everybody did,' and they were told they were wrong."

State of Wisconsin v. Philip Morris Inc., et al.

The landmark case with perhaps the broadest reach—and the most controversy—was the lawsuit led by Bob Habush against Big Tobacco for the State of Wisconsin.

Heavily freighted with political baggage, the claim was handled by three Wisconsin law firms, including Habush's, which put in thousands of hours over nearly two years. The lawsuit culminated in a 1998 national settlement, with the major tobacco companies agreeing to pay Wisconsin nearly $6 billion over twenty-five years and an estimated $160 million annually after that to offset health-care expenses related to smoking.

Despite decades of scientific studies showing a link between smoking and a host of life-threatening illnesses, the tobacco companies had successfully defended themselves in lawsuit after lawsuit that alleged harm to those who used their products. But damning evidence disclosed in secret industry documents and in testimony by former tobacco employees severely weakened the cigarette companies' defense. State attorneys general from around the country began efforts to recoup their Medicaid costs for treating people with smoking-related problems.

In 1994, the State of Mississippi filed the first of the lawsuits, claiming the tobacco companies had concealed the harmful effects of tobacco and the addictive nature of nicotine, had manipulated the levels of nicotine, and had targeted children as potential customers. Rather than contest the suits, the tobacco companies changed direction and worked toward a universal settlement with the states.

Wisconsin came late to the game in 1997 as the twenty-first state to file its claim, due partly to then-governor Tommy Thompson's reluctance to sue. Thompson's critics charged that this reluctance was because of political connections to the tobacco giant Philip Morris, which at the time owned the Miller Brewing Company in Milwaukee and the Oscar Mayer Company, a Kraft Foods subsidiary, in Madison. Thompson, a Republican, reportedly had received at least $55,000 in campaign contributions from tobacco companies and their affiliates over a ten-year period. Phone records later showed he had been in conversations with Philip Morris at the time the lawsuit was being considered.

Jim Doyle, the Wisconsin attorney general, a Democrat and no friend to Thompson, had been a driving force nationally in the effort to sue Big Tobacco while serving as president of the National Association of Attorneys General from 1997 to 1998. He publicly pushed Thompson to join the effort until finally, after Doyle staged two press conferences in one day to promote the cause, Thompson gave the go-ahead to move forward.

"The attorney generals, including Jim Doyle, had decided to prepare a consolidated lawsuit against Big Tobacco rather than lawsuits against individuals, which had not been very successful," Habush explains. "They would sue the tobacco companies for the expenditures that the state had paid out to treat people with heart disease, cancer of the lungs, cancer of the bladder, and all other tobacco-related illnesses."

Wisconsin would hire private attorneys to act as special counsel (as did other states), because Doyle's office did not have the manpower or resources to handle the lawsuit. Doyle had the discretion to select the law firms, but Thompson would have final approval.

Habush topped Doyle's list. He was the dean of Wisconsin trial lawyers and the head of a firm with ample resources and acclaimed expertise. "The choice of Bob Habush and the Habush firm was in many ways obvious," says Doyle, who in 2002 was elected governor of Wisconsin. "This was essentially a plaintiffs' lawsuit, tort litigation. And the Habush firm had the financial resources. They were going to front all of the costs, and they were going to take it on a contingent. There weren't any other firms in the state who had the size and the reach and the kind of power to do that. In addition, Bob had a very significant national profile, and that was very important. It was very useful for us in this litigation to have an attorney of that stature."

As attorneys general in other states were assembling their legal teams, Habush received a call from Doyle. "He invited me to his office," he recalls. "So we meet and he says, 'I'd like to retain you as one of the lawyers representing the state in the tobacco case.'

"I said, 'Great, I'd love to do it.'

"He said, 'You guys have to front all the expenses, and if we win, you get reimbursed. Otherwise you don't.'

"That's the typical contingency fee arrangement, but this would be a huge investment for us. This was a big-time lawsuit, with very rich defendants who were not going to quit so fast. But it sounded exciting."

The selection of the additional law firms became a political chess game. At one point, the process took on a peculiar twist when a longtime Habush rival, Ted Warshafsky, indicated to Doyle that he also wanted in.

Warshafsky was considerably older than Habush, yet their careers in some ways followed parallel paths. Both graduated from the University of Wisconsin Law School. Both were highly successful personal injury attorneys in Milwaukee. Both served as president of the Wisconsin Academy of Trial Lawyers. And both had little use for each other.

As Habush recalls: "When I first got together with Doyle, he said to me, 'I'm also going to ask Warshafsky.' I kind of made a face. 'What's wrong?' Doyle asks. 'Well, number one, we don't get along too well, but that's not a problem, I suppose. Number two, Ted never shuts up. He just talks and talks and talks. It would be very tough to work with him.' Doyle was unmoved. 'Get over it,' he said."

At a preliminary meeting with several lawyers, Habush's warning proved to be right on the mark. "We had our first meeting at the attorney general's office to plot a strategy. Wouldn't you know, exactly what I said was going to happen happened. Warshafsky wouldn't shut up.

"Jim let it go the first meeting. Then at the second meeting the same thing happened. [Warshafsky] just would dominate the conversation, interrupting people left and right. The meeting was in my Waukesha office. Jim and

I both stepped out at one point to go to the bathroom. We're standing next to each other at the urinals.

"'How do I get rid of this guy?' he says.

"'Don't blame me. You're the one that wanted him.'

"Doyle says, 'You've got to come up with something for me. He's driving me nuts.'

"So I thought for a second and said, 'All right. Here's what you do. You tell him that because we have a Republican governor, we need to bring in a Republican law firm. Because Ted and I are both Democrats, you've got to substitute him with a Republican firm to get this approved by Thompson.'

"Warshafsky, of course, believed I sabotaged him, that it was my decision, that I wanted him out of the case. Which was true, but it wasn't me that decided he was a no-go. It was Jim. And I wasn't going to blame Jim."

As a counterbalance to the liberal-leaning Habush, Doyle chose the firm Whyte Hirschboeck Dudek in Milwaukee, known in legal circles as being conservative.

Thompson, to put his imprimatur on the process, added a third firm: Brennan, Steil, Basting & MacDougall, from Janesville, Wisconsin. One of the partners, George Steil, was a Thompson friend.

Habush himself had been friends with Thompson since he was a state legislator in the 1970s and '80s. "Tommy was a lawyer and had a part-time practice in Elroy, Wisconsin, his hometown," Habush says. "He sent me cases to handle that he didn't want."

Thompson was elected governor in 1986, around the same time Habush was battling tort reform in Washington as president of the ATLA. "We maintained our friendship despite the fact that he was a Republican," Habush says. But that friendship ran hot and cold.

Following his term as ATLA president, Habush maintained a high profile fighting tort reform on the state level, forming a Wisconsin "war council" made up of lobbyists and public relations experts who worked to defeat anti–tort law legislation.

As Habush tells it, he and Thompson had an arrangement. "When he became governor, Tommy thought tort reform was bullshit," he says. "But he had all these tort reformers as his constituents. The Medical Society, the Wisconsin Manufacturing Association, the insurance industry—they were his key financial supporters. He told me, 'Bob, I won't promote tort reform as long as I'm governor. But you have got to keep it off my desk. If it hits my desk, I'm going to have to sign it.' I said, 'I will do my best.' And I did my best."

Tort reformers in the Wisconsin legislature introduced a bill that would gut tort law. With support from both sides of the aisle, the bill was gaining speed. Moving fast, Habush leaned hard on Democratic assembly speaker Tom Loftus to bottle it up in committee—and keep it off Thompson's desk, as he had promised. The bill died without coming to a vote, but Habush's political allegiances suddenly were being pulled in opposite directions.

"Tom Loftus, lo and behold, decides to run for governor against Tommy," Habush says, "and he comes knocking on my door for a campaign contribution. In those days, I was writing check after check after check to Democratic legislators and guys running for governor. I was up to my ass in politics. I was chairman of the Jefferson-Jackson Day dinner one year. I'd coached gubernatorial candidate Marty Schreiber on how to give a speech. I'd been asked a couple times to run for office. I had that itch.

"So Loftus comes to me and says, 'All right, Mr. Trial Lawyer, I saved your ass. Now I would like you to raise $25,000 for me from your trial lawyer friends.' I was able to raise something like 20,000 bucks for him. But I didn't make a contribution myself. I didn't want to infuriate my Republican friend, Tommy. Loftus, though, calls me on it. He says, 'I expect a check out of you, too.' So I wrote a check for $2,500 to him and $2,500 to Thompson. Well, it hits the newspaper. Tommy sees that I gave $2,500 to Loftus, and he sends my check back, torn up, with a note: 'I never want to see you again, you traitor, two-faced bastard . . .' blah, blah, blah. That cut me off from Tommy. He won reelection, and I got the silent treatment for years."

Finally, to get back on Thompson's good side and repair the arrangement the two had made on tort reform, Habush went to Thompson's chief of staff, Jim Klauser. "I was teaching at the law school at UW–Madison back then every Monday night," Habush says. "I'd often meet Klauser for dinner at the Edgewater Hotel. We'd talk politics. Jim didn't believe in tort reform either. He was very friendly and always offered to help out if I needed a favor. He became my go-between to Thompson. I kept asking him to set up a meeting with Tommy, and Tommy kept refusing. One evening, Klauser says to me, 'OK, Bob. Tommy will see you, but be prepared. He's going to rip you a new asshole before you kiss and make up.'"

A few days later, Habush was escorted into the governor's office in the state capitol. "As soon as I walk in, he starts ranting at me, on and on. Eventually, he ran out of expletives."

"Are you through?" Habush said to him. "Do you remember when you said to me you wouldn't promote tort reform as long as I could keep it off of your desk?"

"Yeah, I remember that," said Thompson.

"Look," Habush said. "What happened was Loftus kept it off of your desk, and I owed him a favor. So I gave him a campaign contribution. But I gave the same amount to your campaign. In the end, I only did what you told me to do."

Thompson stared at Habush across his desk and suddenly broke into a grin. "You asshole," he said. "I didn't tell you to give him any money." He walked over to Habush and gave him a hug. "Bob, you make a better friend than an enemy. I want us to be friends again."

Preparing the tobacco case was complex and costly. In a contractual agreement with the state, the three law firms had agreed to litigate the case and front the costs in return for contingent fees of up to 20 percent of any possible court victory or settlement. Each firm threw its best attorneys at the suit. "We had biweekly in-person meetings of the managers of the different committees, probably the ten top lawyers," recalls Dan Rottier. At Doyle's recommendation, Habush took on the role of chairman of the legal team. When a lawyer from one of the other firms suggested that the chairmanship rotate periodically, Rottier replied with a smile, "The chairmanship of this group will rotate when Bob spins in his chair."

With his vastly successful trial record, Habush was the indisputable team captain. He ran the meetings, he handed out committee assignments, and he gathered reports. "He was handling the liability. I was charged with developing the damage analysis in Wisconsin," Rottier says. "One of the first things we asked ourselves was, what are we going to do about data?"

Four states had filed earlier than the rest: Florida, Minnesota, Mississippi, and Texas. Each of those early lawsuits generated mountains of files gathered from discovery and depositions. This gave the Wisconsin team a good starting point. Its neighboring state Minnesota had hired an attorney named Mike Ciresi from the Minneapolis firm Robbins, Kaplan, Miller & Ciresi. "He took a different tack," Rottier says. "The other states seemed to be structuring their preparation for a global settlement. But Ciresi thought, 'This is just a lawsuit. We're going to structure this to try the case, to win the case.'"

The approach made sense to the Wisconsin lawyers. After evaluating the state of preparedness in other cases around the country, they decided to run on what they could glean from Minnesota. "Ciresi was generous enough to let us sort of appear as co-counsel for Minnesota," says Rottier. "That allowed us to get on the electronic mailing list for every piece of paper filed in Minnesota. And believe me, there were multiple filings every single day for the year or so after we became involved. One of my jobs was to read every one of those pieces of paper: all the court filings, all the briefs, all the depositions. I went to some of the depositions of the presidents of the tobacco companies around the country just so we would get a jump on the other states."

Minnesota's attorneys had examined thirty-three million documents. Narrowing it down to three million, they created a database. "Bob decided we would try to buy into their database," Rottier says. "We offered Ciresi a million dollars, five hundred up front, five hundred at the end, to share it. That was not state of Wisconsin money. That was lawyers' money. Law firms fronted it. We rented space across the hall from our Madison office. We rented computer systems and contracted good lawyers. At our peak we had about thirty-five lawyers working on the case from different firms. It was a tremendous organizational challenge."

The Minnesota database was gargantuan. Computer systems used by the state of Wisconsin and the University of Wisconsin were too small to run it. Habush and Rottier authorized $1.2 million for computer time for an East Coast consortium to run data to generate reports on exactly what had been paid out in Medicaid claims by the state.

"The data analysis on damages was so complex because we were searching twenty years of medical assistance payments, with the twenty-five diagnostic codes that related to tobacco," Rottier says. "It was for maternity, low birth weight, children born of mothers who smoked, early nursing home admissions for smokers, stroke, heart attack, emphysema, lung cancer, things like that."

The Wisconsin attorneys were moving toward a trial. "We had all our ducks in a row," Habush says. "We found the scientists that were supporting the cases against the tobacco companies in every kind of science: oncology, urology, cardiology, pulmonology, epidemiology. We had what I thought was a terrific case, and we had picked the trial team. I was going to try the case as the lead trial lawyer. Dan Rottier was going to be there with me. Tom Basting from Brennan, Steil, Basting & McDougall and Bobby Scott from Whyte Hirschboeck Dudek were going to be lead trial lawyers. We were all ready to go. I thought this was going to be the trial of the century. And then up pops a settlement."

In November 1998, on the heels of settlements with Florida, Minnesota, Mississippi, and Texas that totaled $36 billion, the tobacco industry agreed to pay $206 billion over twenty-five years to the remaining forty-six states, the District of Columbia, and five U.S. territories. As part of the Master Settlement Agreement, Wisconsin would receive a projected $5.9 billion.

A portion of the settlement would provide funding for a tobacco control program, responsible for creating smoking prevention and cessation projects around the state. In addition to the payout, the settlement included strict limits on how the tobacco companies could advertise and promote their products. For example, the companies would no longer be able to target youth—ad characters like Joe Camel would be banned, and free samples to minors and sports sponsorships with youth audiences would be prohibited.

"Bob and the other firms really had gone to work at putting together a case that would go to trial," Doyle says, looking back. "We were one of only a few states in the country that were in that position. As it turned out, we got everything we would have gotten at trial, and maybe a little bit more, because we were joined together with all the other states. I saw Wisconsin's role and Minnesota's role as sort of the outlier, saying to the other states, look, we'll see how you guys end up on this. And if it's good enough for us, we take it. But if not, we're going to trial. So we really just kept moving, which I think was one of the really critical components of getting a good settlement."

Also in the settlement was a provision requiring the tobacco industry to pay all outside attorney fees out of an account separate from the settlement amount. "The tobacco companies and the attorneys general had agreed to set up an arbitration panel, and the outside attorneys would apply to this panel for their legal fees," Habush says. "We'd have to show the panel why the fees were justified. We were asked to submit a petition, a kind of a brief, if you will, attesting the contingency fee. The panel then would arguably agree to the fee—if they felt like it."

In preparing the brief, the Wisconsin firms calculated a fee of $175 million over forty years, or about $847 million after adjusting for inflation—a figure less than the 20 percent fee that had been agreed upon when negotiating a contract with the state. "I was smart enough to know that probably wasn't going to sail, politically speaking," Habush says. "But we were taking a negotiating position. We were trying to get tobacco's attention. So this is what we submitted, figuring we'd get less. How much less, we didn't know. Well, when this went public, the shit hit the fan."

Local media had a field day, tearing into the law firms for being "greedy." The Milwaukee newspaper, using billing documents it had obtained, estimated the firms made $2,853 per hour on the case. Tommy Thompson, Habush's come-and-go friend, piled on, calling the $847 million bill "excessive" and "exorbitant."

"Of course, they all wanted to know how many hours we worked, how many minutes we worked, how many seconds we worked," says Habush. "'No lawyer is worth that kind of money,' they cried. The fact that it was a contract or that we were successful, everyone forgot about that. So it was open season on lawyers, particularly on Bob Habush. I was the poster child."

Conservative talk radio was particularly brutal. One talk show host at WTMJ, Charlie Sykes, tore into Habush. "Sykes is a right-wing Republican," Habush says. "And as a political force, right-wing Republicans don't like personal injury lawyers. He railed on me and railed on me. Friends of mine who heard it said, 'You better listen in, because this is getting ugly.' So I had my secretary turn on Charlie Sykes and play the show every day.

"On one particular day he's talking about a particular lawyer that did something good—a business lawyer, not a personal injury lawyer. 'Unlike Bob Habush, who is dishonest, this lawyer has integrity,' Sykes said.

"Now in the law of defamation, when you call someone dishonest, it goes into a category where if you claim you've been defamed, you don't have to prove damages. It is so insulting to your core integrity, especially to a professional person, that it's called 'defamation per se.' I sent a tape to a professional at Ohio State University who is a well-known defamation professor, who wrote a textbook on defamation, and I asked him, 'What do you think?' He says, 'You've got a case.'

"So in response to Charlie Sykes's comments, I wrote a letter to WTMJ, saying that I am going to start a lawsuit against WTMJ radio, the general manager, the sales manager, and Charlie Sykes for defamation," Habush continues. "I set forth the defamation, and I set forth the law, and I include a letter from the professor at Ohio State. Twenty-four hours later I hear from the general manager: 'Bob, what can we do to make this right?' I said, 'Come on over.'

So the general manager comes over with the sales manager, and we talk it out. They say, 'We can't control this guy. He's got great ratings. No one wants to fire him, no matter what he says about people. What can we do, Bob?'

"I said, 'This isn't about money, OK? You get me Charlie Sykes in a meeting. And I want you, Mr. General Manager, to be there too so that you're a witness.'

"They set up the meeting the following day in the general manager's office. I walk in; Charlie Sykes is sitting in a chair. He comes over to me and shakes my hand. I could see the perspiration forming on his forehead."

Habush recalls the conversation:

"Do you know me?" Habush asked.

"Of course I know you," said Sykes. "Everyone knows you."

"No, no, no. Do you really know me?" said Habush.

"Well, what do you mean?"

"Do you know that I've been practicing law for forty years and I've never once had a grievance filed against me with the state Office of Lawyer Regulation? I've never had a client file an ethical complaint against me. Nobody's ever accused me of dishonesty, ever, and I've represented some crazy people from time to time."

"I didn't know that," Sykes said.

"Do you know that I teach at the University of Wisconsin Law School? And that I've won every award a lawyer can win from the bar associations?"

"No, I . . . I didn't know that either."

"Do you know anything about my philanthropy? Do you know anything about the scholarships I've created at Marquette Law School? The chair I endowed at the University of Wisconsin Law School? The charity I've given to the community for helping the handicapped? Do you know any of that? No, you don't know me, Mr. Sykes. You don't know me at all. So why did you say over the air that I was dishonest and had no integrity?"

"I said that?" answered Sykes.

Habush pulled a small tape recorder from his jacket pocket and pushed the Play button. Sykes's face turned pale.

"What can I do?" he asked.

"I don't want your money," Habush told him. "But tomorrow on your radio show you're going to tell people you met me for the first time. You're going to tell them what a wonderful guy I am and that you believe I am an honest man with integrity—and that if anyone thought you believed otherwise, they were mistaken. You're going to say that on the air, and you're going to sound like you mean it. And the next time you get angry with lawyers, don't use my name as the poster child. Use one of my competitors'."

The next morning, Habush tuned in to Sykes's show. An hour into the program, he heard Sykes's mea culpa:

"Guess who I met yesterday? Bob Habush, and I want to tell you what a great guy he is. If anyone thinks I believe otherwise, you are mistaken. Habush is a man who's honest, a man with integrity. And I want you to know, if I got hit by a bus, I would hire him."

"Charlie Sykes," says Habush, "never again used my name on his program."

Sykes notwithstanding, the media chewed on the attorney fees story for weeks, hammering away at Habush and the law firms. To put the controversy to rest and expedite payments, he decided to take another tack. Included in the Master Settlement Agreement was an alternative method of payment. Under a "liquidated fee agreement," fees could be negotiated directly between the private attorneys and the tobacco industry. Legal fees would be paid from a $1.25 billion pool of money from the industry over a four-year period.

"The bad press was killing us," Habush says. "On top of that, it was going to take months and months for the arbitration panel to hear us. If we went through the panel, we would be paid with an annuity, paid out over time. I figured I'd be in a nursing home somewhere when my last check came. I'd probably be wiping the drool away with the check. I didn't feel like waiting.

"So I picked up the phone and called Philip Morris's law firm, the Wachtell firm in New York. I told them I wanted to talk about settling our claim. Herb Wachtell himself was the lead lawyer for Philip Morris. What they decided, everyone else went along with. So I went to New York, met with Wachtell, and we went out to dinner. I was able to work out a settlement with him in which the tobacco companies would pay $75 million to our three firms."

The deal quelled the criticism. Wisconsin finally could celebrate the tobacco settlement windfall. "The state's legal team won a major victory for our state," Attorney General Doyle said to the press, pointing out that the firms assumed a great risk in agreeing to take the case on contingency and emphasizing that the fees were not linked to the settlement amount. "None of this money will come from the taxpayers."

Tommy Thompson, who in 2001 was appointed U.S. secretary of health and human services by President George W. Bush, did an about-face, praising the attorneys—albeit subtly—for their work. "National experts credit the strong case brought by Wisconsin with helping bring about a nationwide settlement," he said in a statement. "The attorneys' fees that tobacco has agreed to pay them are commensurate with the result."

The three firms agreed to divide the legal fees 40/30/30. Because Habush led the lawsuit, Habush, Habush& Rottier received 40 percent; and the two others got 30 percent each. "Our firm ended up with a nice fee," Habush says. "I split it up among all the lawyers in the firm pro rata, based upon the percentage of income they had earned over the last three years. We spread it down to the secretaries' profit-sharing plan. Everyone in the firm benefited from the tobacco money that came in."

Additionally, partners at the Habush firm agreed to allocate $6 million to charity, much of it to community foundations, trusts, and nonprofits around the state—donations to law schools in Wisconsin, the state medical society, and health-care projects, for example. "We also asked everyone on staff to spend 10 percent of their share on charity over the next five years," Dan Rottier says. "We got that moral commitment from all the lawyers, all of our staff."

Through the establishment of its own foundation, the firm also initiated an annual program to distribute free bicycle helmets to Wisconsin children. Since 1999, the program has given away more than one hundred thousand helmets through the firm's thirteen offices around the state.

Several years ago, coordinators of the program decided to train Habush employees to fit the kids with the helmets, which are purchased from Bell Helmets. "I thought, 'You know, we ought to get a little more involved,'" says Ken Jarvis, a coordinator and a paralegal at the firm. "Now we have a little table or booth set up, and we have multiple fitters who show a child how to fit it on his or her head. We also show the parent how to properly fit it and how [it should be worn], and we talk to them about the reason why helmets are important."

Today, some 125 separate helmet giveaway events are organized between March and September. Consistent with the safety theme the firm pushes, "it's just one thing the firm's foundation does that gives back to the state of Wisconsin," says Jarvis.

In the aftermath of the Master Settlement Agreement, however, the millions of dollars that were to flow in perpetuity to the state met with a less charitable end, thanks to a failure of the political system. In 2001, Governor Scott McCallum convinced the state legislature to sell off the settlement payments to fill a deficit in the 2001–03 state budget. In a securitization agreement, the state sold bonds that were backed by its $5.9 billion tobacco settlement and received an estimated $1.3 billion to pay its debts. Critics compared the plan in concept to lottery winners cashing in on a smaller jackpot immediately rather than collecting far more money over time.

"It was politically hijacked by politicians who used it to balance the budget," Habush says. "It was a disgrace. It's like winning a great settlement for a client, and they go to Vegas and blow it all at the casinos. There's nothing you can do about it."

While the McCallum deal sucked funds from Wisconsin's tobacco prevention and cessation programs, it fortunately did not affect restrictions on tobacco advertising, promotions, and other anti-smoking laws. Today, fewer people in the state are smoking, and Joe Camel remains banned for life in Wisconsin and throughout the country.

Linda Green v. Smith & Nephew AHP Inc.

By definition, it's the plight of a single individual that is at the core of personal injury law. In Habush's representation of Linda Green, one woman's plight ultimately led to the transformation of the health-care industry and relief for hundreds of thousands of people like her.

Linda Green (Linda Kutz today) was a radiologic technologist at St. Joseph's Hospital in Milwaukee, taking X-rays and CT scans of patients. With a spike in the late 1980s in the number of cases of communicable diseases, health-care workers such as Green were required, under universal precaution guidelines, to wear latex gloves to guard against AIDS, hepatitis, and other contagions. Sometimes she would slip on more than fifty pairs of gloves during an eight-hour shift.

In September 1989, on a routine day at work, Green suddenly felt light-headed. She had trouble breathing and swallowing and asked a coworker to relieve her so she could go home. "I just thought I had an awful cold or an infection," she recalls. "But when my husband saw me, he said, 'Something's not right. This is not a cold. We need to get you to the emergency room.' He dropped me off at the ER and went to park the car, and when I walked in I couldn't even speak. I couldn't tell them what was wrong. They rolled me into the emergency room, and they start hitting me with epinephrine. 'She's going into anaphylactic shock,' they were saying. 'She must have been stung by a bee.' When I could finally speak again, I told them no, I just had a bad cold."

A few months later, it happened again. "Again, I was at work. So I left my work area, walked to the emergency room, and the next thing I know they're admitting me to the intensive care unit. Again, I could not breathe. It got to the point where they were talking about either putting a tube down my throat or doing a tracheotomy because my throat was getting so tight."

Doctors injected her with a number of medications to open her airway, and finally her breathing returned to normal. "I was probably a minute away from them just doing the trache," Green says.

The episodes occurred again and again over the next two years. "No one at the time knew what the culprit was," says Green, who was scared. She had become a walking, talking medical mystery.

In 1991, a pulmonary specialist suggested a bronchoscopy, a procedure in which a video scope is inserted into the air passage. "The airway tightened around the rubber scope, and they almost couldn't get it out," Green says. "The surgeon contacted my pulmonary doctor and said, 'She's deathly allergic to something, and it's going to kill her. We've got to figure out what this is.'"

She was referred to an allergist, Dr. Jordan Fink, at the Medical College of Wisconsin. He had seen similar reactions in children and had begun researching the unusual cases. "At first they thought it was just with spina bifida kids who had been undergoing surgery," Green says. "They thought there was something in the IV fluids that would send them into anaphylactic shock. And then they drew a link to latex exposure because the kids had had repeated visits to hospitals."

Dr. Fink agreed to include Green in his research and tested her for latex exposure. Once again, she had a severe reaction. As soon as the skin-prick test began, her chest swelled and she gasped for air. "They almost lost me during the test," she says. "They needed to call the resuscitation team and stabilize me and get me up to the ICU. But they had their diagnosis." She was highly allergic to latex, the material commonly used in the production of disposable medical gloves.

Green's doctors told her she could not return to her hospital job. She was in her early thirties, with a long career still ahead of her, and wasn't ready to quit. "The hospital put me on workers' comp, and I was eventually told they had no other position for me," she says. "They weren't willing to make any changes in the workplace as far as getting non-latex gloves. I fought very hard for that because it's also going to protect my coworkers as well as other patients. The hospital wasn't willing to do it until they were forced to."

Looking for help, Green contacted Habush. "I was just about beat down to nothing, yet I had to move forward somehow," she says. "I was familiar with Bob Habush through his reputation. Also, working in the health-care industry, he was somewhat of a respected and feared name. And I thought, well, perhaps something can be done. It doesn't hurt to ask. Having this allergy had devastated me. It completely changed my life, took my career away, my earning potential, possibly my life."

Her first meeting with Habush defied her expectations. "When I met with Bob, my first impression was, wow, here's this big, powerful, successful man, and he's a regular guy—very personable. I remember telling my family afterwards, 'You guys would not believe it, he's a different man than what the public sees him as.'

"I know people were a little skeptical because he's kind of a barracuda, and I said, 'No, I've got a whole different impression of him now.' My feelings were, I was very confident because he doesn't mislead you. He told me straightforward, 'We're going to get them. They're going to be made to stop this. It's going to take some time, and it's going to be difficult. You have to be willing to be tough. I'll tell you when things are going good, when things are going bad, and you need to trust me when I'm moving forward for your best interest.'"

Habush and his team of attorneys and investigators began tracking down the manufacturers of the powdered examination gloves worn by Green. "It was a very difficult case because hospitals bought latex gloves from different manufacturers," says Habush. "We had to subpoena the records from each of the hospitals where Linda had worked to get the inventory of the manufacturers' gloves she was exposed to. And as luck would have it, most of her exposure prior to her getting sick was from gloves made by Smith & Nephew. So we were able to target the right manufacturer."

Headquartered in London, Smith & Nephew was, and is, one of the world's largest makers of medical products, including gloves. Like several other manufacturers of gloves, Smith & Nephew located many of its production plants in Malaysia because of cheaper production costs and the great availability of latex, the natural milk-colored sap of the rubber tree. Highly elastic and waterproof, latex was used to make a variety of products, including tires, boots, rubber bands, balloons, condoms, and medical gloves.

As the demand for latex increased with the advent of the AIDS epidemic, thousands of complaints began to surface of users suffering adverse reactions, which ranged from relatively minor rashes to life-threatening cases of anaphylaxis, dubbed "latex shock." Between October 1988 and April 1992, the Food and Drug Administration received reports of 1,036 severe reactions and fifteen deaths related to latex allergies. The most susceptive people were hospital employees.

Habush sent an attorney to Malaysia to take depositions of workers at the latex rubber facilities. "We discovered that, in an effort to meet demand, these factories had eliminated a three-step washing process that was designed to clear the latex of natural occurring allergens," he says. "Up to this point, it had not affected anybody because the gloves had been cleansed of the allergens—an excess of a high-protein content—when they came off the assembly line. It wasn't design. It was a defect in the manufacturing process, which was done intentionally."

An estimated 10 percent of all health-care workers suffered from latex sensitivity. "Doctors, nurses, lab technologists, dentists, and dental assistants—they were exposed to these hastily produced gloves and had allergic reactions. It ended their careers," says Habush. "This wasn't an isolated case. There were thousands and thousands of people who were suffering from this latex allergy merely because these manufacturers in Malaysia had screwed up."

Represented by Habush, Linda Green became one of thirty-three plaintiffs in Wisconsin (there was also one in Massachusetts) that ultimately sued Smith & Nephew and Baxter Healthcare Corporation, another major producer of medical gloves. Green's case, however, became the test case, the first product liability case involving latex sensitivity to go to trial. It would act as a legal exemplar for future trials and settlements around the country.

Don Peterson was the defense attorney who represented Smith & Nephew. He argued that Green was not allergic to latex and claimed instead that she had a vocal cord dysfunction, which impaired her breathing.

"Don was a very good lawyer and a friend of mine," Habush says. "He was one of the few defense lawyers that I was really able to maintain a good relationship with during my career. But in the trial he took a very unusual tack. He didn't defend the case as a product liability, which was how I was presenting it. He defended it as a malpractice case. His tactic was to try to blame Linda Green's condition on something other than an allergic reaction. Essentially he said she was reacting psychologically. He attacked Dr. Fink, saying he made a misdiagnosis, and that everyone had made misdiagnosis. Well, that was mistake. It was just an indefensible defense."

Throughout the three-week trial, Green says, she felt sure Habush would triumph. "He just exudes confidence," she explains. "He's confident in his questioning, he's confident in his manner, and I believe that comes through. Cool, calm, and collected. Even when things get a little tense or heated in the courtroom. I would get a little nervous and wonder, 'How are they going to handle this?' He always came back—very simply, very slowly, very calmly—and turned it around."

In his final argument, Habush reminded the jury of testimony entered by Dr. Dennis Ownby, an allergist from Atlanta who served on the FDA's Allergenic Products Advisory Board:

> Let me read to you what has been read into the record by Dr. Ownby. "Healthcare workers at increased risk. Physicians like other healthcare providers are at increased risk of developing latex allergy. Some physicians have become so allergic to latex that they have to drastically alter their practice, for example, by giving up performing surgery, or delivering children or stopping practice all together."
>
> Physicians are not alone. Dentists, podiatrists, nurses, respiratory therapists, and other healthcare professionals are also losing their ability to practice. "This is clearly a tragedy"—I'm now quoting Dr. Ownby—"especially because it is potentially preventable if latex allergy is recognized while symptoms are still mild. It is usually for individuals that you're working with minor modifications to their work environment. Once latex allergy has become severe, however, it is very difficult to provide a safe work environment. This is clearly a tragedy."
>
> Dr. Ownby is one of the foremost experts in the country. So, members of the jury, don't accept the notion that the defense is trying to give to you that this is no big deal. It is a big deal.

As the jury ended its deliberation, Peterson quickly put in a call to a local television station, Channel 58, the CBS affiliate. "As an indication of how sure he was that he'd win, he invited Channel 58 into the courtroom to await the verdict," says Habush. "I had no idea this was happening. This is something you'd expect me to have done. While we were waiting for the jury, in comes a reporter and a cameraman waiting for Don's victory speech. I'd never seen anything like it in my whole career."

The jury came back with a 13–1 verdict—against Peterson's client. Jurors had decided that the latex gloves manufactured by Smith & Nephew were indeed "defective and unreasonably dangerous" and caused harm to Linda Green. They awarded her $1 million.

"After inviting the TV crew in to celebrate his win, Don ended up losing," Habush says. "But who be it to say I wouldn't take advantage of a TV camera in the courtroom. Don declined to deliver his defeat speech, and I took full advantage of delivering my victory speech, using his TV reporter and cameraman."

Jurors, too, spoke to the media. "We want them to be held accountable," a juror told a reporter after the verdict. "These are used in schools, in hospitals."

"I hope this will awaken the manufacturers," said another juror. "I know something can and will be done."

Green says she expected to win all along. "I always knew that the jury would rule in our favor," she says. "But just hearing it . . . I can't even describe the emotion in the courtroom at the time."

While she remains sensitized to latex today, she seldom encounters latex products. "It gets better over time, after many years of changing what I'm doing, where I'm going, what I'm buying, what I'm eating, things in my environment. I still have to be careful. Simple things like going to a birthday party, and they have latex balloons in the house. I can't go in. Or buying things from the deli. Some places are still using latex gloves to handle food. I've just adapted through the years. It gets easier because it's just an awareness you always have. It's a lifestyle change."

After being denied her old job at St. Joseph's, Green worked in positions she was overqualified for, including answering phones at the hospital. She is now an X-ray technologist at Froedtert Hospital near Milwaukee, a latex-free facility.

"There have been changes in the industry because of this lawsuit," she says. "The manufacturers had to change their products, and the nicest thing to see was, the FDA required warning labels on products. That is a tremendous change for health-care workers as well as patients. Now you're even seeing latex warnings on non-health-care products, things you buy at Walgreens and so forth. That was the satisfying thing that came about from all this.

"I'm just happy that there have been changes so nobody else has to go through what I went through or lose their life. There were quite a few deaths associated with this. I was almost one of them."

The amount of the award disappointed Habush. He had hoped for more, to really turn the screw on manufacturers to initiate changes. But the *Green* case broke new ground on several fronts. It opened the path for dozens of other lawsuits and immediately ratcheted up the pressure on manufacturers and state and federal governments to remove latex products from the health-care industry and other markets. Legislation was introduced in several states to ban the use of latex products in health care. Alternatives were developed. And today, instead of latex, many medical gloves are made of vinyl, neoprene, and other synthetics.

Moreover, as an outgrowth of the *Green* verdict, law was changed in Wisconsin. In an appeal by Smith & Nephew, the company's lawyer, Joseph Kearney (now the dean of Marquette University Law School), argued that the lower court erred in instructing jurors that a product could be found "defective and unreasonably dangerous" based on a consumer's expectations about the product.

"It was an attempt by the tort reformers to discard a concept called 'consumer expectation,'" Habush says, "which is the most lenient pro-plaintiff instruction a jury can receive." As he explained in his final argument to the jury in the trial, the consumer expectation standard asks jurors to put themselves in the shoes of the consumer. "It means if I'm a consumer and using a product, and I'm using it properly, but it contains a harmful characteristic that I have no way of knowing exists, and it occurred during the manufacturing process, then you can find it is defective [and unreasonably dangerous] under Wisconsin law."

The verdict was upheld by the Wisconsin Supreme Court. In the decision, Justice John Wilcox wrote: "Where a manufacturer places a defective and unreasonably dangerous product into the stream of commerce, the manufacturer, not the injured consumer, should bear the costs of the risks posed by the product. . . . The burden then shifts to the manufacturer to prove that the product includes a warning or directions that effectively alert the ordinary consumer that the ingredient can cause allergic reaction in a substantial number of consumers."

The high court's decision embraced and solidified the consumer expectation standard and was cited in courts across the United States. "There were campaigns all over the country to get rid of it because it was such a pro-plaintiff type of law," says Habush. "They thought they were going to get the Wisconsin Supreme Court to abrogate it in this case. But Linda Green was a consumer, and she was dealing with what was otherwise a benign, beneficial product—a latex glove, designed to protect health-care workers and others from blood-borne diseases. How could she possibly have anticipated that this glove contained excessive allergens that caused her to have a terrible allergic reaction and ended her career as a lab tech?"

The commitment to fight to the end for Linda Green is classic Habush, says Tim Trecek, a Habush partner who was involved in the case. "Whenever you're running a case against a manufacturer like this, they are typically multibillion- or billion-dollar companies who don't care about how much time or money they spend in defending a claim. The vast majority of attorneys wouldn't take on a case like this because they couldn't afford it. Bob has always sought justice over monetary contemplations.

"In the scheme of what he had to do, and the time and money he put into the case, if you were looking at it in regards to dollars and cents, it didn't make sense," adds Trecek. "Bob doesn't care about that. Bob knew that this was a defective product. He knew that there were people who were being adversely affected because of the toxins in these gloves. He took on the Goliath. He said safe ways to manufacture products and compensation for someone who's been injured is more important than how much money we do or don't make."

CHAPTER SEVEN

Altruistic Warrior

With their professional skills and the resources available through their law firms, most attorneys are expected to provide services free of charge to clients who can't afford fees. Work that is done pro bono (short for the Latin term *pro bono publico*, or "for the public good") is done at the discretion of each attorney and each firm. Ethical rules of the American Bar Association, for example, recommend that lawyers contribute at least fifty hours of pro bono service each year.

"There is a general obligation for law firms to do pro bono service," says Bob Habush. "Many of the larger firms do fulfill that obligation. Most small firms or single practicing lawyers do not. My firm does not have a pro bono policy, but I know that many of my lawyers from time to time do represent clients or friends for nothing. When I do it, it may not have anything to do with their ability to pay. For instance, I have represented friends in all types of matters when they were in trouble, usually with the law—doctors and lawyers and businessmen. I have represented a judge who was being charged with an ethical violation. I have represented a Jewish day school, which was being sued for a bogus alleged sexual assault by a former teacher/rabbi.

"When I am angry at a perpetrator or feel that a claim is frivolous, or when the cause appeals to me, lending my ability for no fee is an easy call. If the cause is just, and the victim is in need of a good lawyer and can't afford one, and my heart and mind tell me to help, I do it without regard to a fee."

The following three cases illustrate the pro bono work provided by Habush. Each underscores his passion for justice, for making things right.

And taken together, they depict the protean roles he takes on—as an advocate, a teacher, a protector, and, frequently, a champion for those who appear defeated and overcome.

In early 2008, Habush received an e-mail from a woman asking for help. "I need a lawyer," read the e-mail. "I've been sexually abused. Could I make an appointment to talk to you?"

Habush wrote back and told her, yes, of course he would to talk to her. At their first meeting, "in comes this frail-looking young woman, her shoulders bowed, her chin down," he recalls. "And she tells me her story."

Several years earlier, in her first year of high school, Brenda (not her real name) had been sexually assaulted by a man who was her teacher and athletic coach. She had played soccer and basketball and was a student in the teacher's religion class at a parochial high school in Milwaukee.

The abuser, thirteen years older than Brenda and married at the time, preyed on female students he coached and taught. "He had this tendency to befriend the prettiest girls, and they would develop friendships," Habush says. "He would make Brenda stay after class to visit with him, and he'd have her come over to his house and visit with him. And when the sports team would travel to tournaments, he'd sit next to her on the bus. He took her out for pizza, danced with her at school dances, sent her valentines and a Sweetest Day card, sent her letters and e-mails and signed them with 'I love you.' It got to the point where she actually felt she loved *him*."

The sexual contact started in the spring of 2001 when Brenda was fifteen. It continued for nearly a year. Massaging her shoulders in the training room at school, the coach casually slipped his hand under her sports bra.

The abuse escalated. In his van at a park and in his home after school, he fondled the girl's breasts and placed his hand in her pants, penetrating her with his fingers. Brenda said they eventually had intercourse, although he would later deny it.

"She never told anybody," says Habush. "He then dropped her and went on to another pretty girl."

On one occasion, in his bedroom at home, the coach secretly videotaped the other girl removing her clothes to try on a sports bra and spandex gym shorts he had given her.

"Finally, the second victim reported the assaults," Habush says. "So it was not Brenda that did the reporting."

Brent Biesterfeld, high school coach and religious teacher, was arrested in March 2002. He admitted to having multiple encounters with the two girls and to pursuing several others. In a plea bargain, he pled guilty to two counts of second-degree sexual assault: sexual contact or sexual intercourse with a minor. Biesterfeld was sentenced to eighteen months in prison and extended supervision for three and a half years. His name was added permanently to the Wisconsin Sex Offender Registry.

Although her abuser had been convicted and served time in prison, Brenda had difficulty coming to grips with the assaults. "She suffered from tremendous guilt and shame," Habush says. "She tried to kill herself by overdosing on pills. She became an alcoholic and a drug user, and she was an inpatient at a psychiatric hospital in Milwaukee.

"As she was telling me her story, she was crying, sobbing, saying no one wanted to help her. I'm listening to her and thinking, 'I've got to do something. I don't even care if I could just sue that son of a bitch and we don't get a nickel. He's got to pay. Talk about being angry—I was incensed.'"

Habush knew someone who had been abused: "Not an immediate family member but a close relative. I've seen the trauma that it causes and the inexplicable guilt the victim feels. I say 'inexplicable' because even rape victims wonder whether they could have fought more, done more to stop the attacker. When you've got a predator who is an authority figure molesting a younger person, it just magnifies the breach of the trust."

"I'm going to represent you," Habush said to Brenda. "We're going to tell him we're going to sue him and sue the high school, even though the statute of limitations has run. I'll think of some theory that maybe can hold water. The school shouldn't get off scot-free because, from what you said to me, there were telltale signs that this guy acted in a peculiar way with young girls, calling them out of class, going on dates, stuff they had to have noticed."

He told Brenda he would handle the case pro bono. "I'm not going to charge you a fee for this. We'll just see where this goes. I can't make any promises. I'm not sure that we're going to be successful getting any money. But I guarantee you one thing. I'm going to give you some sense of revenge."

He insisted that she stop pitying herself. "I will take the case on one condition: that you straighten yourself out," he said. "You go back into therapy and you clean yourself up, because I'm not going to represent a corpse. I'm not going to represent you if you're thinking of killing yourself. If you want to continue drinking and doping and thinking of suicide, then forget it. Go kill yourself. If you want me to kick some ass for you and teach this guy a real lesson, you let me know, and we'll go that way."

The young woman was taken aback. "She was shocked that anybody would talk to her like that," Habush remembers. "I was supposed to join the legions of people who felt sorry for her. It was like electric shock treatment, and she was just startled. But she said, 'OK. I'll do my best.'"

As he would discover, a criminal complaint had been filed with Milwaukee police in 1999 alleging Biesterfeld had illicit sexual contact with a minor at another parochial school. Brenda's high school principal should have known about this when hiring Biesterfeld, said Habush. "It was negligent supervision, negligent complicity on the part of the school. I could make a case that the school should have found out about it on a background check. Somebody at the prior school had to know about it. But nothing was done."

He took a deposition of the school superintendent, intending, as he always did, to go to trial. "I did a pretty good job on the superintendent," he says. "Then I had my researcher study the law on sexual predators." The researcher learned that Wisconsin law included an extended statute of limitations on civil lawsuits against sexual offenders, which, Habush explains, "allowed me to take the position that the teacher was an agent of the school, and the school should come under the umbrella of the extended statute, and thus would be legally responsible for his actions. It was an interesting theory. I didn't know if it was worth a damn. I didn't know if it would have sustained the legality if an appellate court got a hold of it. But it sure was something I could use as leverage."

What Habush was really after was the deposition of the predator, Biesterfeld. He wanted vengeance. Taking the deposition, he pushed, pried, and vilified Brenda's abuser until he exacted a confession and an apology from Biesterfeld for his loathsome actions.

Q: Let me advise you that I have looked through your entire record. I have information from the people you interviewed with before and after your conviction. There is very little that I don't know about you and what you've done. Let me also advise you, are you aware of what's happened to [Brenda] since your encounter with her?

A: Somewhat.

Q: Okay. Are you aware of what difficulties that she's had since that time?

A: No.

Q: Are you aware that she's had excessive psychiatric help?

A: No.

Q: Are you aware she's been in and out of psychiatric hospitals?

A: No.

Q: Are you aware that she has serious eating disorders?

A: No.

Q: Are you aware this is all the result of your encounters with her sexually?

A: No.

Q: No one has ever told you that?

A: I wasn't aware of these things from her, no.

Q: Do you care?

A: Yes.

Q: Do you feel bad about that?

A: Terrible.

Q: There were multiple encounters with the two girls sexually prior to your being arrested, weren't there?

A: Yes.

Q: You were their religious teacher?

A: Yes.

Q: You were their coach?

A: Yes.

Q: And you realized at that time that both of these girls were young, correct?

A: Yes.

Q: Do you have any reason to believe they were anything other than innocent?

A: No.

Q: Did you know that they were vulnerable?

A: Yes.

Q: Did you attempt to become friends with them in order for you to be able to fulfill some of your sexual fantasies?

A: Yes.

Q: That was wrong?

A: Very wrong.

Q: They weren't at fault, were they?

A: No.

Q: They didn't do anything to encourage you?

A: No.

Q: And would you agree that they shouldn't feel guilty about this, either one of these girls?

A: Yes.

Q: You take full and total responsibility for what happened?

A: 100 percent.

Q: And if [Brenda] feels some guilt and shame about it, you would tell her don't?

A: Yes.

Q: Were you ever bothered by the fact that you were their religious instructor and you were committing criminal acts upon minors?

A: Yes.

Q: It bothered you a lot?

A: Yes.

Q: It didn't stop you, though, did it?

A: No.

Habush shared the deposition with Brenda. "I got him to tell her, 'It wasn't your fault. It was my fault. I took advantage of you. You were young. Don't blame yourself,'" he says. "He did a better job than any shrink could have ever done because he's the guy that did it to her. When I finished with him, the insurance company offered the limits of its policy, $500,000. So the case was settled.

"Brenda returned to the college classes that she had given up on. She stopped drinking, stopped doping, and took her life back."

The case goes to the heart of Habush's convictions as a professional and as a human being, says Benjamin Wagner, a young partner at the firm who assisted with the depositions. "Bob wants to be on the right side of the angels versus the demons. This young lady was rejected by two other law firms [including Cannon & Dunphy, formed by the two lawyers who years earlier had abruptly left the Habush firm with all their client files]. When Bob agreed to represent her, he saw that it was the right thing to do, regardless of the financial reward. I saw him take on the role not only of an advocate, not only of a lawyer, but also somewhat of a therapist, somewhat of a father figure, and somewhat of a champion. It was remarkable to really see him playing all of these roles for this young lady. She needed a champion. It had a powerful effect on her, a cathartic and healing effect."

Brenda's parents called Habush and thanked him for saving their daughter's life. And a few months after the settlement, he received an e-mail from Brenda. In stark contrast to her first e-mail, this one brimmed with self-confidence and joy.

Dear Mr. Habush,

Remember me?! I'm writing this e-mail to say thank you. I'm usually awesome at thank you cards and get them out right away. However, what you did for me, you and your firm, I didn't want to just send a thank you card right away without first seeing all that it's done for me. I wanted to be able to tell you about how great I'm doing. And to be honest, I put off the thank you card because I didn't want to close that chapter in my life. Until I met you I really didn't have anyone on my side. You fought for me when I couldn't fight for myself. And well you taught me, slowly but surely, how to really live my life. Yeah, I had my parents but they were my parents, they were more emotional than supportive. They told me what I wanted to hear. However, when I met you, you told me what I needed to hear. You told me that I needed to move on . . . I would never have accomplished that without you. And, I never would have accomplished what I've done in the past 8 months if it weren't for you either. You'll be happy to know I am back in school. I got a 4.0 this past semester! Straight A's (I haven't had straight A's since first semester in my senior year in high school!) I'm proud of myself. So are my parents . . . I also moved out of my parents' house, so I'm on my own now and I love it. And I also have met someone completely amazing . . . So what I'm trying to say is all that I just told you, you and everyone in your firm were the ones who made that happen for me.

See, this is why I didn't want to write this because I'm crying. Good crying. But nonetheless being a crybaby. So, Mr. Habush, I want to thank you for being an amazing person. You didn't have to do what you did, any of it. But I thank you so much for believing in me. I honestly can say I don't know what I'd do if I hadn't met you! And anyone that knows me, knows how much I value you as a person. I know my case didn't win a lot of money. Well, in my eyes it certainly did, but your firm is known for huge cases that win a lot of money. However, it was never about the money for me. It was just about getting my life back. And that's what you did for me. You gave me my life back. I guess I just needed a little kick in the ass. Well, maybe a big kick in the ass! So thanks.

You will forever be a hero of mine.

Habush printed out Brenda's e-mail. From a wooden picture frame in his office, he removed a photograph of himself with a trophy fish he had caught on a fishing trip in Canada. In its place, he mounted Brenda's note and displayed it on his desk.

"I've done a lot of these cases and made a lot of money," he says. "Some impact me more than others. On this little case, I never made a dime, I didn't do a tremendous amount of heavy lifting, but I was able to focus my anger and get even with that young woman's abuser. This probably will stand out as one of the most gratifying things I've ever done."

* * *

Like all Americans, Bob Habush was jolted by the events of September 11, 2001. Sitting at home in front of the television with his wife, Mimi, and seeing the first plane crash into the World Trade Center shook his sensibilities like nothing else. Who would fly a commercial jetliner into a Manhattan skyscraper? As the second plane hit, and both towers crumbled into dust, the answer to his question became completely unfathomable.

Several weeks after the tragedy, the horrible images still rattling around in his brain, Habush got a phone call from a rabbi in the Milwaukee area. David Cohen, chief rabbi at Congregation Sinai, said his sister's husband had been working in his office on the top floor of the north tower on the morning of 9/11. He had worked for the bond company Cantor Fitzgerald, and he was still unaccounted for.

"Would you be interested in meeting with my father?" asked Rabbi Cohen. "He's a judge in New Jersey, and he'd like to come to Milwaukee to see what you think we ought to do for my sister."

Habush had handled a dozen airplane cases in the past, both commercial and general aviation crashes, successfully representing the families of victims.

"David's sister and her husband were young, in their thirties, as I recall," Habush says. "They had two young children under ten years old. I hadn't gotten over the acute psychological trauma myself. I was still emotionally upset, the same as most people."

He set up a meeting.

"What can we do?" the elder David Cohen asked. "She's a young widow, taking care of two little kids. Her husband was a very successful bond dealer, making $300,000 to $400,000 a year. Now he's gone."

"Well," said Habush, "conceivably she could have a lawsuit against the airlines for improper security measures, because somehow these terrorists got on board. I'd be happy to look into it for you and meet with your daughter when you think it's appropriate."

At the time, the federal government was in the process of setting up the September 11th Victim Compensation Fund to provide compensation for anyone who was injured or killed as a result of the terrorist attacks. The congressionally enacted fund was unlike any other project in U.S. history. It awarded a total of $7 billion to 97 percent of the affected families over a thirty-three-month term.

Habush traveled east to meet the widow. She lived in a Manhattan bedroom community in New Jersey. "It tore my heart out," he says. "It had been extremely traumatic for her. She tells me, 'He goes to work. He never comes back, and I don't even have his body. I have nothing.'

"She was one of those survivors who called all the hospitals to find out if her husband had been brought in. She went down to Trinity Church near ground zero to hang a photograph of him. Very, very sad. But it became evident the people on the top floor perished because they just couldn't get out. They were told to stay put.

"She had to explain all this to her children, who are asking, 'Where's Daddy?' Then to have a funeral with no body, not even an ash? It was just beyond comprehension. Her mental anguish, it just broke my heart."

Habush laid out her options: "We could file a petition with the Victim Compensation Fund, which would be an administrative procedure. Essentially we put together a claim for damages, figuring levels of compensation based upon age, income projections, children, et cetera. With this option, you give up the right to sue, to go to court. The second option is a lawsuit against the airline. But if you take them to court, it will be a long, expensive, protracted litigation."

"What do you recommend?" she asked.

"Let's go for the administrative procedure," he said, "because I don't think you want to go through protracted four- or five-year litigation. I think we can probably get this done in a year or so. I'm not sure we could get as much as we could get from a jury, but I think we could put together enough of a package to do pretty well."

She agreed, and Habush told her he would be willing to file the claim for no fee, only out-of-pocket expenses for travel and hotels.

He began assembling an economic projection to submit to the fund's administrator, which included a narrative of the family's financial loss as well as the suffering that the wife and children had endured. "Most statutes include as recoverable damages the loss of society, the loss of companionship," he notes. "That is, you lost your husband, you lost your companion. But grieving is not considered a compensable item. Whereas, under the Victim Compensation plan, the grieving would be very much compensable."

He scheduled a hearing in front of the fund's special master, Kenneth Feinberg, an attorney who specialized in mediation. Sitting in a New York office at a conference table, the widow and Habush presented the claim.

Feinberg politely and respectfully posed several questions to the widow and then said he would be in touch.

"He came back to me with a preliminary assessment," says Habush, "which I disagreed with. It was too low. And so I had a second hearing with him. This time, he came back with an amended decision, just over $3.6 million, which included amounts for her children. I thought it was very adequate."

Habush met with the widow and her father to recommend the settlement offer. "When you translate money into a loss like this, it's almost obscene," he says. "But finally, she accepted it."

Today, from time to time, Habush runs into Rabbi Cohen and asks about his sister. "He tells me she has no plans to remarry, that she just can't get over it. But she's made an extra effort to constantly remind her children about their father, talking about him around the dinner table, making photos albums and videos of him, things like that. She wants so much that the children not forget him."

The case moved Habush deeply. "I felt pretty good about doing that case because of the emotional impact of it. You know, three thousand people lost their lives on that September morning. I felt if I could help one widow out of hundreds who lost a husband, I was doing my small part."

* * *

At the dawn of the twenty-first century, a time of hope and optimism, a chronic and intractable bigotry raised its ugly head in Habush's hometown, Whitefish Bay. A flicker of anti-Semitism had reignited a flame inside Habush as he was reminded of the slurs and insults he had faced more than sixty years earlier when growing up. That flame impelled him once again to take action, to fight back.

In 2001, Habush sat on the executive committee of the Milwaukee Jewish Federation, an umbrella organization that raises funds and coordinates planning for dozens of religious groups, cultural programs, and service agencies within the Jewish community. The federation owned and oversaw a 26.5-acre property known as the Karl Campus, with all but two and a half acres located on a leafy residential boulevard in Whitefish Bay.

Based on the campus at the time were a number of groups, most of them nonprofits, including the anchor organization, the Jewish Community Center, along with a day care facility, a nursery school, two day schools, the B'nai B'rith Youth Organization, and an athletic center. Most were open to the general public.

Named after Max Karl, a Milwaukee attorney, entrepreneur, and philanthropist, the Karl Campus dates back to 1983, when the Jewish Federation entered into negotiations to buy the property from University School, a private institution that had occupied the space since 1917. The planned purchase was not received with open arms by the Village of Whitefish Bay. To the contrary, a few dozen neighbors who lived across the street from the campus swiftly made their opposition known to village leaders, and in anticipation of the acquisition by the federation, the municipal government changed the zoning of the property and imposed rigid restrictions on the use of the Karl Campus. For example, the Village limited the total number of people on the campus at any given time to no more than 951 and set specific hours of operation for each of the agencies.

"We had a tremendous struggle in the eighties to get the property," says Bert Bilsky, a federation board member and the executive director of the Jewish Community Foundation for many years. "We had to agree to a lot of restrictions. There was a census that we were expected to conduct of our users. This was all because of the residential character of the neighborhood, even though we weren't putting in a new use. The facility had already been part of the neighborhood. In fact, it predated all the houses that were there. The agreement with the Village was probably one of the most restrictive of its kind, certainly in the state, and maybe even the country."

The unwelcoming response smacked of prejudice. "There were overtones of anti-Semitism," says Bilsky. "We always felt that if we had been a different denomination, we might not have gotten the same treatment."

The federation nevertheless agreed to the restrictions, and the Jewish Community Center, known as the JCC, and the adjacent day schools opened in 1987.

By the early 2000s, as more and more members of the Jewish community migrated to Milwaukee's North Shore suburbs, the Karl Campus was experiencing growing pains. Its buildings, most of them outdated and overcrowded, required renovation. As younger families mixed with older members, a need arose for a larger, multigenerational campus.

The Jewish Federation began a capital campaign to raise money for a multimillion-dollar expansion and renovation project. Habush made one of the lead gifts, along with Sheldon Lubar, a venture capitalist and civic activist, and Stephen Marcus, an executive in the lodging and entertainment industry.

In May 2001, members of the federation began meeting with delegations of village officials and holding open houses with neighborhood residents. In May 2002, after months of informational sessions, the federation's real estate attorney submitted plans for a 58,500-square-foot addition, a new parking lot for 205 cars, and thirty additional parking spaces in an existing lot. The federation had operated in goodwill and didn't foresee a problem.

"We were busting out at the seams of both the schools and the Jewish Community Center," says Bilsky, who coordinated the fund-raising. "Our feeling was, look, we've been great neighbors all these years. We're a community asset. There have been very few complaints. We've adhered to the requirements, which were made back in 1987, a long time ago. We're going to go in and have a rational conversation with the members of the village board, and we'll get something between where we would like to go and where we must go."

It wasn't that easy. The village board reviewed the federation's plan and sent it back for major revisions. Meanwhile, a group of neighbors filed a "protest petition," which compelled a 75 percent "supermajority" vote by the village board to approve the expansion.

The federation saw the requirement as a thinly veiled attempt to kill the project. "There were still some very difficult neighbors who seemed to feel that our expanded presence would be a detriment to their neighborhood," Bilsky says. "And they prevailed upon members of the village board."

The neighbors argued that the expansion of the JCC and day schools would add traffic congestion along Santa Monica Boulevard, which bordered the property on the east, and make other adverse changes to the neighborhood, says Bruce Block, the real estate lawyer representing the federation. "They identified seven or eight issues, traffic, noise, increased storm water, all these things, boom, boom, boom, boom. And we addressed each one ad nauseam and in detail. We'd have our experts go through all these issues."

Working sessions with the Village often went late into the evening, sometimes past midnight. "We wanted an outdoor pool, and that didn't fly, and we accepted that," says Bilsky. "But we ended up with what we felt was a fair plan, and they were stalling us. Some of them were saying one thing to us in private and then they would get into a public meeting and say exactly the opposite."

Block recalls discussions he had with the village board and village president. "After months and months of putting this together, the village trustees said, 'We will support you. We're not going to let you swing in the wind on this.' But as soon as that caught any kind of publicity, all hell broke loose. I got a call at home from the village president, Jim Gormley, saying, 'I just want you to know I've got an election coming up. I'm not going to be able to support this plan.'"

Local ordinance required the plan commission to hold a preliminary meeting for zoning changes. The meeting was open to the public at Whitefish Bay High School, Habush's alma mater.

"Seven hundred people showed up," Block says. "This was supposed to be a working session presentation. But before we even started our presentation, the village manager showed a PowerPoint he had put together, stating why the JCC was already in violation of whatever they were supposed to be doing. It was insane. Just a total sandbag. We were furious."

Meanwhile, neighbors up and down Santa Monica Boulevard were posting lawn signs: *Stop the expansion. Stop the JCC.* At one point, they put up For Sale signs, each sign counterfeit, yet a fervent expression of the stiff opposition.

The ill will escalated and spilled over into the public meetings of the village board. Neighbors would dress in red shirts and hold red paper Stop signs over their faces to protest the expansion.

The level of acrimony bothered Katie Pritchard, who was elected village president in the midst of the protracted campaign. "To me, what made it terrible was the presence of pretty blatant anti-Semitism," she says. "When you work with people on tough issues, you always have some irrational, personal conflicts. You have people that aren't basing things on facts, and you have different perceptions and different opinions. But when you add the anti-Semitism, it's a whole different hurtful thing. People would come to speak at public meetings, and they'd talk about this shockingly and unabashedly. They'd say, 'Hello, my name is so-and-so, and I live at such-and-such. And I don't think we need any more Jews here.' That blatant. Some would say, 'These are not Whitefish Bay Jews. These are Mequon Jews who are going to be coming here.' One person said, 'Imagine if the Fox Bay Theater was filled with Jews. People wouldn't want that in their neighborhood.' It was just unbelievable."

Pritchard identified a group of about ten ringleaders who were driving the anti-JCC movement. "There was a small group who organized and intimidated and harassed and harangued and threatened, and people were really afraid of them," she says. "Neighbors would secretly call me or catch me in the grocery store and say, 'It's not that I feel this way. I have to keep living with my neighbors, and they're very intimidating.'"

Pritchard, who also sat on the plan commission, kept a journal of the two-year battle, documenting some of the offensive behavior. "There were swastikas at the middle school," she says. "Every year the JCC would host this Walk for Israel through the neighborhood. And some of the marchers said there were neighbors who would yell, 'Heebs go home. Heebs go home.'"

The attacks got personal. "There were people who went through my campaign list and said, 'Anybody who gives that's Jewish must be motivated by your vote for the JCC.' The opponents wanted to disqualify me from the board because I had worked at United Way, and United Way gave money to the JCC. After me, they tried to disqualify Paul Mathews, who was on the plan commission, because he's president of the Marcus Center for the Performing Arts, which was funded by the Marcuses, a Jewish family. And they tried to disqualify Commissioner Mark Huber because he works at Aurora Health Care, and Aurora provides the sports medicine for the JCC."

The divisiveness began to wear on her. She wrote in her journal: "I so dreaded going to another meeting and accepting public comments from idiots that I thought I'd be better off if I got hit by a car."

In March 2003, nearly two years after the federation first announced its plan, the village board gave "provisional approval" for a much smaller addition: a 42,000-square-foot expansion and a parking lot for 103 cars.

Then, weeks later, something confounding happened. One of the early critics of the JCC expansion was elected to the village board. The woman, who lived across the street on Santa Monica Boulevard, persuaded another village trustee to overturn the provisional approval. In a 4–3 vote, less than a supermajority, the project failed to win the go-ahead. Adding insult to injury, the board then approved a motion to downsize the project even more: a building addition of just 31,000 square feet and a parking lot for only forty-five cars.

The federation rejected the reductions as unworkable. Good neighbors to the community for more than fifteen years, its members felt betrayed. "People were mad," Bilsky says. "There didn't seem to be any rational basis on which they were making some of these decisions. There certainly are standards that have to be followed. You can't just be arbitrary and capricious about saying no. What became clear is that we weren't going to lie down for this. And that's where Bob Habush came in. Bob developed a strategy. I helped develop a legal defense fund, and people contributed significant amounts of money, $200,000 total. We were going to sue them."

Habush until then had been merely observing the federation's struggle. "I sort of heard that they were having trouble getting approval, but I wasn't involved directly," he says. "At that time they had hired another lawyer, named Bob Friebert, a well-known lawyer. He does mostly commercial litigation. I would hear reports that they weren't getting anywhere, that the Village was just yanking Friebert's chain, playing him for a jerk. As I'm hearing all this crap, I'm getting angrier and angrier. I'm reliving my Whitefish Bay days, my anti-Semitic attack as a kid, and I'm thinking, 'Goddamn them.'

"One day, in a federation board meeting, I said, 'That's it. I'm taking over this case at no fee. I'm going to do it for nothing because I'm going to start kicking some ass.'"

He started by joining forces with Bruce Block, the real estate attorney. "I don't know shit about real estate. So I send a letter to Whitefish Bay saying that I've been retained as co-counsel with Bruce," Habush says. "I wanted to give the board a chance to reverse its position and think seriously about allowing the JCC to make the additions. But they had basically said, 'Kiss our ass.' So we drafted a complaint and filed it in federal court, alleging discrimination and asking for punitive damages."

Bruce Block—normally reserved and low-key—also was ready for battle after seeing how the Village had treated the federation. According to Block: "So many folks at the federation were trying hard to be as open-minded and as reasonable as possible, and not to fly off the handle and play the anti-Semitic card, but to say, 'OK, let's give them the benefit of the doubt.' But after that last vote by the board, I said, 'This is just nonsense. It's nuts. Shit, let's litigate. Let's get this over with.'"

The federal lawsuit made constitutional claims under the Religious Land Use and Institutionalized Persons Act, which prohibits discrimination against a religious institution on land-use issues. The claims and Habush's letter recognizing his retainer were forwarded by the Village of Whitefish Bay to its insurance company, and the company's representative soon contacted Habush. They set up a meeting.

"So, what's the story?" Habush asked.

"Well, can we work something out?" said the insurance attorney.

"No, I don't think so," Habush said, staring hard at the man across from him. "Your people have gone too far. They're being influenced by a bunch of anti-Semites, and I don't like it. It's got to stop.

"I don't know if you know me, but I'm a pretty good trial attorney, and when I'm pissed off, I'm *really* good. *And I am pissed off.* So I'll tell you what I'm going to do: We're going to prepare subpoenas for every one of these yokels who live around here, and I'm going to subpoena them all to a deposition. I'm going to ask them questions like 'Did you send out letters disparaging the Jewish Community Center? How do you feel about the Jewish Community Center? How do you feel about Jews?' And I will just tear them a new asshole."

"Well, you won't do that."

"Oh, I won't? Watch me."

And with that, the meeting ended.

Block sat in on the conversation with the outside attorney. "He had a great deal of respect for Bob," he says. "He was also frightened of Bob—intimidated, in my judgment. And I thought Habush was brilliant in his role. He is a very intimidating man when he wants to be, without blustering. He just has a very forceful persona that's very helpful on certain occasions. The attorney didn't feel like he was being disrespected. But he knew that Bob had a great deal of gravitas and that Bob believed in his cause.

"Bob's reputation helps him," Block continues. "You know, it's like Chauncey Gardner in the movie *Being There*. If somebody thinks you have certain power, every time you move an eyebrow, all of a sudden it has significance. And Bob's very effective at using that to his advantage. He may be daydreaming, for all I know, but if he just looks at you with that stern look, you think, 'Oh, my God, the wheels are turning. He's gonna crush me.'"

Habush's presence quickly got the attention of the insurance carrier and the village board. The village attorney saw the need to settle things as fast as possible, before the issue ended up in court. "At the same time, I don't think the federation was interested in embarrassing anybody or tearing apart the community," adds Block. "Long term, the JCC said this is our home. We're not going to sit here and piss these people off for life. But what's happened here is not right. Let's get a resolution, and let's move on."

Village President Pritchard was glad to see the federation push back. "The federation put on the full-court press when Bob Habush got involved. They started bringing in several lawyers, and they would sit in the front row through the board meetings, which sometimes went on until 12:00, 12:30 at night. They hired a court reporter to record the board's comments and the public comments. And they just didn't miss a thing. They were ready to depose every trustee. Everybody. And you know, that was helpful because the trustees weren't listening. They weren't cautious.

"There is no doubt in my mind that when Habush came on and the lawyers started lining up at the meetings, that was a sign," she adds. "Everyone knew they were smarter; everyone knew that they would win."

The day after meeting with the insurance company's attorney, Habush's legal team made a motion for the subpoenas. "I got a call," Habush says. "Whitefish Bay wanted to talk."

The two sides came to a compromise: The federation agreed to certain limitations on when members could use the facilities, and the size of the expansion was smaller than the original proposal. But the deal was done.

"It was stuff we could live with," says Habush. "The biggest hang-up of all was traffic, which in my mind became a legitimate concern. There were going to be religious services, schools, preschools. So I said, 'Well, we've got to find a way to take the pressure off Santa Monica Boulevard. How about building a road that goes out of the parking lot to the west, away from the neighbors?'"

But the final piece of the puzzle—building a road a quarter of a mile long that would connect to a major thoroughfare, Port Washington Road—proved to be more complicated than expected. The problem was that Port Washington Road was in the city of Glendale, and Whitefish Bay and Glendale seldom embraced any kind of mutual cooperation when dealing with civic matters like transportation, redevelopment, or zoning. According to Habush: "Somebody contacted Glendale, who said, 'In a pig's eye. We're not allowing a road in there. No goddamn way.'"

Habush had little interest in the squabbles of two competing municipalities. "So I picked up the phone and I called the head of the state's Department of Transportation, Frank Busalacchi. I said, 'Frank, I've got a problem,' and I told him what it was. 'You're the secretary of transportation. I'd like you to call Glendale and tell them we need approval for this road. I don't care what you say. Just please do it.'"

Busalacchi put in a call to Carl Mueller, a public relations executive who represented the City of Glendale. "At the time, I was watching this very closely because we were in the process of developing a multimillion-dollar plan to totally redo Bayshore Town Center, a regional shopping mall," says Mueller, who also represented the developer. "Bayshore was immediately adjacent to Whitefish Bay and within walking distance of Karl Campus. We knew Whitefish Bay would likely oppose what we wanted to do with the mall. It was not just a makeover but a major expansion, which was likely to bring more traffic, et cetera, into the area. More importantly, we needed an additional freeway ramp in and out of the mall, which required state approval and funding. Even though Whitefish Bay technically couldn't stop what we were doing, they could cause us a lot of trouble and defeat our ability to get the freeway ramp."

Mueller heard that negotiations had bogged down between the Village of Whitefish Bay and the federation over the JCC expansion. "And word came through that Bob Habush had stepped up at a federation meeting and said, 'I will take this on, and I will do it pro bono.' Not long after, I get a call from Busalacchi, secretary of transportation. He told me I needed to get Glendale to approve running a new road from the Whitefish Bay campus to Port Washington Road, basically to move traffic into Glendale off of Whitefish Bay streets."

Mueller recalls the conversation with Busalacchi.

"Frank," he said, "Whitefish Bay and Glendale have had a contentious relationship for years. They don't get along. Why would Glendale do this for Whitefish Bay? And why are you calling me?"

"Bob Habush is all over this," Busalacchi told him. "We have to get him off our back."

"Well, Frank, what about our freeway ramp?"

Busalacchi paused. "We'll talk to you about that ramp."

Mueller contacted the mayor of Glendale with a directive: get the road approved by the Common Council at the next monthly meeting. Mueller vouched for Busalacchi. He trusted him as a man of his word.

"The bottom line is, we got it done," says Mueller, who now also represents Habush and his firm. Glendale approved the road, Habush finalized his agreement with the Village of Whitefish Bay, Busalacchi came through with funding for the freeway ramp, and the Bayshore Town Center was transformed into one of the most successful shopping malls in Wisconsin.

"It was several years later that I explained to Bob how vitally important his role was in all this," adds Mueller. "He didn't know that. He is a great courtroom attorney, but the value of what he does goes way beyond that, sometimes in ways that maybe he doesn't even understand."

As with any case he takes or any issue he backs, Habush was willing to go to the wall. He was ready to go to court. And was fiercely determined to win.

"Because of Bob's ability to communicate this in a very serious way, as only Bob can, we reached a settlement," says Bert Bilsky. "That was much more preferable to us than to engage in litigation. I mean, it's very hard to raise money, and litigation could have made it harder.

"Altogether, we raised close to $41 million for this project. It was all pledges, either cash pledges over five years or deferred contributions from people who made bequests that would be satisfied when they died. So we needed a clear path to being able to do the work we wanted to do. Bob was our bunker buster. Not only did he cochair the campaign, but he also broke through the issue."

Months after the settlement, Habush was presented with the American Jewish Committee's 2004 Community Service Human Relations Award. In a speech at the award dinner, Bilsky praised Habush for being a bridge builder: "Bob created a bridge—girder by girder—stretching from the difficult position we were in to a resolution that left even our adversaries thinking they had achieved a victory."

Today, the Karl Campus is teeming with activity, a vibrant center for people throughout the community, members and nonmembers alike. "Every time I drive by," says Habush, "I smile."

CHAPTER EIGHT

A Plaintiff's Heart

There's a private side to Bob Habush that runs counter to his persona as an intimidating, take-no-prisoners trial lawyer. It's a side with fewer hard edges, a lenient and empathetic side that is purposely hidden from his courtroom adversaries yet widely extolled by those who know him well. In some ways there are two Bob Habushes, each with varying roles: they seem to contradict yet complement each other. It's as if he wants to battle the world and save the world at the same time.

He is the relentless fighter, intolerant of injustice, liars, and bullies; the alienated grade-school Jew who took vengeance against the neighborhood toughs. Since (and perhaps because of) those scrappy beginnings, he has carried in his gut a resolve to get even.

Simultaneously he is a guardian and defender, generous with his time and resources, a personal sponsor and intrepid advocate who will go to the wall to help those in need.

Habush's daughter, Jodi Habush Sinykin, describes her father as a protector, not only of his family but also of his close friends, his clients, and the extended family employed at his law firm. "If there is any perceived crisis in health or in safety or in well-being, he helps in a very concrete, needed way," says Sinykin, an environmental lawyer in Milwaukee. "Many years ago, I was in a gallery of a well-known photographer who had a collection of wildlife photographs, and one absolutely caught my eye because it's very emblematic of my father. It is a picture of a battle-scarred, regal lion close-up, primarily of the lion's face."

She purchased the photo for her father's sixty-fifth birthday.

"He's a caretaker and a champion," she adds. "And he walks the talk."

His role as lionhearted protector is apparent in the imprint he has made as a friend and a boss, and as a philanthropist in his community. It's a character he takes on with a quiet ferocity, seldom marred by show or swagger. He possesses a healthy ego, yet he's not the type to hold press conferences to spotlight his importance. Rather, his actions speak louder than his words. As his daughter says, "He sets a very high bar purely by example."

An early display of his protective nature emerged in the mid-1960s. His daughter Sherri—developmentally disabled by a defective vaccine when she was an infant—was ready to start school for the first time. Bob and his wife, Mimi, decided to enroll her in a public school in Glendale, Wisconsin, where they lived. They were dismayed to find out that the school would not accept children with "learning problems." Although the Wisconsin Constitution guaranteed public education for all children ages four to twenty, those with developmental disabilities or special needs were at the time labeled "retarded" and were ignored by the public school system.

"I read the Wisconsin Constitution, which said all citizens should get a free public education," Habush says, looking back. "They had no exceptions for handicapped kids. So I set up a meeting with Wisconsin attorney general Bronson La Follette, a classmate of mine in law school and the grandson of Robert 'Fighting Bob' La Follette, the famous Wisconsin governor and congressman. I told him my story, showed him the constitution, and said, 'I think that the failure to provide a free public school education to my daughter is unconstitutional.' Bronson said, 'I'll have my people research it.' Two months later I got a call from him. 'Bob, I agree with you. I'm issuing an opinion that all Wisconsin children—blind, deaf, physically or mentally handicapped—are entitled to a public school education.'

"I then made a phone call to the school district that we lived in at that time," Habush continues. "I said, 'I'd like to meet with the superintendent and the school board over possible litigation I'm thinking of filing against you.' That immediately got their attention. So I met with them and passed out the attorney general's opinion."

Habush said, "OK, folks. You've got two options here. One is to create a special ed class for mentally retarded children like my daughter and hire a special ed teacher. Option two is to spend the rest of the year or two in court with me, because I'm going to sue your asses."

"How can we do that?" said an incredulous school board member. "We're going to open a class and hire a teacher for one kid?"

"Let me tell you something," replied Habush. "My wife and I belong to a support group. We see kids who are out there and languishing at home watching television, getting no education. My wife and I can afford to send our daughter to Montessori school, but many parents can't. Their kids are not learning to read, not learning to write, not learning to have intrasocial relationships, nothing. You start this class and I guarantee you will have other handicapped kids enroll."

The school district agreed to start a special education class. "They hired a special ed teacher. They advertised the class and, boom, twenty kids, right out of the gate," Habush remembers. "So Sherri Habush and her dad established special education in the city of Glendale, which then went to Whitefish Bay, Shorewood, and the city of Milwaukee.

"When she was ready to go to high school, there were no special ed classes at Nicolet High School. I had the same meeting there with the school board, and they created a special ed course at Nicolet. It was a terrific program. Sherri did great. She started to do math. She learned to write. Not great, but she learned. And she graduated high school.

"The knowledge that there were tens of thousands of handicapped kids who were not getting educated had picked up some momentum around that time in Wisconsin, and eventually it became part of the mainstream thinking. But prior to that, there was no public school special education at all. Nothing."

After Sherri graduated from high school, she told her parents she wanted to go to college. Bob and Mimi thought a traditional college might be too overwhelming for her. They searched for an alternative. "We found a place in Santa Barbara, California, called Devereux. It provided residential programs for developmentally disabled adults—with vocational training and job training—and kids from all over the country," Habush says. "We enrolled her there."

The Habushes privately hoped Sherri would return to the Milwaukee area after graduating from Devereux. But where would she live? "At that

Figure 9
Habush House
Habush bought an apartment building and converted it into a residence for developmentally disabled adults.
Photo credit: Robert Habush

time, group homes had just started budding up. And there was a lot of resistance among neighbors," Habush recalls. "In Glendale in particular, there had been a big fight, and the city turned down an application for a group home. So I said to myself, 'I'm going to buy my own apartments, and I won't need to get licensed as a group home.'

"I bought two apartment buildings, side by side. Each had eight units. Then I turned it over, mortgage-free, to Jewish Family Services to run and staff it. We called it Habush House. And it's still operating today. It's nonsectarian. You don't have to be Jewish to get in. Many people have lived there since the beginning."

Habush House is on a local bus line and within walking distance of a grocery store, drug store, and movie theater. "There are any number of parents who have developmentally disabled kids who now reach adulthood," says Bert Bilsky, who, as executive director of the Jewish Community Foundation, helped organize Habush House. "The parents age, and they worry very much about where their kids as adults are going to be in the future. To have secure housing and a program for them is extremely valuable. Bob and Mimi's gift to our foundation ensures that they would be perpetually dedicated to this cause."

Sherri, meanwhile, remains in California. "She's 52 and lives on her own," says Habush. "We have a staff person from Devereaux stop in two or three times a week to help her out. She works at a nonprofit travel agency called New Directions that specializes in trips for handicapped adults. Sherri and two or three other people work there. I started it, I support it, but they now have good fund-raising capacity to sustain it. It's a one-of-a-kind operation. It gives these people an opportunity to travel to places they could never go. They travel to Europe, to Hawaii, throughout the United States. It's a terrific organization."

* * *

In giving and philanthropy, Habush's manner is low-key and behind-the-scenes. He offered his services pro bono to help persuade the Village of Whitefish Bay to approve the expansion of the Jewish Community Center. Along with his legal expertise, he served as cochairman of the $41 million capital campaign, contributing one of the lead donations.

Habush also chaired a capital campaign to renovate his synagogue, Congregation Shalom, in Milwaukee. And for years, he and Mimi have supported programs that focus on Israel, including Project Renewal, which helps rehabilitate distressed neighborhoods there, and Operation Exodus, a program that aids in the resettlement of Jews.

"Bob cochaired the Operation Exodus campaign, which we ran in 1990," Bilsky says. "From 1990 to 1993, we helped to resettle almost a million Jews from the former Soviet Union when the Soviet Union was breaking apart and they were allowing Jews to leave. I initially believed his primary interest was in the state of Israel and in creating a safe haven for Jews in Israel. But then I started working with him directly. I got to know his style and his way of working. And I realized that he had a great passion, not only for Israel fund-raising but also for our local community."

One such effort was the Habushes' support of Jewish Family Services, a nonsectarian provider of social services to the Milwaukee area. The agency's building is named in their honor: the Robert & Mimi Habush Family Center.

Benjamin Wagner, a partner at Habush Habush & Rottierabuws & Rottier, has known Bob Habush most of his life, through his father, Jeff Wagner, a Milwaukee County judge, and his grandfather, Marvin Wagner, a surgeon at the Medical College of Wisconsin. Both knew Habush professionally and personally.

"I knew he was a great trial lawyer," says Benjamin Wagner. "But before I was in law school, I knew him more as a community leader, not only within the Jewish community but also society here in Milwaukee."

As evidenced by the Jewish Community Center project, Habush's generosity goes beyond his commitment of financial resources, Wagner says. He commits his time and his loyalty.

"Bob also has been completely selfless in legal philanthropy," he says. Habush has supported Wisconsin's two law schools. As a graduate of the University of Wisconsin Law School, he established the Robert L. Habush Bascom Professorship in Trial Advocacy, as well as the Robert L. Habush Moot Court Advocacy Fund. At Marquette University Law School in Milwaukee, he funded the Habush Advocacy Scholarship in his father's name. He has taught at both schools for years.

Moreover, Habush Habush & Rottier has donated to the Milwaukee Justice Center, a collaborative project that provides court-based legal resources—volunteer attorneys and self-help desks, for instance—to low-income litigants who don't meet the financial requirements to receive legal aid and choose to represent themselves. "It's another marked example of giving back to the community and the legal profession," Wagner says. "And it's another example of giving to the underdog—whether it be financial underdog, injured underdog, or mentally disabled underdog."

In the late 1990s, Habush became friends with Howard Eisenberg, the dean of Marquette Law School at the time. "He was the first Jewish dean at a Jesuit law school," says Habush, "and I thought that was kind of interesting. I was curious as to why he had chutzpah to even apply for the position. So he and I had lunch together from time to time. He used to represent prison inmates and was very passionate man, highly respected at that law school."

Eisenberg was also an emphatic fund-raiser for the school. He persuaded Habush to contribute $500,000 to renovate the student courtroom in the law school building. "It was on the top of that old building, beautiful room, gorgeous," says Habush. "It was going to be the Robert L. Habush Courtroom."

Howard Eisenberg died suddenly of complications following a heart attack on June 4, 2002, before the renovation was completed. "I felt something had to be done to memorialize the only Jewish dean at a Jesuit law school in the United States so that people would never forget that he was there," Habush says. "So I told the law school that I wanted that courtroom named after Howard, not me. It became the Howard Eisenberg Memorial Hall. I just felt so bad that Howard died, and it didn't seem right for me to have my name on it."

* * *

If there is one cardinal principle that forms the cornerstone of Habush's relationships, both personal and professional, it is loyalty. It's a facet of Habush's character that Dan Rottier, president of Habush Habush & Rottier, became aware of months after joining the firm in 1979.

"I was assigned to a significant case to work with another young lawyer who actually is my age but had started with the law firm straight out of law school. I wasn't happy with his work, and I remember reporting on the case to Bob and saying, 'I really have a difference of opinion on how this thing should be handled.' Bob said something like, 'You've only been here six months. Your associate has been here almost four years. I'm not talking to you about this right now.' And he said it in such a fashion that what I took from it was his sense of loyalty to the other lawyer. It was an early message about loyalty.

"I would say loyalty, hard work, and a belief in the legal system has sort of structured his career," adds Rottier. "And, of course, his talent."

Ask Habush to name the things he will not tolerate, and he answers without hesitation: people who are untruthful. And people who are disloyal. "When someone is disloyal—a friend or business associate or whatever—to me that's unforgivable," he says. "I guess it goes under the heading of trust."

Habush parted ways with a law partner and longtime friend because of what he regards as a betrayal of his trust. During the mid-1980s, while battling against tort reform as the president of the Association of Trial Lawyers of America, he would spend two or three days a week in Washington, D.C., overseeing a staff of one hundred and running two lobbying groups.

"At ATLA, the president is the point person," he says. "He's the person that does all the interviews, goes on television, testifies in Congress, and runs the political operation. It's a big job"—a job that effectively removed him from his law firm's daily operations from time to time. That caused a measure of resentment from Howard Davis, his college friend, Army buddy, and law partner.

From the time Habush took over the firm from his father, Davis had handled most of the administrative responsibilities. Habush's role as the very visible face of the firm apparently bred in Davis some dissatisfaction, which was only exacerbated by Habush's involvement with ATLA. When Habush returned to his firm at the end of his two-year commitment at ATLA, he heard through the grapevine that his friend Davis had been suggesting my ATLA presidency was hurting him.

"I could tell that people were treating me differently than when I had left, because Howard had affected how the other attorneys viewed me" recalls Habush. "They seemed distant. I thought maybe I was just imagining it. But there was a whole different feeling. I didn't know why until two of my confidants told me it was because Howard had poisoned the staff against me. He had been disloyal to me and it hurt. But when I think back, there must have been a lot of resentment. He wasn't a trial lawyer and never wanted that role. But he probably felt he wasn't getting enough credit. Yet he was the second-biggest earner in the law firm. He made seven figures for a lot of years."

Habush said nothing to Davis about what he had learned and soon reestablished unity at the firm. But he never forgot the breach of loyalty. Much later, when Davis's production began to slide and he spent more and more time at his Florida home, Habush confronted him. He insisted that Davis retire and reminded him of his disloyalty. "But despite that, you can maintain an office here; you can maintain your name in the letterhead," he said. "I'll pay you a minimum of $150,000. If you work and bring in money, you'll make more."

That night, Davis emptied his office and closed the door behind him. The next morning, he returned to attend a firm meeting. With little explanation, he announced his immediate resignation and walked out. "We haven't spoken since," says Habush.

The parting was painful for both men, recalls Rottier. "The conflict," he says, "was really about someone getting paid merely because he owned part of this firm or having to work hard to earn it. And there was a difference of opinion there. Bob's [view] has always been you work hard to get paid, and I share that belief. I think Howard viewed it more as an entitlement, that he owned a significant part of this firm and should get paid. That philosophy doesn't work."

* * *

A courtroom cross-examination by Habush has caused many in the witness stand to break out in a nervous sweat. The patience and respect he exhibits toward his clients, though, is far less obvious.

Habush partner Larry Fehring remembers a case from 1997 involving eight Wisconsin men who were killed in an auto accident while on a fishing trip. Judy Zwirlein, the widow of one of the men, hired the Habush firm to represent her in a lawsuit against two trucking companies connected to the crash.

"We're at our office," says Fehring, "and the defense attorney is taking Judy's deposition. She breaks down during this deposition, and Bob takes her into another room to console her. Ten minutes go by. Fifteen minutes. Now we're getting close to thirty minutes. The defense attorney wants to get this thing over with, and he tells me, 'Can you do me a favor and go in and find out where we're at?' So I knocked on the door, and Bob took me inside. I told him what the attorney had asked, and Bob said to me, 'All that matters is taking care of Judy. So you go back out there and tell him it'll take as long as it takes.' And Bob was upset with me for interrupting.

"It was a lesson to me: the client always comes first, and screw the defense attorney. I mean, the defense attorney was working for the company that killed this woman's husband. Bob was deeply concerned for her well-being."

"Bob's got a plaintiff's heart," says Ken Jarvis, a paralegal at the firm. "You have to have a plaintiff's heart to work for this firm. You have to want to win for your client as well as for yourself. But you put your client first, and Bob does that. He has a plaintiff's heart. Always has, always will."

Habush's protectiveness extends to the people who work for him. As a boss, he has cultivated a family-like environment at his firm over the years. He acts as mentor and teacher. Disciplining an employee because of a mistake is rare, says Cindy Ferguson, his executive assistant for more than twenty-five years. "That's not how he approaches mistakes," she says. "If you make a mistake, he just wants you to fess up, try to fix it however you can, and do what you can so it doesn't happen again.

"He demands perfection of himself, and that's what he demands of his staff," she adds. "So when you work for him, there are times when he's relentless, and it can be exhausting. But at the end of the day, you'll know that you've been pushed to do the best job that you could do. People that work with him for the first time are pretty intimidated. But when the result is good, and it usually is, he'll thank them and let everybody know what a good job they did. I think it's a sign of a really great leader."

Similarly, staff attorneys who lose a trial never are scorned or penalized. Losses are seen as inevitable, the price of doing business in a law firm. "There is an old expression in trial law," says Jim Weis, a partner, "and that is 'If you don't lose a case now and then, it's because you are not trying enough of them.' That's really true. I give Bob a lot of credit because another great thing he does within the firm is that he promotes people to try cases.

"He makes it very clear that if you lose a case, that's not a problem. You move on," adds Weis, who works out of the firm's northern Wisconsin offices in Wausau, Rhinelander, and Stevens Point. "He's tremendously supportive when a loss takes place. That's a great attribute, particularly for young trial lawyers, whose egos are so fragile. You just need to have that attitude, and most firms don't. Bob really encourages you, win or lose. That's the culture in the entire firm: get in there and try it. You don't get a hit if you don't swing."

Nor does Habush second-guess how a lawyer runs a trial. "It would be very easy for Bob to second-guess or armchair quarterback; he'd have the background and knowledge to do it," says Tim Trecek, a partner. "But

I don't ever remember Bob saying, 'You should have done this' or 'You should have done that.' That would just destroy a lawyer's self-confidence."

Above all, Habush wants the lawyers in his firm to fight as hard as they can for their clients without wavering, says Benjamin Wagner. "I've learned from him that you never shy down from a fight," he says. "You have to be fearless. You have to accept the fact that you can lose, and you can't be fearful of that."

Habush himself can count his losses on one hand. Although losing is a rare occurrence, he pours himself into a case, and when it doesn't go his way, he takes it especially hard.

He remembers one trial from the late 1970s. After a string of wins that went on for several years, he lost a malpractice case involving a motorcycle accident. A young man was thrown off a motorcycle. He appeared to have sustained a back injury, but the doctor who cared for him at the hospital did not order restraints to have him immobilized. Habush argued that as a result of the doctor's negligence, the young man had ended up a paraplegic. The jury, however, decided for the doctor.

Habush was physically sick, so devastated that he thought about staying away from the office for a while. But, deciding he'd better get back on the horse, he returned to work. No one said a word as he walked down the long hallway to his office. Finally, pausing to look around, with a tight grin he addressed his staff: "So much for legends."

He admits that his losses have knocked the wind out of him. "But even when I win, after a trial I get depressed," he says. "I drop off a cliff. It's a post-trial depression. It's the adrenaline drop, and it lasts for three, four, five days, sometimes a week. That's with winning, so imagine what losing is like. It's a physical thing. It's a chemical thing. I can't control it. It's the hangover. Getting back to work is the best remedy. And I've got a wife who gives me a kick in the ass when I start feeling really sorry for myself: *Get over it. Enough!*"

✳   ✳   ✳

Habush's indomitable pursuit of excellence applies to his every endeavor. "Once he takes on a project, no matter what the project is, he wants to be the best at it," Rottier says. "He wants to have done a job better than anyone else could have done it, whether it's heading an organization, whether it's raising money, whether it's organizing a meeting, and in particular, whether it's running a case. Where that motivation comes from, we can only speculate.

"Is the size of an award important? Probably. But more because it reflects on the size of the case, the injury to the plaintiffs, the job he's done. It's not about the actual income that results from it, because I don't think money drives him. When it comes to a case, if you match that inner drive with his commitment to a particular client, if he's your lawyer, you are in a good place. His organizational abilities are second to no one else in terms of managing cases."

The Milwaukee real estate developer Barry Mandel first met Habush when Mandel was a teenager. "I was friends with a nephew of his, and we would visit his office from time to time," says Mandel, who holds a law degree. "I looked at Bob as a figure that I would sort of follow over time because he was a lawyer. But it was this underlying drive that he had for excellence, and his sense of determination that he had, and a persistence that he exhibited, that caught my imagination.

"We used to play tennis. And I saw something that was just unusual about him as a person. It wasn't that Bob was the best tennis player, but it was this drive in him to win, to be the best he possibly could. It almost appeared at times that he could will the ball over the net."

Habush remains a friend and mentor today. "He takes it to a different level," Mandel says. "He has a great deal of substance. He's also very pragmatic and realistic, because without that he would not have been as successful as he is. Don Quixote didn't necessarily take down too many windmills. And Bob doesn't swing at windmills.

"And I would also say that because he is such a protector, a strong advocate, it puts him in a position where at times he may wear that suit of armor more than he would otherwise want to. And so he carries it with him."

His high regard for his clients—injured, vulnerable, and unsure where to turn—feeds his watchful vigilance, to the point where he has become responsible for the personal welfare of his employees. He takes care of his own, particularly in times of crisis.

Habush accepts his part as protector and advocate. "Not only with the people I represent but with my family at the firm I see my role as 'the avenging angel,' if you will," he says. "It isn't something I talk about, but it's clearly part of who I am. I feel protective of the people in my firm. I would stop at nothing to protect them."

When Ken Jarvis, his longtime paralegal, found himself in trouble, Habush lent a hand without delay from a thousand miles away.

Jarvis, sitting at home one day in 2009, noticed that his big toes had gone numb. He shrugged it off. But when he woke the next day, all of his toes on both feet were numb.

"I went to work, toes numb, and didn't say anything to anybody," Jarvis recalls. "I woke up the next morning, got out of bed, and both of my feet were numb up to my ankles. It was almost like I was walking on blocks of wood. My hands, too, were getting numb. I thought, 'Now I better call the doctor.' So I called the local hospital in Waukesha, where I live. They did all kinds of testing for about a week and a half straight. Nerve tests, where they stick a needle in your foot, your hands. I couldn't feel anything. If I picked up something, it was as if my fingers were rock solid.

"By this time I'm missing a few days at work. The doctors didn't know what was wrong. They did a spinal tap, I got brain scans, and they [didn't] know what it was. I thought, 'What's going on here?'"

After he returned to work, a partner at the firm called Habush, who was in Florida, to tell him about his colleague's condition. Minutes later, Habush called Jarvis. "What's going on with you?" Habush asked, and Jarvis filled him in. Habush told him he would make a phone call and get back to him.

Two days later, Jarvis had an appointment with a top neurologist at Froedtert Hospital, the regional medical center for southeastern Wisconsin. He had called the specialist weeks before and was told the doctor had a six-month waiting list. But thanks to Habush's pull, now he was in.

The day before his appointment, however, the inexplicable numbness had progressed to his face. He got on the phone with the specialist, who instructed him to get to the hospital right away. "I get checked in, and it's like the royal treatment," he recalls. "I had testing done until about 6 p.m. that night—all kinds of testing, more brain scans, another spinal tap.

"Finally, they had a diagnosis: Guillain-Barré, an autonomic dysfunction that affects the nerves of your body." That night Jarvis began the first of seven blood treatments.

Ironically, Jarvis—the thorough investigator that he is—had come across a reference to the disease on his own while researching his symptoms. When he mentioned it to a doctor at the Waukesha hospital, the physician dismissed the possibility and missed the diagnosis. Remarkably, at the very same time, a firefighter with the same symptoms was being tested at that hospital, Jarvis says. The numbness had spread to his lungs, forcing doctors to place him on a ventilator.

"He was in the hospital for four or five months, whereas I was at Froedtert Hospital only for a week," says Jarvis. "At some point he was able to come off the vent and take a few steps, as he went through physical therapy and rehab. When I heard about him, I thought, 'That could've been me. It easily could have been me.' So I will forever be grateful to Bob. It's not overreaching to say he probably saved my life and certainly saved me from any kind of long-term affects by getting me into the right hospital."

Another Habush employee, attorney Ralph Tease, witnessed Habush's protective instinct before he'd even begun working at the firm. Tease was a civil defense lawyer in Green Bay, doing mostly defense work for insurance companies and feeling like he had found his niche. "I loved the people I worked with, but defense work is kind of a drudgery," he says. "It's billable hours, and I was keeping the squirrel cage spinning."

Out of the blue, his secretary buzzed him with a call from Bob Habush. "I thought, 'Well, this could be interesting,'" says Tease. "Bob told me that his firm was opening an office in Green Bay, and he wanted to know whether I'd be interested in talking to him about running it. I said certainly I'd be willing to talk. That led to a couple of meetings, and eventually an offer was made. But I wanted to think about it before I accepted.

"I came home from work, and my wife was on the phone with Bob. Unbeknown to me, he had called her to, I guess, relieve any anxiety she might have. He talked to her about the sense of family at the firm—the importance of the role of the spouse in the firm and the importance of just family. So when she hung up the phone, she was fairly impressed and persuaded that this was going to be a good move for me.

"And since that time, I've seen nothing to the contrary," says Tease, now the managing partner of the Green Bay office for Habush Habush & Rottier. "This is his family, and he loves the people that work for him dearly.

And from the very start, when I heard him on the phone with my wife, that was what I sensed."

Years later, Tease again found Habush ready to step in, this time in a more dramatic fashion. The two of them had been litigating a case involving a natural gas leak that had caused an explosion at a condominium complex in Ellison Bay, a small community in Wisconsin's Door County. A husband and wife were killed, and family members were seriously injured. "We had been litigating it in federal court for over a year at a very fast pace," says Tease. "We took over a hundred depositions. It was a monster case."

In January 2008, Tease had a heart attack. "I was out jogging with my partner here at Green Bay and another gentleman," he recalls. "I was fifty-one at the time, and they're both younger than I am, but I could usually keep up. But I was a little winded that day and got to a point where I didn't want to tell them I couldn't keep up. You know, that wouldn't be manly. So I told them I needed to stop and stretch for a while and I'd catch up with them later. At that point I just felt like I was a little fatigued. I did a few stretches on the side of the road and started running again. After about half a block, it hit me."

Deep snowbanks covered the sidewalks, and Tease was afraid that if he fell into the snow he would be hidden from view. So he stumbled down the middle of the street to a nearby fire station and began pounding on the door. "They got me to the hospital," he says. "It was a widow-maker heart attack, and 93 percent of the people don't survive that. I was just in the right place at the right time."

The Ellison Bay case went to mediation and was settled in March. "But there were a couple months where Bob had to take over," Tease says. "And he did it without a complaint or a whimper. It was just another indication of the kind of person he is. Not only did he take care of the case, but he really took care of me. During my hospitalization and my recuperation, he was very attentive to my needs, very protective of me. He was my line of communication to other attorneys at the firm. He waited until I was out of harm's way before he turned loose all the other partners and e-mails and phone calls to me. Just every step along the way, he wanted to make sure I wasn't being pressured or overburdened."

Tease recovered fully from the heart attack. But three years later, his doctors recommended double bypass surgery to treat his heart condition. Again he was working on a case with Habush. And again Habush took over while Tease was convalescing. Says Tease: "I remember telling Bob at one point, 'You know, I feel really blessed to have a partner like you that can step in and do what you did. But it doesn't make me feel that good at the age of fifty-four to have a seventy-five-year-old load me onto his back and carry me to the finish line again.' But that's just him. He's timeless. It's like the old Marines motto: No Man Left Behind."

Ralph Tease has come to understand Habush's drive to remain in the trenches. "People think, 'Why would he continue to work on cases? He certainly doesn't need to do it for the money,'" he says, pausing to reflect. "I've concluded two things: One, he has a burning desire to represent the downtrodden and victims against the giants. He feels that he has a purpose, and that drives him more than anything. But the second is that he has a love for the law and a love for the firm. In Wisconsin, Bob is the father figure of tort lawyers, and he knows that people within the firm look up to him. As a result, he feels that he needs to continue to set an example and to carry the torch. He's going to carry that torch until he can no longer lift it. It has nothing to do with money. It has nothing to do with awards or prizes. It has to do with the people he represents and his colleagues and the law that he stands for."

CHAPTER NINE

Big Blue

Ironworker Jeffrey Wischer let his wife sleep in on the morning of July 14, 1999. Patricia Wischer faithfully would awaken every weekday at 4 a.m. to make her husband an omelet and pack his lunch: two sandwiches, a couple of pieces of fruit, a bag of chips, and five Oreo cookies. But on this particular Wednesday, Wischer slipped out of bed, kissed his wife good-bye, and quietly walked out the door as the sun broke the horizon.

Inexplicably, he left behind the gold serpentine chain he usually wore around his neck—and his wedding ring.

Wischer was part of the construction crew that was building Miller Park, a new baseball stadium in Milwaukee. An employee of Minnesota-based Danny's Construction Company and a member of Iron Workers Local 8, Wischer had ironwork in his blood. His father was an ironworker, as were his brother and his brother-in-law. Occasionally, on weekends, he would drive his three children around town to show them the projects he had helped build. "Look. Daddy built that. . . . Daddy built that," he would say, pointing to a grain silo in the Port of Milwaukee, or an Interstate 94 overpass, or a sprawling Target distribution center.

The Miller Park job was by far the largest he'd ever worked on. Named through a deal with Miller Brewing Company, the $400 million ballpark would replace the still-standing Milwaukee County Stadium, a proud but antiquated open-air facility that had been the home of the Milwaukee Braves in the 1950s and mid-1960s and of the Milwaukee Brewers since 1970.

The new stadium would be state-of-the-art, crowned with a $47 million retractable roof constructed under contract by Mitsubishi Heavy Industries of America. Made of sixteen thousand tons of structural steel, the fan-shaped roof would slide open and closed in ten minutes to accommodate the fickle Wisconsin weather. Seven panels of iron latticework would form the roof's frame. As it was pieced together, each panel was lifted into place by a 567-foot-tall sky-blue crane nicknamed Big Blue. When the roof was opened, the five movable panels would fold into each other and come to rest over two fixed panels on either side of the stadium's outfield.

A ground-breaking ceremony was held in October 1996, with completion of the stadium scheduled for opening day of the 2000 baseball season.

By the summer of 1999, with the project two-thirds finished, more than 1,600 construction workers had worked on Miller Park. Wischer led a small team of ironworkers.

"Jeff liked the work because the old stadium, County Stadium, was such a big part of our life," says his wife, Patricia, known as Trish. "We'd take the kids to Brewers games all the time."

But, like other ironworkers on the site, Wischer had grown frustrated. He believed Mitsubishi's managers had become increasingly lax in following safety regulations so they could meet ever-pressing deadlines. "They're not following the rules," he told his wife one day. "Everything's all fucked up." In early July 1999, Wischer took more than a week off to look for a different job. He wanted to make sure he had work lined up before he quit.

Recently his coworkers had given him a denim jacket embossed with the International Iron Workers emblem. "All of the guys on his team went out and paid for this jacket because they said Jeff was just an amazing boss," Trish explains. She encouraged him to stick it out at the Miller Park project. "I said, 'You have to go back to work there. These guys are counting on you.' So now I have a little hardship feelings because I sometimes feel like I made him go back."

Back on the job site, Mitsubishi superintendents had scheduled for July 14 a crane lift, or "pick," of one of the seven roof panels. As with past lifts, Big Blue—a Transi-Lift 1500 model, manufactured by Neil F. Lampson Inc. in Kennewick, Washington—would hoist the fully assembled panel from the outside of the stadium 330 feet into the air and then swing it into place. The piece, labeled 4R3, was the size of a football field and weighed 450 tons. For this pick, Jeffrey Wischer and two other workers—William DeGrave and Jerome Starr—would be lifted by a smaller crane in a steel cage called a "man basket" nearly 300 feet above the stadium floor. The three men would bolt the roof panel to stadium supports as the crane moved them into position above the right field bleachers.

The job of an ironworker was fraught with risks, and working from a man basket was a particularly dangerous, though critically necessary, task. Jeff and Trish had worked out an arrangement in case anything went wrong on the job. Recalls Trish: "Anytime there was an accident, he always called me and said, 'There's been an accident. I'm OK. Gotta go.'"

Early in the afternoon, Jeff called Trish to tell her the lift had been scrubbed because of high winds. He'd be home soon to watch the kids. Trish decided to go to work early. She was the bar manager and a hostess at a Mexican restaurant in Waukesha, about twenty minutes west of Miller Park.

As the dinner hour approached, the restaurant began to fill up. Trish was at the hostess desk talking to a coworker when the phone rang. The hostess on duty took the call and handed the phone to Trish.

"They went ahead with the lift," the caller said to Trish. "Something got screwed up, and Big Blue went down! Workers got hurt, some might've been killed."

Trish couldn't breathe. "It's Jeff, I know it is!" she cried. "He didn't call me to say he was OK. He didn't call me!"

She dialed his cell phone number, desperately hitting the speed dial over and over and over, but there was no answer. Feeling dizzy, her head spinning, she fell to the floor.

Hours passed with few details. She made frantic trips to Miller Park and the local hospital to check on the status of her husband. But no one would tell her what she needed to know. No one would say anything.

That evening, emotionally exhausted, she huddled with family members at Froedtert Hospital, waiting for any news. Someone noticed a clipboard on a nurse's desk and pointed it out to Trish. Printed on the clipboard were the names of three deceased Miller Park workers: William DeGrave, 49; Jerome Starr, 52; and Jeffrey Wischer, 40.

The dreadful news—there in black and white—was now too much for Trish. The walls suddenly closed in on her, and everything went dark.

Light rain had fallen that morning. According to early weather reports, it would be windy throughout the day. In fact, the National Weather Service had issued a small craft advisory for boaters on Lake Michigan. Temperatures rose from the mid-60s in the morning to the mid-80s in the afternoon.

Previous crane lifts at the Miller Park site had been postponed because of bad weather, and wind in particular could create problems. By noon, it was questionable whether the pick would take place. (One worker later said that at a practice lift in the morning, he saw the roof section, 4R3, swing side to side as it was being raised; Big Blue's operator lowered it to the ground to adjust the load.) But later that day, supervisors ordered the work to proceed, despite ongoing sustained winds above twenty miles per hour.

Forty-five stories tall, Big Blue towered over the site, an engineering marvel, one of the five largest construction cranes in the world. Visible for miles, it had become a source of awe for the locals and motorists passing along the nearby interstate highway.

The pick began about 3 p.m. Foot by foot, Big Blue hoisted the panel—equal in surface dimensions to almost four wings of a 747 jetliner—over the outer wall of Miller Park until it hung suspended over the bowl of the stadium. To the east, the orange man basket dangled from a smaller crane, with Wischer, DeGrave, and Starr inside, bunched together and watching.

At 5:13 p.m., from out of nowhere, a sound like a crack of thunder ripped through the air. Workers on the ground scattered for cover. Pitching to the east, Big Blue's long boom suddenly buckled as a gust of wind caught its 450-ton load. The wind tugged at the boom until it crashed through the stadium wall and tumbled like a broken toy to the stadium floor, its load a jumbled wreck.

On its descent, the boom sliced the cable that held the man basket, sending the three ironworkers plummeting to the infield. As they fell, their screams could be heard by the crane operator, Joe Edwards, over their walkie-talkie radios: "Joe, get us out of here! Get us out of here, Joe! Get us out of here!"

As Big Blue toppled toward him, Edwards was sure he was going to die. He grabbed the control levers in the operator's cab of the smaller crane and waited for the impact.

"I mean, I could feel it," he said later, describing the crash. "It sounded like a war zone. I could hear small pieces of iron just zinging and popping and banging and slamming. I could hear concrete exploding. I could hear the heavy iron crushing and mangling and twisting. The cab was getting beat around so bad. Picture some insane man in his maddest rage taking a pillow and just beating it out of control against the wall. That's the way that rig was getting banged around. I mean, I was getting beat all over.

"And I just sat right there getting ready to die. I said, 'I know I'm going to go away from here, and I know I ain't going to suffer. But I wonder what the hit is going to feel like, if it puts me into the other world, in the other dimension.'

"And then all of a sudden I heard this *crrrrr*. All this iron is screeching and piling up, and just at the last second, that piece just tailed away from my operator's section of the crane and hit behind me. I could reach out and touch that pile of mangled iron, that sixty-, seventy-foot iron. I could lean out and touch it. I said, 'Holy Christ, I lived through this.' I was shocked I was alive.

I ended up with a piece of Lampson's boom lacing in my lap, about an eight-foot section. And I kind of sliced my Red Wing boot and sliced my thumb a little bit.

I looked around. I couldn't see for a minute, because it was nothing but a cloud of dust in there. I vaguely heard some noises outside, somebody screaming my name. And I threw out the piece of tube lacing and said, 'Well, I guess I better get out of here.' So I climbed down and jumped out and went looking for the guys. And that's when Danny, the foreman, grabbed me and kind of block-tackled me and wouldn't let me get over there.

I found the basket. I mean, they were faced my way. But Danny tackled me about ten feet away. He wouldn't let me go over there and look at them.

Everybody else thought I was dead, and I couldn't believe I was alive. So the shock didn't hit for about—it was probably five or ten minutes. I mean, it took five minutes just for the dust to settle. It was a big push of wind, like a twister went through."

A mass of steel, glass, and concrete was strewn across the floor of the unfinished stadium. Lying in the infield, entangled in cables and useless harnesses, were the mangled bodies of the three ironworkers.

Figure 10
Fatal judgment
Killing three workers, a giant crane toppled into an unfinished stadium during high winds.
Photo credit: Robert Habush

* * *

In the early morning hours of July 15, Trish Wischer sat in her kitchen. The house was silent, her children asleep in their beds. The reality of her husband's death began to hit home. The shock was hard to take, but she remembered something he had said to her just a few days earlier.

They had had a number of what-if discussions about the possibility of him getting hurt or killed on the job. How would Trish and the kids get by? They had talked about the family finances, about setting up trust funds for the kids. And they had talked about contacting an attorney.

"Two or three days before the accident, Jeff said, 'If anything ever happens to me, before you even talk to anybody, you call Bob Habush,'" Trish says, looking back. He had known the Habush name from the TV ads. "Jeff knew something was going to happen, and he was preparing me."

Now she needed to follow through. She reached for her phone.

The next morning, as the sun began to climb, Trish's phone rang. Bob

Habush was on the line, calling from San Francisco. "I understand you need to talk to me," he said to her, and he listened as her heartbreaking story spilled out.

"I'll have a couple of my people at your house within the hour," he told her. "Don't go anywhere or talk to anyone until they get there."

Moving quickly, he called his associates and instructed them to ask Trish about her husband's safety concerns. They arrived at Wischer's home before investigators from the Occupational Safety and Health Administration got there to question her.

Habush returned immediately from California. As the plane wheels touched down, he was on the phone, making arrangements for Trish to come into his office as soon as she could.

A day later, Habush met with Marjorie DeGrave, who hired him to represent her. The third widow, Ramona Dulde-Starr, the wife of Jerome Starr, would retain David Lowe as her lawyer, but eventually Habush would represent all three widows as lead attorney.

Thinking the crane could have been to blame for the accident, Habush asked one of the researchers in his office to find the top expert on construction cranes. The researcher came up with the name Howard Shapiro. Based in Long Island, New York, Shapiro had written a reference book on cranes and derricks and had drafted industry standards for the technical performance and safety of cranes.

"I picked up the phone and called him," Habush says. "'I just got in from vacation. What's up?' he said, and I filled him in about Big Blue and the Miller Park tragedy. 'I want to find out if the crane failed because of some design defect,' I said to him. A defect in the crane was all I was thinking about at that point. Shapiro listened, then said to me, 'I'm onboard.'

"As he told me later, it turns out there were a dozen phone calls on his voice mail that he never got to because I had caught him just as he walked in the door. He'd come from Europe on an overnight flight and went straight to his office. Other people were calling to hire him—the insurance companies, the defendants. I got to Shapiro first."

Habush pulled together his team: investigator Terry Tadysak, paralegal Ken Jarvis, and attorney Mark Young. "I immediately knew I was going to throw this into a lawsuit right away because I had to get protection to maintain the evidence, a court order to not destroy anything, not to move anything from the scene. I also knew immediately that I'd have to start discovery, get depositions from witnesses before they were compromised by anyone else." Through Tadysak, he informed OSHA—which had had safety officers on-site when the crane went down—that he was on the case and collecting evidence.

Fast out of the gate, Habush also had luck on his side. Within a week of the crash, the Milwaukee County district attorney, E. Michael McCann, launched an investigation to determine whether criminal negligence was a factor. The probe put pressure on the would-be defendants: Mitsubishi, the firm hired to build the retractable roof, and Big Blue's owner, Lampson Inc., which had leased its crane to Mitsubishi.

"There were police and district attorney investigators all over the place," says Habush. "I'm only surmising, but I think the executives at Mitsubishi, who had numerous engineers on-site, became terrified over the prospect of going to jail over this accident. They knew better than anyone that they had been rushing things and could very well be held accountable for doing a lift on that date when it was unsafe.

"Within days," Habush continues, "Mitsubishi was pointing to the Lampson's crane as being defective, which of course made the press. Well, Lampson didn't take kindly to its crane being defamed all over the media. So Lampson, in its defense, pointed its finger at Mitsubishi, saying Mitsubishi's employees were wrong to order the lift that day. The two defendants are killing each other in the media while I'm forming my case. It's the perfect storm for a plaintiff's lawyer like me—two defendants fighting each other before I had even made a move."

The defendants hired John Bell, a well-known defense attorney whose Chicago firm, Johnson & Bell, promoted itself as the go-to firm for insurance companies facing large claims as a result of catastrophic events. Joining Bell was Kevin Owens, a product liability attorney at Bell's firm, and Ralph Weber, from Reinhart Boerner Van Deuren in Milwaukee. Meanwhile, Lampson hired as its lead attorney Don Carlson, with Crivello Carlson in Milwaukee.

Damage to the stadium was estimated at $100 million. As Habush and the defense attorneys put together an agreeable plan to preserve and examine the massive amounts of evidence, he was still unsure of the culprit. "I had no idea whether there was something wrong with the crane, whether it was lifting too much or not, or whether the crane operator was negligent," he recalls. "The guys who operated the crane were Lampson employees, but they were loaned to Mitsubishi. So Mitsubishi was in control. I thought there was a possibility that they did something wrong, maybe lifted too fast. I didn't know."

Beginning the discovery process, Tadysak and Jarvis assembled records, reports, photos, and interviews. (They would eventually amass more than one hundred thousand documents.) Dan Rottier, the firm's CEO and a partner, studied the defendants' insurance policies.

Habush, meanwhile, started issuing subpoenas. "I knew immediately I'd have to start getting depositions from witnesses before they were compromised by anyone else," he says. "It was the fastest I've ever moved in on a case, because I had all these targets, people who were identified and interviewed by the police and district attorney. I did one deposition after another after another. Every damned deposition I did myself, all the depositions for the liability part of the case. It wasn't that I didn't have confidence in anyone else, because I do. But no one does them better than me. My rule of thumb on discovery is a double strategy. I want information. I don't leave any stone unturned. But I also want the witness to feel he got bruised in the deposition, so when he leaves, he'll say to the defense lawyer, 'Holy Christ, I don't ever want to see that guy again.' That plays into the defense attorney's head."

In forming his pretrial strategy, Habush was setting up a case for punitive damages. "That was my sole purpose in the Miller Park case, because proving negligence, in my mind, would be pretty simple."

Under the common law, punitive damages could be awarded for "outrageous" conduct that was "malicious" or "in wanton, willful, or reckless disregard of the plaintiff's rights."

"Under the common law, the conduct did not require 'intent to injure,'" Habush explains. "So if I punched someone in the eye and I blinded him, the fact that I didn't intend to blind him is inconsequential. It doesn't matter. Defense attorneys and their clients were afraid of punitive damages because juries could go wild. Verdicts could be huge amounts. So there was a big push from the tort reformers to either eliminate punitive damages or restrict punitive damages.

"Many punitive damages cases went to the U.S. Supreme Court, and the court established a rule of thumb. It looked at the ratio of the punitive damage to the compensatory damage, and if excessive, they would knock it down. For example, if you got $100,000 in compensatory damages and one hundred times that amount in punitive damages, the punitive damages would be considered 'unreasonable punishment' and thus unconstitutional, and they would reduce the punitive damages."

In 1995, in the tort reform era, the Wisconsin legislature passed a law that said courts could allow punitive damages when "evidence is submitted showing that the defendant acted maliciously toward the plaintiff or in an *intentional disregard* [emphasis added] of the rights of the plaintiff."

"The legislature thought adding the word *intentional* would raise the bar on proof, but it made things confusing," Habush says. "The phrase *intentional disregard* is what I would call the ultimate oxymoron. *Intentional* is when you're paying attention to someone, and *disregard* is when you're not paying attention someone. So how can you be intentionally disregarding someone? It always puzzled the hell out of me. It seemed so inconsistent. So that was put to the test in the Miller Park case. There had never been a case tried to test the limits of that statute—that is, determining what kind of conduct would qualify as intentional disregard."

Habush had never pursued punitive damages. "I had numerous cases before Miller Park where I thought the conduct was what I called gross negligence," he says. "Under gross negligence you could get punitive damages. But instead, I used the degree of negligence to increase the amount of my compensatory award from a jury. I was very good at getting the jury angry with the defendant. But strategically I never used punitive damages. It's too risky. Punitive damages are always subject to judicial review and more often than not get cut or eliminated. Consequently I was able to get larger jury awards with negligence and not take the chance that I would have it cubbyholed into punitive damages that I would lose on appeal."

A punitive damage claim permits the introduction of evidence of conduct prior to the time of the damage-producing event and after the event as well. Neither would usually be admissible in a negligence-only case.

As Habush took depositions—more than one hundred total—his road map began to unfold, shaped by a pattern of safety rule infractions and a climate of intimidation by work site supervisors.

"I took the depositions of every Mitsubishi employee and every Lampson employee who was on that site," he says. "We also got the names of witnesses who called themselves 'sidewalk superintendents'—citizens with cameras and two-way radios who observed the lifts. They had gotten access to the radio channel that Mitsubishi employees used to communicate with each other. The conversations that were overheard turned out to be critical."

Tactically, pitting Lampson against Mitsubishi paid big dividends. "Lampson and Mitsubishi were still at each other's throats," Habush says. "So the Lampson people were quick to tell me what was wrong on that work site prior to the collapse of the crane. I had an instinctive feeling that there was going to be an easy negligence case one way or the other, whether it was the crane or the operator or the supervisors. But if I could get Mitsubishi, it would be a slam dunk as far as negligence was concerned."

He learned from Lampson about the transfer of Milo Bengtson, a crane operator on loan from Lampson and the first supervisor of the Big Blue operating crew. Bengtson, who had helped build the Grand Coulee and Hoover Dams decades earlier, told Habush he'd had arguments with Mitsubishi's roof construction supervisors over safety and the operation of Big Blue. According to Habush: "The site supervisor for Mitsubishi, Victor Grotlisch, was annoyed with Milo Bengtson because he was causing too many delays for them—requiring Mitsubishi to make lifts only in good weather, not to lift in the middle of the night, commonsense precautions. So they got rid of Bengtson."

In another deposition, Bengtson's replacement, Allen Watts, told of how he was instructed not to make waves when he started work at Miller Park, to stay out of trouble and take orders directly from Grotlisch. Giving an example of Grotlisch's power, Watts said the site supervisor refused to postpone a July 1 lift that had run into the evening, because he wanted to impress members of the media and baseball fans who were attending a Brewers game at County Stadium nearby.

More and more evidence pointed to Grotlisch as the person responsible for bad decision making and high-handed control. It seemed no one wanted to cross him.

"The intimidation on the work site was awful and pervasive," Habush says. "Employees were afraid they'd get fired. Once Milo Bengtson got transferred, the word got around at the work site: don't complain or you're going to be out of work."

The trial was set for October 16, 2000. Habush and his team were prepared months in advance. "Four months out, I am ready," he says. "I've got all my exhibits done, my research done. I have met with the witnesses I'm going to use. I've had my experts in town to prepare the exhibits they want to use with their testimony. The exhibits are marked, indexed, and loaded on my computer. I'm thinking about my opening statement, and I'm already sketching out an outline for my final argument. I am not a seat-of-the-pants kind of guy. Preparation is 90 percent of success in trial. And I'm General Eisenhower and it's D-day. The only difference is I didn't have George Patton off somewhere pretending he was going to land at Calais rather than Omaha Beach. I didn't try to fool the enemy into thinking I was going to settle the case."

Dan Rottier has seen firsthand what Habush puts into his preparations. "He pays tremendous attention to detail, to the point of—after doing it fifty years—if he has a significant witness, he still writes out questions, which astounds me. He will read and read and read and ask for more material and more material. It's unbelievable, his commitment to absorb information, to be prepared. I think he has a mind that allows him to evaluate information and determine fairly quickly whether something's important or not; and if it's important, he does retain it. It's remarkable."

In prepping for the trial, Habush developed a keen understanding of the subculture of ironworkers. He familiarized himself with their lingo and their nicknames—Diver, Nooner— and with the technical nomenclature used in their trade. He appreciated the "brotherhood" of these union workers and understood the bravado and stoicism they displayed as they answered his questions about the deaths of their three colleagues. The ease with which Habush could relate to them stemmed from the factory and construction jobs he'd had in high school and in college and from the blue-collar workers he had befriended.

As the trial date neared, several partial settlements were made. "Mitsubishi had different insurance companies at different levels, and the general contractor did as well," Habush says. "I was able to settle with them prior to the start of the case for $19.7 million. They wanted to get the hell out of the way, get out of the case. They figured their policies were history. We were able to take some lower-level coverages to put in the bank before the trial." After the trial and before the appeal, an additional $7.3 million was paid, making the total $27 million.

The partial settlement assured that the three widows would be compensated. But the women insisted that the jurors, as well as the media, hear the evidence of the case, the multitude of complaints about safety and management. They wanted someone to take responsibility for causing their husbands' deaths. Habush was ready and willing to lead the charge.

"This really was part of a push to get this case tried," he says. "I had three clients, three widows, who didn't want to settle. They wanted revenge. They wanted punishment. They wanted me to verbally hurt people in the courtroom. This relatively paltry amount we got from those lower layers of insurance were never enough to satisfy them. They were not afraid to testify. They *wanted* to go to court, just like me. And they wanted to get even, just like me. We were on the same page."

* * *

Habush had Mitsubishi in the crosshairs. The roof was over budget and months behind schedule; it was supposed to have been completed by the summer of 1999. When the lift of 4R3 was ordered for July 14—the day before Governor Tommy Thompson was scheduled to pay a visit to the work site—Mitsubishi supervisors had little patience for delay and little concern for safety. The lift was set, a foregone decision, weather be damned.

"I had established this solid case against Mitsubishi for their gross negligence and the arrogance of their site supervisor, Victor Grotlisch," Habush says. "That lift never should have taken place. It was a high risk on a highly windy day."

Meanwhile, the defense attorneys representing Mitsubishi—John Bell, Kevin Owens, and Ralph Weber—would try to knock down the contention that the wind was excessively strong. Instead, they would go after the crane, arguing that the Lampson Transi-Lift 1500 was defective, that a giant copper spacer at Big Blue's base had broken and sent the crane tumbling, and that the ground beneath it was soft and improperly prepared. They would lay the blame on the Lampson workers who controlled the crane.

Habush, however, launched a counter strike. "I went to Don Carlson, the lead defense attorney for Lampson, and I said, 'OK, here's the skinny. If you were the only defendant around, I'd go after you. But I don't have to. I've got an absolute slam-dunk negligence case against Mitsubishi and a good shot at punitive damages. So I'm not going to target you, but I'm not going to dismiss you either. Nor do I want a settlement out of you. What I want is for us to cooperate on strategy so you know where I'm coming from, and so your people know they're not dealing with the enemy.'"

He told Carlson he would treat Lampson employees, including the company president, Bill Lampson, as "friendly witnesses" in his cross-examinations. He would save the Lampson employees for last, using their testimony to impeach Mitsubishi's witnesses and indict the mega-company with his claim of negligence. "Of course, Carlson was thrilled," Habush says. "This made his job a lot easier. And it fit my strategy perfectly."

Jury selection began at the Milwaukee County Courthouse on October 16 for what would become a six-week trial. Meanwhile, three miles away at Miller Park, the last of seven panels that made up the retractable roof was lowered into place by a replacement crane—the thirtieth and final lift.

In a highly publicized case with numerous parties, the selection of a jury was lengthy. Starting with a pool of 190 prospective jurors, about three times the usual pool in a civil trial, the judge and attorneys had to narrow the list to just sixteen: twelve regular jurors and four alternatives.

To systematically weed out biases as best as possible while trying to determine who would be most sympathetic to his clients, Habush devised a questionnaire for the prospective jurors, asking questions such as *Have you ever been hurt in a car accident? Have you or a relative ever been sued? What is your level of education? Do prefer Fox News or CNN?*

"It took us two days to pick a jury as opposed to two hours," he says, "and many of them had to be interrogated separately because we didn't want them poisoning the rest of the pool by making a big speech about the judicial process or something. We had to eliminate people who could not sit because their employers would not pay the difference between the jury fee and their wages. But some who could have used that as an excuse didn't. They really wanted to be on this jury. They knew instinctively this was one of those real cases, not a frivolous case. So from day one, we had involved, excited, committed people. It was a nice mix, eleven women and five men, and they were good."

The case would be heard by Milwaukee County circuit court judge Dominic Amato, a judge known for his fairness and for sometimes making offhand and controversial remarks from the bench. Previous to his election to the court in 1988, Amato had been a trial lawyer for fifteen years, doing criminal and personal injury cases as a plaintiff's attorney and a defense attorney.

"There were sixteen-plus lawyers ready to litigate," Judge Amato remembers. "All of them knew their way around the courtroom, but there were two lawyers that really, really did a good job, and that was Bob Habush and Don Carlson. These two lawyers had the ability to nonverbally interact with the jury and everyone else in the courtroom. They had the correct demeanor. They chose their words carefully. They showed respect at all times. They didn't lose their cool. There's no perfect trial, and there's always some genuine operatic sharing. But they established themselves as no horse manure."

Habush was especially nimble, says Judge Amato. "He had the speed of a cheetah, but he could walk a tightrope like the Flying Wallenda Brothers."

Located on the fourth floor of the historic courthouse, Judge Amato's courtroom had been radically transformed for the trial. Normally a stately hall of justice with twenty-foot ceilings and hand-carved wood trim, the room now took on the appearance of a high-tech government office. Computer monitors were everywhere: on the judge's bench, the court reporter's desk, the witness stand. Attorneys from each side sat elbow to elbow around three long wooden tables, laptops shining brightly before them. A huge viewing screen hung to the right of the judge, while television cameras on tripods lurked from the rows of benches in the back.

Judge Amato took the bench, shunning the customary black robe for a suit and tie.

Habush was the first attorney to deliver his opening statement. He stepped slowly toward the jury box and immediately, dramatically, introduced the families of the ironworkers, compelling jurors to personalize the case:

On July 14th, 1999, James, age 4; Maggie, age 2; Miranda, age 15, lost their daddy and Marge lost her husband, Bill DeGrave, age 49.

On July 14th, 1999, the children of Mrs. Wischer, Roland, age 9; Zachary, age 11; and Shawna, age 17, lost their daddy and Trish Wischer lost her husband Jeff, age 40.

On July 14th, 1999, Ramona Dulde-Starr lost her husband, Jerry Starr.

And the evidence will show, members of this jury, that this event on July 14th was a totally preventable accident. How do I know? Because we've spent 15 months, all the lawyers, taking over 122 depositions, we've gone through thousands and thousands of documents, we've spent months hearing testimony, retaining experts and consultants. So all of us pretty much know what you're going to hear over the next few weeks. But it's important to remember at the onset, this is not a criminal case. I don't have to prove beyond a reasonable doubt what we're claiming happened that day, and the judge will instruct you at the end of the case what our proper burden is.

Simply put, members of the jury, Big Blue went down on July 14th because of high winds. The decision on July 14th to lift a roof piece the size of half a football field weighing 450 tons with a surface area about the size of three and a half 747 airplane wings, the decision to lift that piece that day was made by one Victor Grotlisch, who was the site superintendent for Mitsubishi Heavy Industries of America. This decision was made intentionally and his decision was made in the face of what the evidence will show were hazardous conditions, and this decision, members of the jury, was made in violation of the manufacturer's specifications of what type of winds this crane should operate in.

This lift was made in violation of OSHA regulations and this lift was made in violation of Mitsubishi's own safety manual with respect to following the manufacturer's specifications. . . .

We believe the evidence will show that both Lampson, by their employees, and Mitsubishi were negligent that day, but with respect to Mitsubishi, we believe the evidence will show more. The evidence will show that the decision to lift that day was done intentionally, was done consciously, was done in violation and disregarding the rights of the three men who were killed, their rights to life, their rights to safety, their rights to a safe workplace.

As the trial commenced, Habush scrolled down his list of the depositions he had taken—supervisors, crew leaders, ironworkers, crane operators, company executives, independent engineers, sidewalk witnesses—calling each to the witness stand to testify. "We had built this huge foundation of evidence," he recounts. "Everything that occurred at trial was developed during my pretrial discovery work. My investigator had taken written statements from everybody that was deposed so they couldn't deviate later on in court."

Habush called to the stand Milo Bengtson, the fired Lampson crane supervisor. Bengtson repeated with even more sting the criticisms of Mitsubishi that he'd made in his deposition, saying that site supervisor Grotlisch "had no common sense whatsoever." He recalled the first lift of a roof panel in the dead of winter, January 8, 1999, painting Grotlisch as autocratic and irresponsible.

A: In the pre-lift meeting, I was concerned that we would not be able to get this piece tied down, secured. It was the first one; no one really knew what they had to do. So I went to Victor and asked him if he would guarantee me three days, that he would keep the men on site for three days and work steady to secure the piece. He said it was only going to take eight hours. I said, "Well, if we get it done in eight hours, that's fine, but we should plan on three days." It was real cold, it was dangerous, hard to work in the air. . . .

Q: And what happened?

A: It went up about approximately noon. Got it into position. It took about an hour, 1 o'clock. I'm not sure what time Victor left, maybe within a half hour. He got on a plane and went to Denver to a football game. . . . The men stayed approximately two more hours. It was not secured at all. We had one guy-line on one end. There were no bolts in the truss columns.

Q: Now, as I understand it, he ordered you to do this lift and then he took off and went to Denver to watch a football game?

A: Yes.

Q: And how long did that piece hang in the air?

A: By the time it was secured good enough to where we could cut the crane loose, I believe it was 11 days.

Q: Eleven days. Did that present any potential danger to the workers at that worksite?

A: Yes. The way it was left for the first three days, if we would have had any kind of a windstorm, we would have probably lost everything.

As he built his case, Habush again and again guided the jury's attention to wind speeds that were recorded on the day of the accident. He called to the stand John Malan, a meteorologist at WTMJ-TV in Milwaukee, who said he recorded gusts of twenty-seven miles per hour at Mitchell International Airport and thirty-two miles per hour at WTMJ's studio at the time the crane collapsed. Habush brought in William Keefe, an engineer who had investigated more than sixty crane accidents, who condemned Mitsubishi for ignoring wind conditions that were "obviously" unsafe. Habush played videotapes recorded at the construction site that showed flags flying straight out in the wind. And, in a novel use of demonstrative evidence, he used the Boy Scout Handbook that shows how Scouts gauge the force of the wind by observing flags extended at different degrees.

Habush also called the equipment operator, Connie Urick, a skydiver familiar with judging wind speeds, who estimated the winds were twenty-five to thirty miles per hour that afternoon. "Sand was blowing in my face, and my hard hat flew off," she said. "I saw the piece coming. I saw the basket. . . . Then I heard a cable pop, and I turned around and heard another pop. I didn't see the guys in the basket. It was gone," she said, and started to cry.

Critical testimony came from the "sidewalk superintendents" who had been monitoring the progress of the construction. Lynn Sidabras, who lived just minutes from the ballpark, had begun videotaping the project at the ground-breaking ceremony as a hobby and kept a home radio scanner tuned to the on-site chatter at all times. On July 14, he overheard a conversation between Allen Watts, the supervisor of the crane crew, and Big Blue's operator, Fred Flowers.

"On that particular day, I heard Fred talk on the scanner quite a bit as far as giving wind conditions," Sidabras said. "There's one thing that stuck out in my mind that I know for a fact was early in the afternoon. Fred had mentioned that it was a twenty-six-mile-an-hour wind and gusting to thirty or thirty-two miles an hour. That sticks in my mind like glue."

Another spectator, retired autoworker John Thraen, said he heard Flowers an hour before the accident say on the radio that he had a wind gust of thirty-two miles per hour. "I could tell his voice was quivering," Thraen testified. "He was frightened."

The jury listened to Habush as he questioned Robert Becker, an ironworker, who said he heard safety director Wayne Noel on a two-way radio one hour before the crane failed.

Q: And at that time where was the crane and the roof piece?
A: It was approximately 20 feet from the target area.
Q: And had you, on prior occasions and on that day, heard Wayne Noel's voice over the radio?
A: Yes, I had.
Q: And were you able to recognize his voice?
A: Yes, I did.
Q: What did you hear from Mr. Noel over the radio at that time?
A: He stated that we had sustained winds at 26 to 28 miles an hour.

Habush cross-examined Wayne Noel, trying to nail him down about the reported wind speeds. But like other Mitsubishi employees, Noel repeatedly denied that wind speeds were a factor in the July 14 tragedy. In court, he was reluctant to provide direct answers to Habush's questions. Habush kept pushing, repeating his questions in a controlled yet unrelenting manner, never raising his voice. Finally he asked the judge for a little help in shaking loose the witness's response.

"I wouldn't invite the judge to get involved until I'd had several rebuffs," explains Habush, "because the jury doesn't think that's bad. They give the witness favors over the lawyer because they sympathize with the witness during a cross-examination. They're never rooting for the lawyer. They're rooting for the witness, until they start to feel the witness is being evasive and uncooperative. As soon as you get the judge involved, then it tips the other way. It's a technique I've used hundreds of times."

With steady prodding by Habush and a helpful admonishment by Judge Amato, Noel admitted that a man basket should not be used in sustained winds in excess of fifteen to twenty miles per hour. Noel testified, though, that he had not taken wind speed measurements on the day of the crash, saying he did not have his handheld wind speed gauge, called an anemometer, with him at the time.

Based on depositions of other witnesses, Habush knew Noel was lying and called his bluff, artfully challenging his testimony by bringing Kirt Upton to the witness stand. Upton, a veteran ironworker, had supervised Wischer, DeGrave, and Starr.

Q: Mr. Upton, you were on site on the day of the incident on July 14th?
A: Yes, sir.
Q: And tell us whether you had occasion that day to see Mr. Wayne Noel.
A: Yes, sir.
Q: Could you tell us if you saw Mr. Wayne Noel just prior to the time the crane went down.
A: Yes, sir, I did.
Q: Tell us what you saw.
A: I saw Mr. Noel with his arm extended over the edge of the building taking a wind reading.
Q: With what?
A: With a hand-held anemometer.
Q: And what did you say to him?
A: I asked Mr. Noel how the wind speeds were.
Q: Okay. What did you see him do with the hand-held anemometer as you approached him?
A: He pulled it back in and placed it in his pocket.
Q: Did you have any more conversations with Mr. Noel about the weather?
A: No, sir.
Q: Did you see the incident happen?

A: Yes, sir . . . I felt the crane travel abruptly to the south, at which point I heard a bang. I looked up. I was very close to it. At that point in time I heard another bang, and I seen the boom begin to deflect, seen the load shift back to the north. And I turned and ran.

Q: Were you able to see what Mr. Noel was doing or what happened to him?

A: Mr. Noel fell down.

Q: And what did you do?

A: I helped pick Mr. Noel up.

Q: And what did you say to him then?

A: Well, there was still stuff falling. I mean, the boom came over, the cables came over. I took Mr. Noel behind the pivot point. He was very winded, very upset, as we both were, and he began to use his cell phone to call 911.

"That testimony was key," Habush recalls, "because it showed that Mitsubishi was in fact monitoring the wind. Of course, the position of the defense was that the wind wasn't that bad, and they denied Noel was up there with the anemometer. But Kirt Upton impeached him. So they knew exactly that the gusts were thirty-two miles an hour then. That was a big impeachment."

Several Mitsubishi witnesses unabashedly tried to sidestep questions when cross-examined. One witness, Osamu Hashimoto, an installation construction engineer from Japan, seemed to suffer from a sudden case of amnesia when asked by Habush if he told the Miller Park project manager, Kano Saito, that the lift had been suspended because of the wind.

Q: Do you remember telling Mr. Saito that the lift had been suspended?

A: I don't remember.

Q: Do you remember discussing the wind with Mr. Saito?

A: I don't remember.

Q: Did Mr. Saito ask you why the lift had been suspended?

A: I don't remember.

Q: Did Mr. Saito discuss with you what he saw about the wind?

A: I don't remember.

Q: Did you tell Mr. Saito that you had observed the flag and the trees and that you believed the wind was going about 22.4 miles per hour?

A: I don't remember.

Q: Who told you to say "I don't remember?"

A: I don't remember.

His response to the question caused several jurors to break out in laughter.

Each day of the trial, new information was revealed. A round of damning testimony against the defense came from Habush's witness Howard Shapiro, the New York crane expert who had written the bible on crane design and safety. Habush asked Shapiro to walk the jury through the knotty calculations that must be made to determine the safety of a lift as critical as roof panel 4R3. Shapiro explained in his testimony that a wind-sail calculation combines the manufacturer's specifications of the crane with the surface dimensions and weight of the load. It is critical when deciding whether to perform a lift or not. Habush asked Shapiro to do a wind-sail calculation for the July 14 lift.

Q: And what did you determine, for the size of that crane and the size of piece being lifted, what, if any, safe wind speed not to exceed with 4R3?

A: Eleven-and-a-half miles an hour.

Q: And so if this operation had taken place on a calm day with winds not in excess of, say, 12 miles an hour, this accident never would have happened.

A: That's correct, yes, sir.

Q: Are you aware that nobody had done wind-sail calculations not only on July 14th, but apparently for the previous nine lifts?

A: Yes.

Q: In your opinion, was the failure to do wind-sail calculations on July 14th a violation of industry standards?

A: Industry practices, yes.

Q: And a violation of OSHA requirements?

A: Yes.

Nor was there a "lift plan" for July 14. Rather, notes and "odds and ends" were jotted down on a single piece of paper by Mitsubishi's crane crew supervisor, Allen Watts, nearly ten hours before the lift began, said Shapiro. "The behavior on the 14th I feel was unconscionable," he said. "I don't really understand how Mr. Grotlisch could have permitted that operation to go forward in the face of those winds."

In his questions to Shapiro, Habush drove hard to pin negligence on Grotlisch, summing up the site supervisor's most egregious sins.

Q: By proceeding with this lift of 4R3 on the day of the incident, without having done engineering calculations, without ascertaining that anyone else had done them, with knowledge that winds in excess of the load chart could cause the crane to tip over, with an admission that there was a probability that a tragedy could occur by doing the lift of 4R3 without wind-load calculations, in the face of the evidence by weather reports, by observation on the site, by reported wind speeds overheard of those reading anemometers, what is going on that afternoon before 5 o'clock in your opinion due to all the evidence available to you?

A: In my opinion, Victor Grotlisch was playing Russian roulette. But not with his own life.

Shapiro's dramatic statement made headlines and was repeated two days later by Judge Amato while making a ruling on the defense's motion to dismiss the lawsuit.

"The evidence does clearly show a lot of affirmative acts," Amato said, denying the motion, with the jury out of the courtroom and out of earshot. "Not only do we have affirmative acts on the part of Mitsubishi, but what they did—and I'd have to agree with Mr. Shapiro—is play Russian roulette with a lot of people's lives out there."

Responding to his comments, Mitsubishi's attorneys quickly charged the judge with being biased. "I can assure you," Amato replied testily, "that I have been fair and impartial throughout all these hearings, and I continue to be fair and impartial. And if I felt at any time I could not be fair and impartial, I would recuse myself."

The disagreement was one of several legal brawls between the judge and Mitsubishi's defense counsel. Just days before, Amato had rebuked the lawyers for making an objection that he claimed bordered on "frivolous . . . game playing." He threatened to force Mitsubishi to pay attorney fees for any motions that he ruled frivolous. And earlier in the proceedings, he had denied a mistrial request by Mitsubishi's attorneys after a witness said the scene in Miller Park after the crane collapsed was "like Hiroshima." The attorneys claimed the characterization could prejudice the jury against their client, a subsidiary of the Japanese corporation Mitsubishi International.

The tension was thick between the judge and the defense counsel, particularly the lead attorney, John Bell. Day after day, throughout the trial, the Mitsubishi lawyers flooded the courtroom with objections, raising speculation that they were laying the base for an appeal. Don Carlson, the lead attorney for Lampson, recalls: "What I heard from somebody on Mitsubishi's side of the fence was that Mitsubishi decided they needed to get error into the records. I think they knew they were going to lose, and they wanted to figure out some way to get an appeal. So they were going to be really aggressive with their objections. And they just followed that strategy all the way through."

The cold war finally erupted into a thermonuclear firestorm when Bell again accused Amato of bias—this time in the presence of the jury. "I would renew a motion for a mistrial, because we are not getting a fair trial in this courtroom," Bell complained in open court. "You have prejudged this case. You keep saying you're going to give us a level playing field, and there is no level playing field."

The judge immediately instructed jurors to disregard Bell's comments and sent them out for an early lunch. Quickly seizing an opportunity to puncture his adversary's credibility, Habush asked to weigh in on Bell's behavior. "In over thirty-eight years of trying cases in this state and around the country, I have never witnessed a more outlandish and outrageous conduct by an attorney in front of a jury," he said. "He continues to goad you and bait you. . . . It's reprehensible, and he should be sanctioned severely."

Judge Amato leveled his sights at Bell and indeed imposed sanctions: "You will be barred from objecting or making any arguments during the

Figure 11
Cross-examination
At trial, Habush grilled Victor Grotlisch, site supervisor for Mitsubishi Heavy Industries.
Photo credit: *Milwaukee Journal Sentinel*, with permission.

course of the trial, which includes closing arguments," he told the defense attorney. The next day, Bell filed a motion for Amato to declare a mistrial or recuse himself. A statement in the ten-page brief said, "He has made up his mind that Mitsubishi is responsible for the Miller Park accident." Days later, with little comment, the judge denied the motion.

"John Bell was trying so bad to provoke Judge Amato, and Amato took just so much," Habush says, looking back at the spectacle. "But I was bothered that he said he wouldn't let Bell make the final argument. I never thought that would happen. I thought that some appellate judge might say, 'You went a little too far, Amato. You could have fined him. But preventing the defendant from having their key lawyer argue their case? We're going order a new trial.' So I went up to Bell repeatedly and said, 'John, apologize. I'll back you up. I don't want to argue the case against the B team. I want to argue it against the A team.'

"As the case wore on, I finally convinced John that he should apologize, and he did after court session one day. Amato looks at me and I say, 'I think he's apologized enough. I think you should let him argue the case.' So Amato knew where I was coming from and let him argue the case."

If there was a smoking gun in Habush's indictment of Mitsubishi, it came when he put Victor Grotlisch on the stand. As a reminder to the jury, Habush read aloud meteorologic reports that showed winds blew steadily at 20.7 miles per hour and gusted to 26.5 miles per hour just before 5 p.m. Yet, he pointed out, those who were in charge of the lift—principally Grotlisch—did not implement a system for calculating the effect that wind would have on the crane and its load. In setting up his cross-examination, Habush referred to the spoken answers Grotlisch had given in his depositions, drilling him over and over for details of his neglect.

Q: You told me, did you not, Mr. Grotlisch, that when you proceed with a lift at Miller Park, due to variable winds, the topography, the size of 4R3, the size of the crane, without doing calculations of the effect of wind on the load, that this could be a dangerous practice?

A: That is correct, you asked me that question.

Q: And by a dangerous practice . . . a practice that could lead to the crane being affected, its stability being affected; isn't that right?

A: That is correct.

Q: It could lead to the crane tipping over. Isn't that an effect?

A: That's an effect.

Q: And it could also be a dangerous practice because it could fall over and kill people; isn't that also true?

A: Correct.

Q: People such as the plaintiffs?

A: That is correct.

Q: You were reasonably certain, were you not, prior to July 14th, 1999 that if these wind load calculations were not being done with a piece the size of 4R3, that not only was it a dangerous practice, but there was a probability that a tragedy could occur?

A: That is correct.

Q: Now, you told me, Mr. Grotlisch, that it was your responsibility. That if you knew no one at Mitsubishi was doing these calculations,

and you were unsure if Lampson was doing them, that it was your
responsibility to ask, "Did you do them?"

A: Yes.

Q: You didn't, did you?

A: No, I did not.

Q: You dropped the ball, didn't you?

A: Correct.

Grotlisch's response was startling: *You dropped the ball, didn't you? Correct.* It was as if the entire trial was mere pretext, a setup to this one short
exchange between accuser and defendant.

The magnitude of Grotlisch's admission was amplified by Habush's
suggestion of a cover-up by Mitsubishi managers. When questioned by
Habush earlier in the trial, the structural engineer in charge of the project described how he and Grotlisch had returned to a construction trailer
to check the wind radar just minutes after the crane crashed. The trailer
housed a computer that monitored weather conditions. When police investigators inspected the trailer, they found the computer unplugged and all
the recorded data lost.

Yet Grotlisch, under cross-examination by Habush, denied checking the
wind speeds, still adamant that overseeing the wind was not his duty.

"Weren't you a little bit curious to see what the wind speeds were?"
Habush asked him.

"No, sir. That wasn't my concern," said Grotlisch.

His blunt answer provoked quiet sobs from the ironworkers' widows.

* * *

While assigning blame to Mitsubishi managers for their reckless conduct,
Habush steered the jury's attention to the victims and their families to build
his argument for punitive damages. He called the ironworkers' widows to
testify. Each gave short, anguished accounts of how the men were missed.

Marjorie DeGrave, struggling to maintain her composure, told of her
unending grief over the loss of her husband, Bill DeGrave. "Fifteen and a
half months I've been waiting to let you know the pain that my children

and I deal with every day, multiple times a day," she said to the judge and the jury. "The pain is an open wound that some days you sprinkle with salt and other days it's doused. It doesn't stop. It doesn't stop. My children—I take my daughter to the cemetery to my husband's grave site. She sets her dolly down, and she kisses the face of my husband that's etched in stone. And as I cry, my children comfort me and tell me it's going to be OK.

"A trip to the grocery store, riding down the highway, my son spots a crane with its boom up and says, 'Mom, do you think perhaps Daddy's working on that job site?' And my three-year-old daughter looks at her brother and says, 'You know Daddy's working by God in heaven now.' And James replies with, 'Mama, he sure has been gone a long time. Don't you think God can let Daddy come back now?'"

Ramona Dulde-Starr described her husband, Jerry Starr, as her soul mate. "Jerry and I were together for many years before we were married, and we just sort of were like one person. I miss everything about him. He just was everything to me."

Trish Wischer's testimony was particularly heartrending as she explained how her family's life had changed. "I was very active with the school. I was a soccer coach for two soccer teams for four seasons. Jeff was my assistant coach. I was the Cub master at our son Roland's school for four years. Jeff was one of my den leaders. I was involved with the PTA over at the school, and since then I don't do any of it. He was my partner. He did it with me, and it's not the same."

Wearing her husband's wedding ring on a chain around her neck, Wischer told how her teenage daughter, Shawna, was in denial over her father's death and needed therapy to help her cope. "My daughter started having nightmares. She had a dream that she was walking down the aisle. She's seventeen and she's thinking about those things. She was walking down the aisle. Her dad was walking her down. And halfway down the aisle he disappeared."

She recalled how her eleven-year-old son, Zach, had liked to snuggle with his father on the living room couch when he was small. "He told me now that sometimes he wishes he was dead too so that he could lay on the couch with his dad again."

There was no tactical reason for the defense attorneys to cross-examine the widows. Their testimonies were emotionally intense, moving some of the jurors to tears at times.

To in some way quantify the conscious pain and suffering experienced by the ironworkers as they fell to their deaths, Habush hired as an expert witness a psychiatrist and former U.S. Air Force officer who had studied what people go through when they're confronted with impending death. Dr. Richard Levy, an aeromedical consultant, had interviewed children with terminal leukemia and air force pilots who survived fighter jet crashes in the Vietnam War. He also had listened to dozens of recordings of the final words of aircrew as their planes went down in fatal crashes.

Habush had come across the expert's name before the trial began while reading *USA Today* one morning at breakfast. "He had a database that would have survived any attempt to discredit him as an expert," says Habush. "So I called him, introduced myself, and told him I knew that he'd testified about what passengers experience in air crashes. I said, 'I have a similar situation. It's not an airplane crash, but I've got a case involving three guys who fell nearly three hundred feet to their deaths, knowing that they were going to die. It's part of proving conscious pain and suffering and contemplation of death, which is a permissible piece of evidence in a case.' I forwarded him the depositions I had, and he became a witness."

Dr. Levy reviewed a gut-wrenching videotape that had been recorded by OSHA safety officers who were standing fifty yards from the base of Big Blue when it collapsed. As Levy gave his graphic, chilling testimony, the recording was played frame by frame, eliciting looks of somber disbelief from jurors and a flood of tears from the ironworkers' families.

"That video got played three or four times during the trial," Habush notes, "and the widows would become hysterical. It was such a metaphor for the tragedy. They were watching their husbands about to die. Finally, before the third time it played, I asked them to leave the courtroom."

The video shows the roof panel hovering high above the stadium bowl. The crane jerks slightly as the wind catches the airborne panel. Suddenly a loud bang is heard. "What the hell is that?" asks one of the OSHA officers. A series of ground-shaking bangs follows, and an OSHA inspector asks in an agitated voice, "What's going on here?" Someone calls out a warning—"Watch it! Watch!"—and, seemingly in slow motion, the roof panel and then the crane's boom disappear from sight. In the background, against a sky of blue, a second crane falls, yanking a man basket wildly at the end of its cable until the basket drops from view in a cloud of dust and debris.

Levy calculated that as the three ironworkers watched the crash unfold beneath them, they were aware for fourteen long seconds that they were going to die—from the sound of the first loud bang, through a free fall from twenty stories up, to the moment they hit the ground below.

> Q: Doctor, have you reached an opinion to a reasonable degree of medical certainty as to whether or not the men as they fell to the ground were conscious until they struck the ground?
> A: Based on the autopsy findings, I agree that these folks were alive until they hit the ground. . . . I'm sure they were terrified and knew they were going to die, and it must have been a terrible experience for them psychologically, emotionally, spiritually. I would call this terminal pain, terminal psychological pain.

Habush had presented a strong and nearly flawless case—no stumbles, no surprises. In his artful cross-examinations, he had exacted admissions from key Mitsubishi supervisors, and he had used his expert witnesses to paint the defendants as deceitful, power-hungry, uncaring bosses who ran roughshod over standard safety regulations and ignored common sense.

"This was the best I've ever been," says Habush, in retrospect. "It was the accumulation of all those years, all those cases, and all that craft: how to deal with the judge, how to deal with defense lawyers, how to speak to the jury. I felt no adverse tension. I felt strong and vital, using my talent and my years of experience to help people who desperately needed help. It was a joy to serve that purpose. I was energized, totally invigorated. I knew this trial was going to last two months, and I had to prepare mentally and physically as well. I was what, sixty-four? But I felt like a forty-five-year-old. I felt spry and never felt my age during that case. I think I wore the other lawyers down rather than vice versa."

The attorneys for Mitsubishi and Lampson put on a ponderously slow defense of their respective clients, constantly attacking each other. The defense was so prolonged, in fact, that Judge Amato threatened to hold a separate second trial to decide the incessant cross-claims between the two companies.

Mitsubishi relied heavily on its star witness, an accident investigator and engineer, who disputed charges that Mitsubishi supervisors were to blame and instead faulted Lampson for the careless operation of Big Blue. Yet by this stage of the trial, Mitsubishi appeared to be locked in the throes of desperation.

Looking back, Don Carlson, the Lampson attorney, questions Mitsubishi's strategy. "If I had Mitsubishi's case, there's no way in the world I would want to try that thing," he says. "Personally, I don't understand why Mitsubishi didn't admit liability and just let them try to impanel the jury to try to develop the punitive damage case. That, to me, was the only strategy— admit liability, try to keep the damages under control, and say, 'We're really, really sorry. This never should have happened. We never should have picked up that lift. It's all our fault, and whatever you, as the jury, think would be an appropriate amount of damages, and even punitive damages, we will accept.' But I think there was some corporate backroom stuff going on that prevented that from happening. Somewhere in an office in New York or in Japan, somebody made a decision to fight liability. And maybe they thought they could introduce error into the record and get it up on appeal and try to settle. But I just thought they had the wrong strategy.

"You got to understand," Carlson adds, "Johnny Bell is an extraordinarily good lawyer. He's a better lawyer than I am. But he just got caught with a really bad hand. And Bob was sitting there with four aces."

But it was not only about being dealt the right cards. Habush was ready to go, ready to fight in this case, more than in any other case he had tried. He missed the battle. He missed getting even.

"I wanted to punch someone out again," he confesses. "It felt too good, and it had been a while. I hadn't had a jury verdict for several years before this case was tried. The companies I sued and their defense attorneys got smart after a while. They said, 'Let's keep this guy out of the courtroom. He'll kill us.' So they offered huge settlements, and how could I turn down all that money for my clients?"

Habush wondered whether his peers thought he was getting old and had lost his touch and didn't want to try cases anymore. "Some of my colleagues had retired. Some of them had given up trying cases when they got into their mid-sixties. They'd said, 'That's it. I've had enough.' And me, I felt I was kind of redeeming my reputation. 'Hey, guys, this guy's still alive. He's still got a big bite.' Most importantly, I still had the fire in my belly to punish wrongdoers. I was still getting even, going all the way back to my daughter Sherri."

The case was tailor-made for the return of the redoubtable Bob Habush, with all the elements to cap off a brilliant career: strong evidence, unimpeachable witnesses, innocent victims, pitiable clients, a claim for punitive damages, and the potential for a verdict that would attract attention from around the country. This was Habush's Super Bowl, his World Series, his battle for the championship title.

It wasn't his ego. He wasn't doing it for the money. It was for the ironworkers' families. He would win it for the three widows and for every worker's right to a safe workplace. That had been his overriding goal from the very beginning.

* * *

In late November 2000, with Thanksgiving Day over and the results of the 2000 presidential election heading to a U.S. Supreme Court showdown, the Miller Park trial passed the six-week mark. Testimony concluded and closing arguments began.

As expected, John Bell maintained that punitive damages were not justified. "This was an accident," he insisted. "There was no intent to operate unsafely."

Likewise, Don Carlson repeated his claim that Mitsubishi supervisors should be blamed for Big Blue's crash, not Lampson's crane. "The crane," he said, "was safe to use."

Habush was up next. The stage was set.

"The courtroom was always packed throughout the trial," recalls Judge Amato. "But when Bob was going to make his closing argument, the courtroom was really packed, and mostly with other lawyers, even members from out of the district attorney's office. When you have a good reputation to begin with, that builds as the trial goes on. He would catch the attention of everybody in the courtroom, especially the jurors. It's a persona. He had a charismatic draw, like a Clarence Darrow."

Habush stood to approach the jury box, greeting the sixteen jurors with a smile and a nod. "Seems like we've been together a long time," he said warmly, casually sliding the podium closer to the jurors. Every seat in the courtroom was occupied; dozens of rapt observers standing along the perimeter leaned in to hear his words.

Focused and deliberate, making eye contact with each jury member, Habush began his closing: "There was an empty chair at the Thanksgiving table in the Wischer, DeGrave, and Starr homes this Thanksgiving."

In his argument to prove Mitsubishi's liability, Habush swiftly and methodically led the jurors through the complexities of the marathon trial, reminding them of the wind speed reports, the discrepancies by expert witnesses, the incriminating admissions of mistakes, and the flat-out mistruths by Mitsubishi supervisors. Without hesitating, he cut to the heart of the matter:

Victor Grotlisch, when the workers made safety complaints, what did he think about those? Oh, they're just trying to dog it. They're just making up these safety complaints because they don't want to work. That shows his attitude about people complaining about safety problems.

Oh, and this is the best one. Victor Grotlisch: "We hire you from the neck down." What does that tell you about the man? Contempt, disrespect, the men are nothing but beasts of burden. "I don't want to hear from your brains. I don't want your suggestions. You do what I tell you." And that was testified to by both Mr. Watts and Mr. Upton.

Victor Grotlisch—who had to be shown safety standards that were obtained by Milo Bengtson so that he wouldn't have people under the loads. Victor Grotlisch behind schedule, over budget. His expertise and the expertise of Mitsubishi being challenged with financial consequences he knew existed if he didn't go ahead. And Victor Grotlisch, who trumped up a case against Milo Bengtson to get rid of a thorn in his side. The only one who had the guts to stand up to him and to argue with him, who had the courage. He got rid of that thorn in his side. What does that tell you about the man?

He knew that MHIA [Mitsubishi] wasn't doing the wind calculations. He says, "we didn't have anyone who could." But you may have forgotten that Paul Deasy, the fella you saw that was testifying from the Far East. He said, "I can do the wind sail calculations." Apparently no one ever asked him. "I can do them," he said.

Grotlisch admits that although he thought Lampson was doing them, he never saw it on a lift plan. He never picked up the phone and said, "Hey, are you doing them? I haven't seen them on any lift plan." No one ever told him that Lampson was doing these calculations. He didn't know that anyone was doing the calculations. So he says. And so he tells us, "Well, it was my responsibility to find out." And what does he say to you? After great hesitation, "I dropped the ball." Do you remember that testimony? "I dropped the ball."

He's too easy on himself. He didn't just drop the ball. He knew that these calculations were not being done, and he didn't care. Because if they had been done and you would have had restrictions on what kind of winds you can lift in, his style would have been cramped. His unbridled power would have been limited to make decisions. . . .

Working mostly from memory, Habush paused to check his notes on a legal pad on the plaintiff's table. As he moved, the jurors' eyes followed. When he spoke, the jurors listened intently to the narrative.

So Allen Watts arrives. Milo Bengtson's out. Allen Watts is told by his bosses, don't make waves. He knows why Bengtson was pulled off the job. So he arrives, and he's greeted by Mr. Grotlisch. And what is the first thing he says to him? "No politics here. Just follow my directions." From the neck down.

And remember the foreboding that Jeff Wischer felt before this fateful day when he came home and told Trish instructions and directions, the kind of things a person would say if he doesn't expect to be there?

Bill DeGrave came home and told Marge, "Somebody is going to get killed." He didn't know how true his concern was and that it would be him.

And so, members of the jury, before July 14th of 1999, we had the perfect recipe for a disaster. A man in charge of operations who is intolerant of other people's advice, who is contemptuous of the men who worked under him, and who was pushing the envelope of safety again and again and again. . . .

Common sense. Anyone with a whit of common sense, with or without calculation, with or without engineers, would know that if you double the surface that the wind can hit, you've got to reduce that wind speed.

Grotlisch knew that. Noel knew that. The other Mitsubishi engineers knew that. They didn't care. They were going through with this lift no matter what. . . .

This was a windy, gusty day. Dust was blowing. Helmets were blown off. The trees were moving. The light poles were swaying. People felt the effects on the crane.

What were the wind observations? At ten o'clock the crane operator, Joe Edwards, notes estimated winds of 20 to 25 miles an hour, a crane operator who looks and can compare his estimates over years of experience. Again, you don't have to be a wind engineer to know and make estimates. We're not talking about 23.1. We're talking about winds in excess of 20 miles an hour. Edwards notes again at 12:30, 25 to 30 miles an hour.

The citizen Lynn Sidabras, who was watching from County Stadium at the end, experienced 26 miles an hour, with gusts of 30 to 32 at 12:35.

At one to two o'clock, Mr. Hashimoto from Mitsubishi makes an estimate of the wind from looking at a flag of 22 miles per hour.

John Thraen, a sidewalk superintendent, who has the scanner, overhears Flowers say that he has gusts of 25 to 26 miles an hour and steady wind speeds of 17 to 19. . . .

For Victor Grotlisch to come before you and this honorable court and say the winds were minimal at 5:13, that the winds were less than 15 miles an hour, insults your intelligence.

Were all these people nuts? Was Victor Grotlisch blind? Was he walking around with a bag over his head? He saw what everyone else saw. He knew what everyone else knew.

And remember the series of Noel versus Grotlisch? Mr. Noel says, "I talked to Mr. Grotlisch in the afternoon. I told him I was concerned about the wind. I told him about the gusts. I told him about the weather. I talked to him two times between four and five o'clock," Mr. Noel says.

What does Grotlisch say? "I never talked to him. I never heard from him." Why would he say that? Why would he deny knowing what Mr. Noel says he told him? Because he wants to hear nothing and see nothing. He's covering himself. He's running from cover. This is the story he's made up after the tragedy occurred. . . .

Habush looked briefly into the audience for the faces of the widows, and then he pivoted toward the jury.

And now it gets real ugly. The cover-up. While the bodies are still laying there, Victor Grotlisch and Moto Baba go back to the trailer. Moto Baba tells you that Victor said, "Let's go look and see what the winds were on the Doppler." Victor: "I can't recall that." As if this happens every day. He can't recall that. But you can believe Mr. Baba, that that's what Victor said to him.

But let me suggest another story to you. Victor Grotlisch did not have to go back to that trailer to find out what the winds were on that Doppler radar. He knew what the winds were. He went back to that trailer to destroy the evidence. And at the appropriate time, that Doppler was unplugged at 8:30 at night while he and others were still in that trailer. You know darn well if that Doppler had shown wind speeds minimal or decreasing, that we would have seen that in this courtroom.

But we do not have the benefit of what was on that Doppler because somebody unplugged it at 8:30. We know it was 8:30 because when they re-plugged it in the next day, up popped 8:30.

Now, who would have a motive to do that? The sheriff? OSHA inspectors? Ironworkers? There's only one person who had anything to hide, to protect himself after three men were killed and huge damage was caused to the stadium. And so that evidence was destroyed.

Now Mr. Noel. He doesn't let anyone know he has a hand-held anemometer, does he? He doesn't tell the sheriff. He doesn't tell OSHA investigators. He doesn't tell the City of Milwaukee Police Department. He doesn't tell OSHA under oath. He doesn't tell me under oath. He denies it.

Why? Because he knows if they find out that he had a hand-held anemometer that afternoon, he can't say, oh, I was just making estimates or I was getting information from other sources. He has the evidence in his hand. It shows he knows what the wind speed was on the money.

Moving closer to the jury, Habush slowed his speech to an even, instructive pace, using his power of persuasion to steer the sixteen members on a path toward what he believed was the right decision. He was functioning on natural instinct.

On the question: Was Mitsubishi negligent, Question No. 1. The answer to that should be, obviously, yes, although we're claiming that their behavior was even worse than that. They were negligent in the sense of violating the load chart, violating their own safety manual, on following manual specifications, by putting people in harm's way, by not doing the sail calculations, by operating in the conditions. Of course they were negligent. They didn't act as a reasonably prudent person. And it was causal. . . .

With respect to the Question No. 11, did Mitsubishi Heavy Industries act in an intentional disregard of the rights of the decedents, I'm sure you know how I feel about that. I think that should be an easy question for you to answer. Yes. They certainly did.

Certainly all the objectives of answering that question for punitive damages, to punish, to correct behavior, to make sure it doesn't happen again, not just to them, but to others as well, requires that question to be answered yes. . . .

You heard the judge tell you a few moments ago the objectives of punitive damages. One, to punish. Two, to correct behavior so it doesn't happen again, not only of the person that's involved in the lawsuit, but others who may be listening to what you're saying, members of the jury, and observing what's going on in this courtroom, to correct behavior of Mitsubishi and others. Finally, to send a message, a clear and unmistakable, unambiguous message to people who come into our community, to contractors who come into our community, that they will not put our men and women in harm's way. That's the three goals of punitive damages.

I believe the evidence has shown to you that there was intentional disregard of the rights of the three deceased ironworkers. The intentional part is easy. They intended to do the lift. They made the decision to do the lift. It was an intentional decision. They didn't stumble into it. It was an intentional decision in the face of hazards and obvious wind conditions, and in doing so, they ignored, they disregarded the rights of those three men.

What were those rights? The right to a safe workplace. The right to life. In so doing, they intentionally disregarded those rights of the three deceased ironworkers.

We don't have to prove that Victor Grotlisch intended to kill these guys. This is not a criminal case. We don't have to prove that they knew for sure that crane was going to go down.

Let me give you an example. A person decides to run the stop sign, and in running that stop sign crashes into a crossing vehicle, killing the occupants. Would we hear that driver be able to say, I didn't intend to kill those occupants, I didn't know Sally, I didn't know Bill, I didn't intend to kill them?

But that person intended to run that stop sign and, in so doing, must bear the consequences of an intentional disregard of the rights of any other vehicle or pedestrian that might have come into harm's way by that intentional act. . . .

Remember this: Mitsubishi, Mr. Grotlisch, they've accepted no responsibility. Instead they've blamed others. They didn't come here and say, "All right, we blew it. We were negligent. We're sorry." They didn't do that. They've shown no regret. They've shown no remorse. They've given no apologies. They are defiant.

No one needs a stronger response from you, a clearer message, a sharper wake-up call, than this group. Maybe then future tragedies can be avoided.

Before his argument for damages, Habush asked the widows to leave the courtroom. "These poor souls have suffered enough during this trial," he said to the judge and jury, "and what I'm about to discuss with you is going to be extremely painful for them to hear."

As he paced in front of the side of the defense table, allowing the jurors to fix their gazes on the Mitsubishi lawyers, he reminded the jurors of the losses suffered by the ironworkers' families and of the duty of a jury to make things right.

Everyone in their life will experience a loss of a loved one, I would think, and the pain and emptiness that comes with that does not need any elaboration. But the loss of a loved one due to a stupid and outrageous act brings forth some anger that makes the grief even worse.

When someone you love is taken from you by someone who commits a stupid or outrageous act, and when that person, who you love, suffers—whatever period of time—before they die, that haunts you, and you live with that every day, and that makes the grief even worse. We have all of that here, the loss of loved ones caused by a stupid and outrageous act, and they suffered before they died.

Trish Wischer has told you about a loving relationship she had with her husband, he was a caring father, the trauma that's been caused to her and the children: where they need psychological counseling; Little Zacki, who thought the only way he could ever lie with his daddy again is to die; R.J., who's afraid that he couldn't cry, that he would forget his daddy. Shawna, who was walking down the aisle in a dream with her daddy, and he disappeared, and she had to be hospitalized; Trish, who describes his strong arms and beautiful eyes. This is a tiny, tiny bit of what they've gone through.

Ramona Starr, who said that Jerry was the center of the family, how he's sorely missed, of all the years they spent together. And like lovers, "we are one person, one body, and he was everything to me."

And Marge DeGrave: very strong relationship, a proud father, two little babies, four and three. And as she said, their loss is my loss. James spots a crane, and he said, "Is Daddy working on that crane?" And Maggie says to James, "James, Dad is working for God now." And James says to his mommy, "God's had him long enough. Can't he send him back?"

And Marge says to you—and I think this is true of all of the women—"Fifteen months I've been waiting to let you know the pain that I have every day, that I and my children deal with. The pain is an open wound. Some days it feels like there's salt on it, and other days it's dull."

In command of the room, Habush held up the only exhibit he used in the final argument: photos of the three families.

This is what this case is all about, ladies and gentlemen. Jeff Wischer and Trish, Bill DeGrave and Marge, Jerry Starr and Ramona. It's not about tilt meters. It's not about copper spacers breaking. It's about the destruction of three families by an individual, power hungry, intolerant, who pushes beyond the edge of safety. That's what this case is about. . . .

Let's talk about the conscious pain and suffering. When you know you're about to die, it adds an element of suffering. We've all thought about these people in these airplane crashes that know they're going to die, what terror they must be going through.

You heard the testimony: "Get us out of here, get us out of here, get us out of here!" These men knew what was happening.

You recall Mr. Edwards's testimony, the crane operator, how he thought he was about to meet his maker, the man-basket being wildly thrown about, Jerry Starr being thrown out of the basket.

And there's no way to distinguish between the suffering of these three men. There's no way to say one suffered more than the other. So they should be treated equally by you.

And we brought you Dr. Levy, a man who's made a specialty of how people experience contemplation of death. And he told you they were terrified, they knew they were going to die, it must have been a terrible experience, psychologically, philosophically, spiritually, and emotionally.

He went on to say, "These are experienced ironworkers. They knew what kind of trouble they were in. I'm sure they expected to die. And based on my experience, they had adequate time to experience all the things I talked about, unfortunately."

There were no "good-byes," no "I love yous." Only "Who's going to take care of my babies? Who's going to take care of my wife?" I suggest in that line that a reasonable figure for these men would be the sum of two million dollars each for those 14 seconds of hell.

This is where you can speak out, members of the jury, in indignation. This is where you can punish the wrongdoer and send a message so it won't happen again to other families. The law says, as the judge told you, "consider the grievousness of the action." How much more grievous can it be? The law says, "consider the actual damages." How much more serious can death be? And the law says, "consider the potential of what might have happened if there had been more people under that roof piece." Dozens could have been killed.

I bring you no appraisers. There are no appraisers I can bring to you to tell you what to do on this question and how much to insert. All I know is it can't be a slap on the wrist. They've got to get a clear message from you. Otherwise they'll shrug it off and go about their business.

Every day we hear numbers, stadiums costing $350 million, $250 million, ballplayers who play in these stadiums making tens of millions of dollars to play baseball or football or basketball.

Mitsubishi's contract was for $47 million. I think there's some poetic justice that they should be assessed for the death of one of these men to the extent of the bargain they got from their contract.

These men had a contract also—to live, to live a full and free life. And if I was representing one of these people, not three, but one, and speaking for one and not three, I would say that would give them a clear message.

The $47 million of their contract for punitive damages, for the punishment for their behavior, to make sure they don't do it again, but more importantly, that other contractors coming into our town will know how you feel about people who play fast and loose with the lives of our men and women on construction sites.

But we have three men here. So you should consider a multiple of that 47, and I leave that to your discretion. Remember, you've heard that the steel, the bricks, and the mortar had a hundred million dollars in damage. I don't know if you can do less for three human beings than the loss in the property damage in this tragedy.

Judge Amato ordered a short recess. Habush walked over to where the widows were sitting. "You're doing fine," he said them. "You're all doing just fine."

Following the break, the defense presented its case.

Mitsubishi's lawyer John Bell stood before the jurors and began to lay out his argument. There was no cover-up, he said, no malice on the part of the Mitsubishi managers toward the employees. Mitsubishi did nothing that would warrant punitive damages. Victor Grotlisch was being made into a scapegoat. The deaths of the ironworkers were caused by a tragic chain of events, Bell claimed. It wasn't just the wind. The ground was unusually soft at the base of the crane, he said. When the copper spacer on Big Blue broke, the crane's boom was weakened and vulnerable to wind gusts.

"The wind alone did not bring down the crane," Bell said at one point. "This was an accident. There was no intent to operate unsafely."

With Bell's conclusion, the judge motioned toward the plaintiff's table. "Mr. Habush? Rebuttal?"

Habush pushed his chair aside and again stepped toward the jury box. An anger burned inside him. He swept a hand in the direction of the defense attorneys and delivered a final condemnation of Mitsubishi and its managers.

Mr. Bell suggests that Mr. Grotlisch and Mr. Noel somehow didn't know the crane was going to go down and they were putting themselves in harm's way. The law does not require us to prove that Grotlisch and Noel knew the crane was going to go down or that they intended to kill these men. The law is clear. They intended to make the lift. They made the decision. It was intentional. They disregarded the rights of the deceased ironworkers, the rights of life, the rights to limb, the rights to a safe workplace. It's as simple as that.

They have a virtual brigade of people who are strangers to the truth. Mr. Bell couldn't even stand up here and defend them. He couldn't defend Mr. Grotlisch's conduct before the 14th, and he didn't other than saying that Mr. Bengtson deserved what he got. He didn't defend Mr. Grotlisch's conduct on the 14th. He didn't defend Mr. Grotlisch's conduct in destroying evidence. He didn't defend Mr. Grotlisch's conduct after the 14th in continuing to try to raise wind speed and ignore the safety of workers. He's pretty much given up arguing about the wind. There's too much evidence. There's too much evidence that the wind was in the high 20s and wind gusts in the 30s.

Oh, they tried. They tried hard to pretend that gusts weren't important, including with their meteorologist. But there on their own safety manuals, when you are close to the capacity, gusts can tip over the crane. Do you remember that?

Ladies and gentlemen, I told you a while back, several hours ago, that you had a rare opportunity as a jury. Most jurors up here on the fourth, fifth floor of this courthouse, they decide questions of who's at fault in automobile accidents, slip-and-fall cases, medical malpractice, sometimes products liability cases. Rarely, rarely can they do some good that really can affect the future. Rarely.

And the only time that a jury gets a chance to do that is when they're faced with a fact situation where the conduct is so much more than negligence, so bad, that they, as a jury, can punish, and they can attempt to correct behavior.

Understand, Mitsubishi is responsible for Victor Grotlisch. They support him. They still have him employed. They've had him sitting here in this courtroom as their representative during the whole trial in front of these widows, which is their right to do that. But they're responsible for him.

It's not just Mitsubishi, folks. All the workers in this town, all the workers at Miller Park, need to have someone say, if you come into my town, you don't come into my town with people who don't give a rear end about safety, who are arrogant, who think of men as beasts of burden, who don't listen to advice, who are only anxious to get things done, regardless of the dangers, who disregard the safety and rights to life.

So it's not just them. Your message will ring out across this city, across this state, and across this country, and you will be applauded for it, because no one deserved, more than the defendants, to have their behavior described as you should describe it, and you should punish them for it.

It's not profits before safety. It's safety before profits. And maybe, folks, maybe if the lesson is clear enough, the message is clear enough, maybe there won't be three more widows, three more kids that have to lose their daddies or their husbands due to the outrageous conduct that we saw in this case.

And then maybe the lives will not have gone in vain. Maybe some good can still come out of this. I am the voice for these men, who are not here to talk to you themselves. If they were here, I'm sure they'd say, "thank you," and place their trust and their prayers with you that you do the right thing.

In his conclusion, Habush eloquently and ardently reflected on the civil justice system.

Members of the jury, this is the kind of case this courthouse was built for. This is the kind of case that this courtroom was designed for. This is the kind of case that I became a lawyer to handle. Something special can still come out of this tragedy. Some good may still come out of these losses. It's in your hands, and you can ensure and send a message so that other families will not have to have me or any other lawyer standing up here talking with you like this today.

We are confident, on behalf of the families, that you will do the right thing, and I thank you.

✳ ✳ ✳

The jury remained in deliberation for nearly three full days. Bob Habush sweated out every single minute. Were his witnesses credible? Was his argument forceful enough? Did he make any missteps? Did he have the jury's approval? Did they like him?

As he waited, he couldn't sleep, and he didn't want to eat. He barely spoke to anyone, not even his wife. Mentally, he was still in the courtroom with the widows, and he couldn't leave until his work was completed. He couldn't be interrupted.

As with every case he ever tried—going all the way back to the auto accident cases he had worked on for his father, the unbearable "cadavers"—the second-guessing and self-doubt just would not let up. Throughout the trial, he had been poised, confident, unshakable. Now he was a nervous wreck, a prisoner of uncertainty.

Finally, relief. On Friday, December 1, 2000, he got the call. The jury had reached a verdict. He hurried back to the courthouse.

As the jurors filed in to the courtroom, he tried to read their faces, looking for a sign—anything that would give him hope and reassurance. But their faces were blank. Their eyes avoided his.

"Has the jury reached a verdict, Mr. Foreman?" asked Judge Amato.

"Yes, sir," answered the foreman.

For what seemed like hours to Habush, Judge Amato reviewed the verdict in silence. Then he looked out at the courtroom and read the verdict aloud:

Question 1: Was the defendant Mitsubishi Heavy Industries of America, Inc. negligent?

Answer: Yes.

Question 2: Was such negligence of the defendant Mitsubishi Heavy Industries of America, Inc. a cause of the plaintiff damages?

Answer: Yes.

The jury, in a unanimous verdict, found Mitsubishi Heavy Industries of America 97 percent negligent in the Miller Park accident and Neil F. Lampson Inc. 3 percent negligent.

For the pain and suffering of the ironworkers, the jury awarded $4.2 million, or $1.4 million to each widow.

For loss of companionship, the jury awarded $1.05 million, or $350,000 to each widow, the maximum allowed by Wisconsin law.

And for punitive damages, deciding that Mitsubishi had in fact acted with "intentional disregard" of the rights of the ironworkers, the jury awarded the widows a stunning $94 million, or $31.33 million to each widow, the largest jury verdict ever awarded in a Wisconsin civil case.

Habush heard the number, but it didn't register. "Did you hear that?" he said, turning to his associate, Mark Young. "Did you hear that? Ninety-four million? Holy shit. Holy *shit*."

Behind him, at the table of the defense counsel, there were gasps of surprise and long, anguished sighs.

A flock of TV cameras, bright lights blazing, descended upon the three widows as they hugged and clapped and laughed and cried in a torrent of emotion. Across the courtroom, cheers resounded for the victors.

"I've been through a lot of successful cases and a lot of verdicts, but with this one I felt a feeling of self-satisfaction that I'd never felt before," Habush says, remembering the moment.

Standing with Habush among a bank of news reporters, the widows commended the jury for its decision. "I'm certain, with what happened today, that that will reflect for years to come on the safety of families out there," said Marjorie DeGrave.

"It's a great day for worker safety," Habush added. "The verdict sends an unmistakable, unambiguous message to companies that Milwaukee will not tolerate playing fast and loose with workers' lives."

As the crowd thinned out, jurors explained how they had reached the amount of the awards. The total punitive damages were double the amount of the $47 million contract held by Mitsubishi to build the retractable roof. The award for compensatory damages to each widow—$1.4 million—equaled $100,000 times each of the fourteen horrific seconds the workers experienced from the time of the loud banging of the crane to the time they came to rest on the infield ground.

"We were thinking about what these gentlemen went through in those fourteen seconds," said a juror somberly.

The widows left the courthouse and returned to their homes. Habush and his team walked to the nearby Wisconsin Club for drinks and a celebration.

Meanwhile, down the street at the Pfister Hotel, the Wisconsin Academy of Trial Lawyers was holding its annual meeting. Later that night, in Habush's honor, it would present for the first time a new award to one of its young members: the Robert L. Habush Trial Lawyer of the Year Award.

Word of the Miller Park verdict spread through that meeting like wild-fire. "And by total coincidence, they were announcing the award after me," Habush says. "It was total elation. I don't know how I could ever top this again. This was all in one night—a night to remember."

A few months later, the *National Law Journal* named him one of top ten trial lawyers in the United States.

✻ ✻ ✻

Weeks after the verdict, Habush got a call from Mitsubishi's defense attorneys. They wanted to meet to talk about a settlement. "Why not?" Habush thought. "I'll hear them out."

He set up a meeting in a large conference room at his firm's office and had his secretary order a buffet lunch: ham and turkey sandwiches, a vegetable platter, fresh fruit, and cheese. Seated at the table were the defense lawyers, representatives from Mitsubishi's insurance carriers, and two or three partners from Habush's firm—a group of about a dozen.

Habush got straight to the point. "So what have you guys got?" he said, before most of his guests had taken a bite of food. "What's your best offer?"

Their answer? Ten million dollars.

He looked around the table at each of Mitsubishi's attorneys, the collegial smile gone from his lips. He stood up, politely excused himself, and left the room.

His partners quickly followed. "I'm going back in there," he told them, his voice thick with rage, "and I'm going to tell those sorry assholes to get the hell out of my office!"

The Mitsubishi team marched out afterward, struck dumb, and hungry. "They had never been kicked out of an office before without lunch," Habush recalls with a grin. Once again he had followed his fighting instinct, making it abundantly clear what he thought about their so-called settlement offer.

The punitive damage verdict was an especially sweet victory, a barrier-shattering achievement. "It was satisfaction plus," Habush says. "You see, the beauty of a punitive damage case is you can say things that would not be permissible in a nonpunitive damage case. You can talk about punishment. In your final argument, you can talk about messages that should be sent to the community, to the country. That's improper in a regular negligence case. You can't send a message. You can't talk about a lack of contrition. You can't talk financials. You can't talk about how rich a company is. You can't talk [about] how the company should be punished. But in a punitive damages case, you can.

"My point is, I could be articulate in expressing not just my thoughts but my emotions as well," he continues. "All this passion that I've had to contain in the courtroom all these years I finally was able to release in this case. It was like a minister who all his life has harbored an intolerance and hatred for bigots. Then something happened that provoked him to really let loose in a sermon how he felt about things like that. That's what it was like. For the first time before a jury, I was able to express my anger against people who don't give a damn about injuring other people and who never learned their lesson."

(The Miller Park verdict rankled tort reformists. Years later, in January 2011, Wisconsin's newly elected Republican governor, Scott Walker, signed into law a bill that imposed a cap on punitive damages of two times compensatory damages or $200,000, whichever is greater. One year later, Walker signed a new law that completely stripped away compensatory and punitive damages awards for violations of Wisconsin's Fair Employment Act. Under the old law, persons who had been discriminated against in the workplace could sue for up to $300,000 in damages.)

Failing to negotiate a settlement, Mitsubishi eventually appealed the verdict, and the payoff of the punitive damages was put on hold.

Before the Wisconsin Court of Appeals, Mitsubishi's attorneys argued that in the 1995 law, the Wisconsin legislature intended to limit punitive damages by requiring evidence that showed "the defendant acted maliciously toward the plaintiff or in an intentional disregard of the rights of the plaintiff." Under that standard, Mitsubishi supervisors did nothing wrong to warrant punitive damages, claimed the attorneys. Victor Grotlisch, they said, was merely a scapegoat.

Habush acknowledged there was no malicious act on the part of Mitsubishi, but he argued that the supervisors—specifically Grotlisch—showed an "intentional disregard" for the safety of the ironworkers because they knew high wind speeds could imperil the crane's lift and result in harm to the workers. "I'm saying, under the new law, there is no requirement that you have to show that the actor intended bodily harm," he stated.

The court disagreed. In September 2003, in a 2–1 decision, it reversed the punitive damages award.

Habush wasn't about to admit defeat. "They interpreted that statute as saying it should only apply to defendants who intend to injure," he says. "I would have had to show that Mitsubishi supervisors woke up one morning and said, 'Let's go kill some ironworkers,' as opposed to intending to lift the roof panel in the face of risk, which is what I argued. Well, that was so far off the wall. It went up to the Wisconsin Supreme Court."

The supreme court sided with Habush, reversing the appellate court. In its 2005 ruling, it concluded that the law does *not* require a plaintiff to show that "a defendant intended to cause harm or injury." Added the court: "We further conclude that the evidence was sufficient to submit a punitive damages award question to the jury."

The supreme court sent the case back to the court of appeals to resolve other outstanding issues.

"I couldn't take the risk of an unfriendly court of appeals finding some ruling of error on Amato," says Habush. "So before the appeals court got the chance to take another shot at me, I agreed finally to settle the case." Mitsubishi and its insurance carriers agreed to pay significant additional damages that, when combined with the earlier settlements of $27 million, brought the total monies recovered closer to the jury's verdict.

The three widows approved the settlement without hesitation. They had placed their trust in Bob Habush, and he had prevailed. He had come through, as he said he would.

Yet while the women welcomed legal closure, Habush knew they were accepting an open wound that would last a lifetime. He himself had endured such a wound since his daughter's trauma.

Through his firm's charitable foundation, Habush in 2001 commissioned a sculptor to install a piece of artwork at Miller Park as a memorial for the three ironworkers. It was later decided that the statue would be a tribute to *all* the workers who helped build Miller Park.

"It was impossible for me not to get emotionally involved in this case with the families," Habush says. "You get to feel you're almost part of the

Figure 12
Tribute
Honoring the ironworkers killed at Miller Park, Habush paid for a sculpture of three ironworkers, now displayed at the stadium.
Photo credit: Robert Habush

family, which certainly gave me motivation. And I adopt the anger as well, the indignation about the unnecessary deaths of these three men. So when it was over, I felt that something should be put in place at that stadium to remind people of the sacrifice that these three men made—the ultimate sacrifice—during the construction of a sports stadium. I mean, they weren't constructing a missile base. It was for people's entertainment that they gave their lives.

"And I thought statues might be a perfect thing to do. I contacted an Israeli artist, Omri Amrany, whose work I'd seen before. He had done all the statues at Detroit's baseball stadium, Comerica Park."

Standing outside Miller Park is a life-size bronze casting of three iron-workers: a woman, an African American, and a Native American, who is pointing proudly at the ballpark's main gate, as if to invite fans inside. The statue, titled *Teamwork*, has a cast-iron plaque bearing this dedication: "In appreciation of all the Miller Park workers, and in memory of Jeffrey A. Wischer, William R. DeGrave and Jerome W. Starr."

CHAPTER TEN

The Courtroom Avenger Looks Back

For Bob Habush it's all about the law, even today, more than fifty years after his first trial. With the record-breaking Miller Park case under his belt, he could have gone out on top and closed the door on future litigation. Yet he continues to work, still itching for a fight.

"Being in the courtroom is a place where I will always want to be," he says. "It's a place where I never feel better psychologically. It's always been this way. To me, it's what I was put on this earth to do."

Bert Bilsky, an attorney and a senior legacy adviser with the Jewish Community Foundation, has known Habush as a philanthropist and friend for decades. His wife, Marlene, is Mimi's cousin. "I remember when I was first graduating from law school and I sat down with him about personal injury law," Bilsky recalls. "It turned out not to be the thing that I would have been good at or wanted to do. But he made it very clear that personal injury law is a calling, and that if you are called and you have the skills, you can make a real difference.

"I have a good friend who's a personal injury lawyer in Boston, and he came to one of my kids' weddings. He met Bob and he was bowled over. He was like, 'Wow.' He knew his reputation, big-time.

"I think Bob's name would appear on any top ten list in the country. He is recognized by his peers. That's part of the reason he loves his work, part of the reason why it's a calling for him. Because in every situation he deals with, he's fighting for the little guy against the big pocket. If ever a person was doing the job that he was meant to do, it's Bob Habush."

While refining his skills as a topflight personal injury trial lawyer nationally, Habush raised the bar within the profession. "Among other contributions, Bob elevated personal injury law as an important part of the justice system and not some orphan to be ignored," says Dan Rottier, president of Habush Habush & Rottier. "Early on, within the firm, he assembled lawyers who were of sufficient quality to do any kind of law they wanted to do. It no longer was 'personal injury is what you do if you can't get a job.' He hired quality people, and we continue to this day. So most of our lawyers, if they choose to, could work in any major business firms or corporate firms. There are other firms that have done the same thing, but I think he's largely responsible for that. The top lawyers in this field right now are capable of doing any kind of law. That may not have been true fifty years ago."

Active and engaged, Habush keeps his hands in the game while keeping an eye on the horizon. But what he sees for the future of the legal profession, and the civil justice system itself, troubles him. Civil law today is practiced on a vastly different playing field than the one he knew as a young and ambitious trial attorney. It's become a field corrupted by corporate interests and unabashed party politics, he says.

"I fear for the preservation of the jury system," says Habush, reflecting on the profession. "A lot has been written recently about Thomas Jefferson, but one of the things most people do not know about him is that in writing the Constitution he was a staunch holdout to permit trial by jury for civil cases. That right is guaranteed under the Seventh Amendment.

In recent times, however, with the tort reform movement and the effort by big business to curtail its accountability, the attack on the jury system has been increasing. That has had a chilling effect on young lawyers who are considering personal injury as a practice area. It's become much more difficult to practice as a plaintiff's lawyer, Habush says—so difficult, in fact, that personal injury trial lawyers might be a dying breed.

"In some ways, we became victims of our own success, because we got so good at protecting the rights of people that our potential enemies had to find ways to fight us. Which they did," he says. "Using tort reform, such as caps on pain-and-suffering awards, they found ways to beat down small, independent trial lawyers who didn't have the resources to take on corporate giants and well-funded industry groups. They put these measures in place to discourage the future Bob Habushes from going to trial.

Another thing that's changed the system is mediation, he adds. "It used to be if you wanted to settle a case, it was face-to-face with the other lawyer. Or maybe a judge in a pretrial hearing would hammer you to settle. But with the advent of mediation—and lawyers who specialize in mediation—settlements just proliferated. Now the courts usually order it. You have to mediate."

The devil's advocate would ask, doesn't mediation serve a useful role by cutting down on the number of prolonged and costly trials? "In my area, the lawyers are going to get paid regardless," Habush says. "We get a third of the award whether we settle the case or try the case. I can make the argument: at least let the lawyer work for it a little harder, do some heavy lifting, rather than make a quick settlement. It's gotten to the point where cases are more about completing a business transaction than about protecting the safety of consumers and workers. And that's not good.

* * *

In October 2012, Habush was one of three lawyers honored by the Inner Circle of Advocates, an elite group of trial lawyers from across the country. He had been invited to join the Inner Circle in March 1975, following his $1.86 million verdict in the Totsky case. At the time, he was one of only fifty members nationwide.

While he remained an emeritus member, it had been a long time—ten years, in fact—since he had participated in an event with the Inner Circle. The group invited him to deliver a speech about his career in a program that included other speakers who also had emeritus status. Habush decided to travel to New York City with Mimi to rekindle old friendships, meet young lawyers who were new to the Inner Circle, and talk about his years as a personal injury plaintiff's attorney, a subject that could fire him up regardless of the occasion. This occasion, though, was special. The annual convention was held at the Plaza Hotel in Manhattan.

Habush was introduced by Michael Koskoff, the president of the organization.

I think for every one of us who has a father who is a lawyer, your initial thought is you're going to do something else. But then you sort

Figure 13
Honoring a friend
After the dean of Marquette University Law School died, Habush funded the renovation of a court-room into what was named the Howard Eisenberg Memorial Hall.
Photo credit: Marquette University Law School

of say, OK, I will give it a try. But one thing that Bob was not going to do was to go into a personal injury practice. He was going to go into the area of tax law. First he went to business school. Then he decided to go to law school at the University of Wisconsin. But there was a transformative event in his life. His wife gave birth to their first child. And the child received a vaccine manufactured by Parke-Davis. But the vaccine was unstable and the child was seriously damaged. It was a transformative event. Suddenly Bob understood what it was to suffer the kind of pain that our clients suffer. He dedicated himself from then on to representing people who had been through events like he had gone through.

And what a career he has had. He is still active today. He has been honored by every bar association in his state. He has been honored by the Association of Trial Lawyers of America on numerous occasions. He is just the most outstanding lawyer. Recently, in the state of Wisconsin an award was established in Bob's name, the Robert Habush Trial Lawyer of the Year Award.

And with that, I would like to introduce you to Bob Habush.

[Habush speaks.] First let me thank you, Michael, for inviting me, for bringing me back out of the wilderness. It's been wonderful seeing old friends here. And the warm reception that Mimi and I have got made me feel kind of guilty that I haven't been here as much as I should have been. I have never felt that way about ATLA or the International Academy. It's just something about this group. It's hard to define. The friends and the respect that you develop here is deeper and more enduring than any other organization I have ever been in.

I want to thank the Inner Circle for creating the Legacy Opportunity for the old relics like me to come back and talk about the past. I thought I knew what "legacy" meant, but I looked it up in the dictionary and it's "offering something from the past to people in the present and in the future." All of us who have been around as long as I have, fifty-one years this year, we've done things that have left legacies. We've taught at law schools. We've written books. We've taught at seminars. So practically everyone in this room I think has given back something to our successors.

The members of this organization in particular are great sharers, and nobody comes here and brags about why they got here. I remember, 1975 was my entry year, and we had to get up and introduce the case that got us here. And I remember coming to this group and meeting lawyers I had never met before. Many of us in this room have been American trial lawyers all of our lives. But I met men who had been legends. And I remember being in such awe because here I was, I'd had my one big verdict over $1 million, which was the ticket into the club, and I had been looking at all of these guys from California and New York and Philadelphia, with five, six, seven 7-figure verdicts.

I never considered myself a legend. I still don't. That's probably because one time I had an article written about me in the Milwaukee newspaper, and in the title it said, "Legendary Lawyer." I came home from work that day and I said, "Mimi, do you see the article in the paper? You know, it said I'm a legendary lawyer." Well, she looked at me just like a wife will look at you when she thinks your head is about to explode. And she says, "Take out the garbage, legend." From that point on, it reminded me, don't put labels on yourself and don't start feeling that you're so damn important. Of course, I continue to take out the garbage even today.

Let me just say a couple of things about what I can offer you. I'm not considered very humorous. In fact, most defense lawyers don't think I have a sense of humor at all. And I'm not very spectacular. I am more like an auto mechanic on putting a case together. But I thought I'd give you kind of a "The Way We Were" type of talk. It's important for some of you younger people to realize that in the 1950s and the 1960s personal injury lawyers were considered the rump of the profession. We were not respected by the general bar. Labels like ambulance chasers and everything else were placed on personal injury plaintiff's lawyers. It wasn't a very popular part of the practice in those days.

But when the American Trial Lawyers Association was born, people got out on the road. We had caravans. We lectured all over the country. And the trial bar started getting better and better and better. The '60s were rough with juries. But in the '70s and the '80s, let me tell you, it was Camelot. Those were the Ralph Nader years. The juries were consumer-conscious. It was easy to convince them about the bad guys. So those of us who were starting practices in the '60s and the '70s and the '80s, we had a terrific advantage with really receptive juries. It was a whole different time.

This was before class actions. This was before mass torts. This was before computers. There was no e-mail. Hell, we were still using carbon paper. Many of us, we were trying garbage cases. Those were the cases we were training on. And we got better trying all of these garbage cases. And then as time went on, if you were lucky you started getting some bigger cases.

Of course, no one offered you anything as a settlement. There were no offers. We didn't have ADR, alternative dispute resolution, or mediation, where you were forced into a situation in which someone had to make an offer and their client felt pressured and they had to accept it. So we were at trial all the time. Why? Because no one respected us. Because we never got offers. And that is how we built this tremendous inventory of substantial verdicts.

And then there was an intermediate time in the mid-'80s when many of us in ATLA were in a damn war. We were in the first wave on D-day. We spent a tremendous amount of time fighting the good fight. Of course, it still lasts today, with respect to what you've got facing you. You know why that has happened? Our young trial lawyers can't get to trial. They don't have the kind of luxury of trying a lot of cases like my generation had and the generation after me. And so it's preventing tremendous opportunities for young lawyers to get to trial.

And you've got legislation that restricts our practices; and then you've got pre-emption, which restricts our practices; and then you've got decades of propaganda from our enemies that have poisoned our jury pool. It's hard to go to trial without some people on that jury thinking that lawsuits are a lottery, that lawsuits are frivolous, that you're causing their health care costs to go up, that you're ruining their business community. We're now being blamed for everything that is bad in the economy.

These are tough times for you people to be trying cases, for any of us to be trying cases. But you still have to do it. We still have to represent the people who have no voice. It's only us. They don't have a lobby in the state legislatures. They don't have a lobby in Washington. If they don't have us, they've got nothing. We are the lobbyists for the people that get injured by negligent doctors and by defective products. And there still are defective products and negligent doctors.

Let me tell you that my success—and the success I'm sure of all of you—depended on good support from partners. And mine—certainly the best law partner I've ever had—is here in this room, Dan Rottier, one of your members. He's now running the operation, thank God.

But *the best* partner I have ever had is my wife, Mimi. Married now fifty-five years. You all know the times that we were not home with the kids, when we weren't the best fathers, the best mothers. You all know the times that we were so preoccupied that we wouldn't communicate with our spouses, where we were trying cases out of state. This woman has been to every final argument I have ever made: Sitting in hotels, in places like Menomonee, Wisconsin, the middle of winter, forty degrees below zero, playing gin rummy and waiting for the jury to come back. Always trying to console me because I was convinced I lost every damn case I ever tried. "I should have said this. I should have said that," I would say to her. But she refused to buy into it. "You did not lose the case," she'd say, calming me down.

So that is my greatest partner. And all of us who have had partners like this know that without them we wouldn't have been able to do what we're doing. Mimi, stand up and be recognized, please. . . .

Let me give you one last piece of wisdom: nobody on their deathbed has ever wished that they had spent more time at the office. So all of you remember what it all comes down to: it's family, it's friends, it's people who love you and care for you. Yeah, this has all been glorious, but that is what it's all about.

So thank you for having me. And keep up the good fight, because there's no one else that is going to do it.

If there were skeptics that night in the audience, dubious trial lawyers who felt uncertain about the future of their practices and the law profession itself, Habush surely eased their doubts. Here was a voice of confidence, of perseverance; here was a shot in the arm from a guy who had been around the block, a preeminent take-no-prisoners plaintiff's attorney who had been a fighter almost since he could walk, who had learned how to stand up for himself and so many others against misdeeds and injustices.

Demonstrating that he was better than his father, he enhanced the reputation and influence of plaintiff's lawyers in his home state and around the country, leading by example as a political activist and fearsome trial attorney, scoring victory after victory for the vulnerable and afflicted.

Throughout it all, his motivation was constant: to win a measure of justice.

Justice for the young sawmill worker who lost his legs to a recklessly designed buzz saw.

Justice for the insurance agent who, on the eve of his retirement, was infected with the AIDS virus by a contaminated blood additive.

Justice for the high school girl who was sexually assaulted by her trusted coach and religion teacher.

Justice for the sixty-one-year-old grandmother whose scalp was torn from her skull by a conveyor built without a safety guard that would have cost just five dollars to make.

Justice for the four-year-old girl who suffered severe burns when her pajamas, manufactured without flame-retardant, caught fire.

Justice for the twenty-year-old woman who was paralyzed in a car accident when her seat collapsed, snapping her backward against the rear seat.

Justice for the widows and children of three ironworkers killed when their safety cage was knocked from the sky by a tumbling construction crane in hazardous winds.

Justice for the tens of thousands of people who were injured, maimed, or killed by improperly designed automobiles, airplanes, recreational vehicles, child car seats, and farm and industrial machinery, along with numerous unsafe household products—extension cords, garage door openers, high chairs, camping stoves, imported bicycles—that were sold throughout the marketplace.

Justice for his daughter, who suffered brain damage from a defective and dangerous vaccine when she was two months old.

Plaintiff's trial lawyers a dying breed? Not if Habush can help it. The magnitude of his victories proves otherwise. "Through my profession," he says, "I've been lucky enough to be able to channel this deep-seated anger I have into a productive force. And that, I'm proud to say, has had profound consequences."

Index